"It's wonderful to be surprised by the facts. What a relief to read something this important, based on research, in a language I can understand. Thank God, somebody wrote a book for me."

> —An incest survivor

"Gene Abel and Nora Harlow offer a bold new approach to the prevention of child sexual abuse. In addition to helping parents protect their children from becoming victims, they give parents ways to talk to their children that may prevent them from becoming molesters. These are hard conversations to have. Here, for the first time, parents learn words to say and how to say them. It could make a big difference."

> —Lucy Berliner, M.S.W.
> *Associate Editor, Journal of Interpersonal Violence*
> *Board Member, Journal of Child Abuse and Neglect*
> *National Center for Missing and Exploited Children*
> *National Resource Center on Child Sexual Abuse*

"The work on molesters in the family is hard-hitting. Clean, clear writing presenting factual information . . . it grips the reader."

> —George W. Counts, M.D.
> *Former Director*
> *Office of Research on Minority and Women's Health*
> *National Institutes of Health (NIH)*

"Groundbreaking is the only way to describe it! The research facts are shocking, but that's exactly why we need to know them. I was moved by all the families' stories. To, at last, learn what causes someone to molest a child was phenomenal. This book will lift the scales from the eyes of many people. The three steps to protect children are powerful. The Stop Child Molestation Book gives such hope."

> —Claire U. Hertzler, Ed.S.
> *Victim Assistance*
> *Citizens for Community Values*

ALSO BY NORA HARLOW

Sharing the Children: Village Child Rearing Within The City

Lover to Lover: Secrets of Sex Therapy
with Gene G. Abel, M.D.

Gene G. Abel M.D.

Nora Harlow

THE
STOP
CHILD
MOLESTATION
BOOK

WHAT ORDINARY PEOPLE CAN DO

IN THEIR EVERYDAY LIVES

TO SAVE THREE MILLION CHILDREN

GENE G. ABEL, M.D. AND NORA HARLOW

Cover and Book Design by Abby Drue

This book was printed in the United States of America.

To order additional copies of this book, contact:
Xlibris Corporation
1-888-7-XLIBRIS
www.Xlibris.com
Orders@Xlibris.com

THIS BOOK IS DEDICATED

TO
*the three million American children
who are at this time victims of sexual abuse,*

TO
the 39 million adult survivors of sexual abuse alive today,

AND TO
the millions of child victims of the past.

CONTENTS

INTRODUCTION

A FACT

We now have new tests, new medicines, and new treatment therapies that, with early diagnosis, will effectively stop the men and women who commit 95 percent of all sex acts against children.

YOUR OPPORTUNITY TO SAVE CHILDREN

Even if you do nothing else, if you tell this fact to one other person you will be a force to stop child molestation.

── Introduction ──

How can we protect our children from child molesters? Thirty years ago Dr. Gene G. Abel started searching for the answers. Since he was a physician, he approached the problem of child molestation the way physicians approach health problems: Find the cause and figure out what to do about it. How do you determine the cause of a problem? You start by finding out as much information about it as you can.

The first thing Dr. Abel discovered was odd. Child molesters were not the people parents warn their children against. They were not strangers with candy bars. Instead, child molesters were almost always people that the parents knew very well. In fact, more often than not, the child molester was someone the child's whole family trusted. Why? Because the child molester was most often part of the family—a cousin, an uncle, a father, a stepfather. Or he or she was someone close to the family—a best friend, a pastor, a teenage babysitter.

Then Dr. Abel discovered something even odder: The people who sexually molested children were neither uneducated, nor poor, nor crazy. Most of them came from ordinary families. They were educated, married, religious, working, and responsible in their interactions with adults. They were people like us. In fact, they came from solid families, had good parents, and were surrounded by solid, respectable relatives—brothers and sisters, aunts and uncles, cousins and grandparents.

With this information, the question now became: What makes the one member of the family who molests so different from the rest of the family?

Dr. Abel continued his research. He built testing machinery that measured sexual interest. He measured a molester's sexual interest in adults against his sexual interest in children. Measurement, he felt, was the key: If we could measure a person's sexual interest in children, then we could diagnose it. And most important, once we had a way to test for a person's sexual interest in children, we had a way of finding out if any medicines or treatments would control or extinguish that interest.

During the time Dr. Abel was researching and developing ways to

---

diagnose a sexual interest in children, Nora Harlow started a daycare center and wrote two books, one on families taking care of their children and the other on how couples can resolve sexual difficulties. She became the editor of two national publications for physicians, one on psychiatry and one on sex. As an editor, she became interested in Dr. Abel's work to prevent child molestation. They met, they married, and between them they raised four daughters. Nora Harlow joined Dr. Abel's efforts to stop child molestation in 1988.

After years of research, Dr. Abel and his colleagues realized that their findings revolved around the family—child victims molested by their fathers, brothers, cousins, or uncles, or by other children and adults who were frequently in their homes. The threat to American children, rather than coming from unknown men and women, who spurned religion and habitually disregarded the law, was close at hand—usually in their own homes and neighborhoods. Dr. Abel and his colleagues also discovered that children from all walks of life and in families with all levels of malfunction became victims. There was no family so ordinary that its children were never molested. What's more, when they were molested, even children from ordinary families—with parents who told them they would gladly answer any sex questions, or help them with any sex problem—saw their parents as the last people they would ever tell about what was happening to them. That's when Gene Abel and Nora Harlow decided to write a book for ordinary people in ordinary families, outlining how they can protect their children—and almost everybody else's children—from ever being molested.

The Stop Child Molestation Book is that book.

——The Collaboration——

How did Dr. Abel, the physician-scientist, and Nora Harlow, the medical writer, become the "we" of this book?

Out of frustration.

Dr. Abel had published well over 100 scientific papers in medical and criminal justice journals, and chapters in psychiatric textbooks. He had also completed six research studies for the government that produced significant findings leading to advances in child protection. His colleagues had done the same. Still, the people who could most use the new information—families—had no idea that it existed. They went about their daily lives as though no medical advances to protect their children had been discovered or proven effective.

So, we determined to change that. As part of that process we began The Abel and Harlow Stop Child Molestation Study. We analyzed information from child molesters in a new way—looking for the newest facts, facts that would help—not physicians and therapists—but *families* to understand how to protect their children.

Out of our Stop Child Molestation Study came our Stop Child Molestation Plan. Together, we would design a plan for families to use to protect their children. And this plan, when used by families in ever-increasing numbers, would in fact save three million children from *ever* having to face a child molester. That is the three-step plan we describe in this book.

Why is this book important? Because the information it contains is new, it's based on proven and accepted scientific findings, and most important, families can put it to immediate use to provide a barrier between a child molester and their children.

—— THE RESEARCH ——

The research for *The Stop Child Molestation Book* is the most comprehensive ever conducted on how to prevent child molestation. We started by analyzing the records of over 16,000 men and women in 41 states who were evaluated for possible sexual boundary violations. This is the first time that so many thousands of people have answered the same set of questions concerning their sexual activities with children. All 16,000 answered more than 600 questions originally administered by either mental health or criminal justice professionals as one part of The Abel Assessment *for sexual interest*™. From this group of 16,000, more than 4,000 men and women admitted to being child molesters. We then developed The Abel and Harlow Stop Child Molestation Study from information collected on these admitted child molesters. It's published here for the first time.

This huge number of molesters gives us new information vital to the protection of our children. The admitted molesters answered questions about their attitudes and behavior on a wide variety of molestation issues. To devise the questions, we used the findings from six national studies on sexual violence that Dr. Abel directed for the Center for Studies of Antisocial and Violent Behavior of the National Institute of Mental Health (NIMH).

The molesters gave us information about their families, their incomes, their religious beliefs, their marriages, and whether they were in trouble with the law. They answered questions about their childhood and if they were molested. They answered questions about their sexuality, adult sexual preference, adult affairs, acts of exhibitionism, voyeurism, and obscene phone calls. They answered questions about themselves as child molesters: how old they were when they started molesting, how many victims they had, how many acts they had committed, if they had used force and if so how much, how they were related to the child (parent, stepparent, older brother, cousin, grandfather, uncle, aunt, family friend, caretaker or stranger).

To keep *The Stop Child Molestation Book* easy to read, we've collected most of the scientific details of the Study and other molestation subjects in the Appendix section in the back of the book.

In addition to this new research, this book is also based on the insights Dr. Abel has gained from evaluating and treating over one thousand adult survivors and their families and several thousand child molesters and their families.

──── WHY WE'RE WRITING THIS BOOK NOW ────

We wrote this book as soon as we could. We couldn't write it any earlier because the technology that makes it possible to stop child molestation did not exist. Just as technology is changing our personal lives, it has also given us new testing capabilities. Dr. Abel has used these advances to invent The Abel Assessment *for sexual interest*™. Seven years in the making, it improves on the testing device he built 30 years ago. This new test, "The Abel," has been in use nationally since 1995. It is noninvasive, fast, and gives extensive information.

While the Abel does include the more than 600 questions we used in our Stop Child Molestation Study, it goes beyond that. It also includes several additional testing components. Most importantly, The Abel Assessment *for sexual interest*™ helps the professional come to a more accurate diagnosis and come to that diagnosis *early*.

With early diagnosis, we can drastically reduce the number of children molested. How early? We now have the technical capability to test for evidence of the disorder *before* the teenager actually molests.

We have the test, and we have the medicines and the therapies. So what's to stop us from saving children from 95 percent of the sexual abuse acts now committed against them?

Their families.

Most people still believe child molestation is a big mystery and that nothing can be done about it. They believe that there is nothing they themselves could possibly do that would ever make a difference. They are wrong.

We are asking you to change those beliefs in your family.

To help you, we show you in chapter after chapter what real families have done to protect their children. We've changed their names and identifying features to protect their privacy. We chose them because their stories are not unusual. All the events in this book have happened, not once to one person, as they appear in this book, but many times to many people. We've presented these very real families because they offer examples of actions you can take to stop child molestation in your family.

It is our belief that nothing of major consequence can or will be done to remove sexual molestation from the lives of children until ordinary people in ordinary families—people like you, in families like yours—move forward to act.

The Stop Child Molestation Book will take your hand and help you go down that path step by step.

1

THE STOP CHILD
MOLESTATION PLAN:
INTO A NEW ERA

A FACT

Today, at least two out of every ten little girls and at least one out of every ten little boys are victims of a child molester. From this day forward that can change. We now have the power to prevent the child molesters who molest 88 percent of our children from ever approaching them. In addition, this same category of child molesters commit 95 percent of the sex acts against our children. We know who this child molester is, where to find him (or her), which children are most at risk, *and* how to protect them.

YOUR OPPORTUNITY TO SAVE CHILDREN

If you are an ordinary person in an ordinary family, you have the most power of anybody to save the children around you. Every time you tell your child or your sister or your husband or your friend a fact about what causes child molestation, every time you tell them about what we can do now to stop it, you build a stronger safety net for your child.

1

"I'll never ruin my mother's life by telling her"

Cyndy, a beautiful young woman of 31, has that sparkle in her eyes that makes everyone want to talk to her. She's the girl we see across the room that everyone believes has it all. Beauty. An ivy-league education. An easy laugh. Charisma. She says she'll never tell her mother what her stepfather did to her . . . or why her marriage broke up over it.

Cyndy: My life is a soap opera. After my dad died my mother and I lost everything. My mother got a secretarial job at a factory. The owner was 40. My mother was 28. They married and we moved into his big house. I loved him so much. He tucked me into bed every night.

After my mom and I had lived there a year or so, he started being sexual with me. He told me there was no use telling Mom, because she'd never believe me. He told me that without him Mom and I would be poor as church mice. At that young age I was afraid —because I knew what that was, to be really poor. So, I started to take care of my mother and to hold this new family together by doing what he wanted.

When I was 13, when I started to develop, he stopped. We went on as a picture perfect family, as though those five years never happened. Except for that, my stepfather was good to me. He paid for me to go to the best schools. I watched my mother adore him. He told me many times that he loved my mother. Today, when I visit, I can see he loves her. They have a sweet life together. Now, I hate him, I love him — maybe more love than hate, I think. No, maybe more hate.

We want everyone to know—and especially Cyndy and the 39 million other adults who were molested as children—that from this day forward child molestation can end.

Who's going to put an end to it? You are.

But why you? Shouldn't stopping child molestation be left to profession-als—physicians and therapists? Better yet, shouldn't the police and the courts take care of it?

Professionals—physicians and therapists—can *never* put an end to child molestation, neither can the police or the courts. Why? Because they come on the scene too late. By the time they get there, the children have already been molested. Only you can get there in time.

There's a bigger reason why the professionals and the courts can't put an end to child molestation. They have no permission to talk to a child about sex—unless, of course, they talk to the child after the fact, after the child has already been sexually abused or has abused another child. Only *you* can talk to your children before anything happens, before any damage is done—to anyone.

——— INTO THE NEW ERA ———

At the heart of our power in this new era is The Stop Child Molestation Plan. We're going to ask you to use The Stop Child Molestation Plan to protect the one child, the five or ten children closest to you.

Does following this plan mean no child will ever be sexually abused again? No. What we *can* do is stop the molesters who commit 95 percent of the acts against our children.

THE STOP CHILD MOLESTATION PLAN

1. **Tell others the facts.**

2. **Save the greatest number of children in the shortest possible time.**

3. **Focus on the cause: Start saving children at the beginning — before a child becomes a victim.**

As long as we have a nationwide failure to know the most basic facts about our molested children and their molesters, every child is at risk.

How do we remove that risk? You step forward when the subject comes up, to tell your family and your friends the facts.

THE STOP CHILD MOLESTATION PLAN

1. Tell others the facts.

What are the first three facts you can tell others? Fact one: Today, child molestation can be over. We have the knowledge to end it. Fact two: Today, living in the United States, there are 39 million adults who have survived child sexual abuse. Fact three: Today, more than three million American children are victims. Most of them are like Cyndy when she was a child, struggling alone, believing there is no adult who can help them.

—— NOT IN MY FAMILY ——

Cyndy's stepfather convinced her that it would be useless to tell her mother because her mother would never believe her.

What if, like Cyndy's mother, you are certain there has never been a child molester or a molested child in your family?

You are probably wrong.

Like Cyndy, most of today's children will never tell. They feel ashamed that this has happened to them. They are protecting their molester because he or she is part of their family. They are protecting other members of their family—saving them from the pain of knowing.

In spite of the millions of victims in our families, many people stick to their mistaken belief that child molestation has nothing to do with them.

An estimated one in 20 teenage boys and adult men sexually molest children, and an estimated one teenage girl or adult woman in every 3,300 females molests children. Although that's well over five million people, most families mistakenly believe that as far as molesters go, there has never been one in their family, and what's more, there never will be. Add together the child victims, the adult survivors, and the molesters, and that's 15 out of every 100 Americans who have been either a molested child or a molester.

To help stop child molestation from happening to the children closest to you, begin by telling others the basic facts.

—— IN THIS CHAPTER ——

"The Stop Child Molestation Plan: Into a New Era" tells you about the basic facts of child molestation and presents a plan to save children from sexual abuse. In it you will learn:

- the definitions of child molester and child molestation;
- the damage caused by child molestation;
- the characteristics of a child molester;
- the four general causes of child molestation;
- the four general remedies;
- why The Stop Child Molestation Plan will work.

—— WE START BY SPEAKING —— THE SAME LANGUAGE

If we're going to work together to stop child molestation, we have to speak the same language. We have to mean the same thing when we say "child molester," "child molestation," and even "child."

Moreover, all of us have to understand the basic facts: What exactly is child molestation? How many of our children are sexually abused? How seriously are they damaged? What are the characteristics of a child molester? What causes someone to sexually abuse a child? Which of our children are most at risk? We also need to know some minor facts, such as, "What is the difference between hugging children and sexually abusing them?"

A *child molester* is any older child or adult who touches a child for his or her own sexual gratification.

Child molestation is the act of sexually touching a child.

A *child* is a girl or boy who is 13 years of age or younger.

What's the *age difference* between a molester and a child? Five years. A

14-year-old "older child" sexually touching a nine-year-old, for example. This is the accepted medical definition.[1]

Sometimes, a professional will consider that a molestation act has occurred when the older child is only three years older—a sixth-grader with a third-grader, for instance. The crucial element here is the lack of equality between the two children; the sixth grader is clearly bigger, more powerful, and more "adult-like" than the third-grader.

In this book, however, we avoid definitions that are ambiguous by sticking to the medical definition. *We define "child molester" as an adult or child, who is at least five years older than the child he or she has molested.*

At this point you have learned the language of this book.

—— CHILD MOLESTATION: WHAT IS IT? ——

We've said that child molestation is the act of sexually touching a child. But what *exactly* is sexual touch?

Notice that our definition requires the teenagers or adults to put their hands on the young child, to sexually *touch* the child.

Of course there are many more forms of child sexual abuse. The molester may flash his penis to the child, masturbate in front of the child, or show the child pornographic material. While we recognize that these acts are valid forms of molestation and that they have serious consequences to the victim, in this book we have chosen to focus on the type of molestation that parents and society are most concerned about. In this book, then, we define *child molestation* and *child sexual abuse* to mean the same thing: an older child or adult sexually *touching* a child for his or her sexual gratification.

At this point, it's necessary that you understand the exact definitions of the two kinds of sexual touching that occur in acts of child molestation and the important distinctions professionals make between them. These two kinds of touching are *sexual fondling* and *sexual penetration*. The definitions are, by necessity, sexually graphic.

In 75 percent of molestation acts, the child molester sexually fondles the child, touches the child's chest and buttocks, fondles the genitals, and sometimes asks the child to touch his genitals.[2]

Acts of penetration include vaginal or anal penetration with the finger and oral, vaginal, or anal penetration with the penis. Child molesters molest much less often by penetration than by fondling. If you ask a molester if he's ever "had sex" with a child, he may answer honestly that he never has. However, if you ask if he has sexually touched a child, the answer is yes.

For this reason, when we talk about acts of child molestation we use the phrases "sexual touching" or "sexual interaction" rather than "having sex."

Sexual fondling may sound as though it could be misinterpreted. Don't all families fondle their children?

Yes, but not *sexually*. Fondling a child for sexual gratification is vastly different from hugging a child, cuddling a child, holding a child on your lap, or touching a child in any of the hundreds of ways that families touch their children to show love. There's no mistaking sexual touch. The molester sexually fondles the child's genitals for the direct purpose of sexually exciting himself and the child.

———— TELLING OTHERS THE FACTS ————

Now you've read the most sexually graphic material that appears in this book. We included it only because we believe it is absolutely necessary for you to know. If we're going to save our children from sexual abuse, all of us have to understand exactly what we mean by the act of sexual abuse. Why? Because one of the greatest obstacles we face is people's fear of the facts about child molestation.

For instance, some people who have no idea that sexual touch is vastly different from hugging are afraid to hug a child—especially one who isn't theirs—because someone might think they are child molesters. You can calm their fears by telling them this fact: Hugging is *not* molesting. Sexual touch is when an adult fondles the child's chest, buttocks, or genitals with the direct purpose of sexually exciting himself or the child.

Can you tell your husband that fact? Can you tell your sister, your cousin, or your best friend? If you can, then you can easily tell others all the rest of the facts in this book.

The beauty of spreading these facts is this. The less people know, the more anxiety they feel, and the more they want to run away or pretend that today's estimated three million sexually abused children don't exist. Every fact has a calming effect. By telling the people closest to you the facts, you can help those same people become strong adult protectors of the children closest to you.

—— How Many Children —— Are Sexually Abused?

"Three million children! I don't believe it. How can you possibly know that there are *exactly* three million child victims?" As you begin to tell others the facts, this is the first question they may ask you. The answer: Of course, we don't know *exactly*.

Women's role in child molestation research

Dr. Gene Abel: I was lucky, because I was a young researcher at a time when women came forward to demand that the government support research to stop rape and child molestation. I owe most of my early scientific career to the forceful lobbying efforts of the National Organization for Women.

Children seldom tell. Those millions of children are a secret. They are the secret in family after family after family. Even adult survivors of childhood sexual abuse seldom tell. What we do know from studies of adult men and women is that the number is *at least* three million. At least three million children are molested before they finish their 13th year.[3,4] In 1998, there were 103,000 reported *and confirmed* cases of child molestation.[5] For comparison, at the height of the polio epidemic that struck children in the 1950s, there were 21,000 cases reported in a year. For rubella, there were 57,000 cases reported.[6]

For child molestation, those numbers of reported and confirmed molestations are only the tip of the iceberg. For every case reported there are at least two and maybe three more cases that never get reported.[7]

That's why we may never know the exact number of child victims. We do know that if we use the conservative estimate that two in every ten little girls and one in every ten little boys are victims (based on the population reported in the 1999 U.S. Census statistical abstract) well over three million children are victims.

Take a moment to think about that. Three million children is a staggering number of children. *That's 46 National Football League stadiums packed with children who are, today, being sexually abused, and who believe they have no adult to go to for help.*

They are like Cyndy. Like many child victims, Cyndy believed that very bad things would happen to her family if she told. She believed that it was useless to go to her mother. Even today—more than 20 years after the fact—she continues to keep the secret about her stepfather and about her marriage.

—— How Severe is the Damage? ——

Cyndy: I would never ruin my mother's life by telling her. And I'll never tell her what happened to my marriage.

I had a lot of sexual experience before I was 13 — more than many women have in their whole lives. Dad taught me a lot. Men like this. And this. And this. It was as though, when I was with him doing sexual things, I wasn't me — I was another girl acting in a play.

For me, having sex was no big deal — in high school or in college. By the time I got to college I was a real sex bomb. I had sex with a lot of college guys. They would follow me around the campus with lovelorn eyes. Lots of guys were after me, but no one could catch me. I chose Rob. Tall, dark, handsome, sweet. Stable and a caretaker of others, like my step-dad. We had sex all the time. I loved having sex with Rob. Our honeymoon sex must have stood up there in the sex Olympics.

Everything seemed perfect for the first six months. I thought I loved him. I did have this small idea that he loved me more than I loved him. It was toward the end of the first year of marriage that I changed. I was overwhelmed by a whole new set of feelings for Rob. I began to feel deep, soft feelings for my husband. I loved him more than I had ever loved anyone. And as soon as that happened, my marriage fell apart. I lost interest in sex. And worse.

> The last night I let him touch me, he was holding me in his arms. He was talking about how much he loved me. I felt his hand slide onto my breast — just like my step-dad's hand — and I bolted. I remember sitting on the cold bathroom floor vomiting into the toilet. The second I felt close to Rob, sex with him revolted me.
>
> Since our divorce, I've been to a string of therapists. I can't do it — love and sex. Some days I miss Rob so much. I'll be driving along in the car alone, not even thinking about him, and I'll suddenly start crying. I want a baby, but I can't do it. I can't be in a family of my own.

Some people will say that sexually touching a child does no harm. Some adults will even tell boy victims to "act like a man" and "stop whining." Other adults are unsympathetic about the experiences of adult survivors. They will say that, no matter what happened in childhood, that is the past. You're an adult now, so get over it.

The facts are that sexual abuse does harm the child and that the damage often carries over into the child's adult life.

Studies show that this damage can include [8] [9] [10] [11]:

- difficulty in forming long-term relationships;
- sexual risk-taking that may lead to contracting sexually transmitted diseases, including AIDS;
- physical complaints and physical symptoms;
- depression, suicidal thoughts, and suicide;
- links to failure of the immune system and to increases in illnesses, hospitalizations, and early deaths.

In the following chapters, you will get to know child victims in ways that will give you a clear understanding of the abused child's experience. For now, to quickly understand how sexual abuse damages the child listen to the stories told by Helen and Steve.

In addition to the tangible physical and emotional damage that sexual abuse does to the child, that terrible secret that is held close by two or three family members can go on to tear at the fiber of the family in generation after generation.

"Take this secret to your grave"

Helen is in her 70s. She calls herself a baby nurse. That's because she's always worked with babies. First at the one hospital in her town and after retirement at the office of the town's baby doctor. She tells the story of her older sister, Margaret.

Helen: My older sister Margaret was 75 when she died. On the day of her funeral, I let her down. Me and my big mouth. She had a daughter, Susan. At the funeral, Susan was stern-faced as usual. Susan is an injustice collector. For as long as I can remember, I've never seen her in the same room with her mother when she didn't have her whole body set and ready to be critical of Margaret for something.

Back at the house this child — who was over 50 — said something snotty about her mother. She said it to one of her kids, one of Margaret's grandchildren, and I blew up. Later, Susan wanted to talk to me. She wanted me to know that she always loved her mother, *but . . .*—she could never forgive her mother because of the way Margaret had mistreated her own father.

According to Susan, who was so sure she had *everything* all figured out, her grandfather was the nicest man in the world and her mother made everyone's life miserable because she was so eaten up with jealousy. Even as a little kid, Susan said she knew her grandpa liked her best. But her mother was never going to let her have any time with her sweet grandpa, according to Susan. If her mother wasn't going to be the center of his attention, then nobody was.

"Anytime he started to pay attention to me," Susan said, "anytime he started to have a conversation, mom would start barking at the poor man about how she had things to do and had to go home. Once, when I was little, grandpa said he would take me to see the new baby ducks at the city park pond. I cried to go and mom slapped me so hard my teeth rattled. When I got home there was still a big red mark on my face. I bet you didn't know that." When

Susan said this, she had that look. I swear she looked just like a six-year-old about to show me she was right and I was wrong.

You have to understand I had just watched my sister's casket being lowered into the ground and I was in no mood for an "I love my mother, but . . . —" conversation. She was going on about how her mother was always jealous of her. She said she'd never forgive her mother for refusing to take in grandpa when he was dying.

Then, God forgive me, I blurted out my sister's secret. She'd taken it with her into her grave and I was supposed to do the same. But I just blurted it out. "Your mother was never going to let that man into the same house with you. He made her have sex with him when she was a little girl."

I've never felt so guilty. I promised my sister I'd never reveal her shame. When she was ten and I was seven, she put my hand on the Bible and made me swear. Margaret said as long as she didn't tell, our dad agreed to never touch me.

I had the room next to Margaret's and I remember hearing her cry after he left her room. I'd knock on her wall with our special knock. I'd knock over and over to give her comfort.

Another mistake Susan made about her mother was to "know for sure" she was a hypochondriac. Margaret was susceptible to every cold, her colds turned into bronchitis, turned into pneumonia. Her poison ivy required antibiotics. Her headaches sent her to bed. While Susan may have been right, there's another possibility. Perhaps, as is true for some sexual abuse victims, the abuse had weakened her mother's immune system so that, in fact, she was more susceptible to colds, pneumonia, and poison ivy, simply more susceptible to physical illnesses than most people.

Cyndy and Margaret had no one to tell who could rescue them. We're going to change that. And we're going to change what often happens when children do tell. Usually, boy victims keep the secret of their molestation even more closely guarded than girl victims do. In Steve's case, he considers the day he did tell as "the worst day of my life."

"The worst day of my life"

Steve is in college part-time. He works delivering pizzas. At 19, he already knows the exact day that was the worst day of his life: The day he got up enough courage to tell his father a "deep, dark secret" about this "real popular" guy—the boys' activities director at the church—who was molesting him

Steve: The guy who did it was young, a little older than I am now. He supervised these activities for nine, ten, and eleven-year-old boys in our church. Real popular guy. He carried a briefcase. I guess I was the only one who saw the gun in it. He never said he was going to kill me or anything; he just let me see the gun.

It started when I was eight; I had this idea in my head that I'd be the sacrifice. Like if I did it with him, he'd leave all the other kids alone. I was ten when I found he was doing it to another boy and I told my Dad.

Jeez, was that the worst day of my life. My dad started yelling he was going to kill the guy. He said if he had to spend the rest of his life in a jail cell, it was worth it.

My dad promised me we could talk private. Dad and me were down in the basement. I didn't know it, but Mom was hiding on the stairs listening. So she started carrying on. She was screaming and holding her heart. Said this was the worst thing that ever happened to her. She locked herself in the bathroom and was moaning and crying.

The activities guy sort of got to be this hero —can you believe it? Like at church. He lied his head off, saying he never touched me. Turns out there were two more boys he was doing it to. The one I knew about never told. The other guy came up to me years later at a party when I was, I think, fifteen, and said he wished he'd told, but back then he didn't want all the crap he saw happening to me to happen to him.

Back then, the activities guy was telling everyone he always knew I was a troubled boy. He said I was a liar but it wasn't my fault. And he made up some other stuff about me, too. Like how he noticed I followed him around and how I was a needy kid . . . and stuff. A couple of the mothers took my mom's side and defended me. People were fighting. I never went back to that place; I didn't want everyone staring at me. I felt Mom and Dad and everyone would have been happier if I didn't exist.

One day, I cut my wrists. There was this big rush to the emergency room —where they said it wasn't all that serious. 'Cause, I guess, I was this little kid. I was only ten and didn't know the right way to do it.

Three heartbreaking stories. For adult survivors there is damage. For today's children, sometimes in addition to the difficulties that may affect their adult lives, there is direct physical damage.

Why I've dedicated my research to stopping the sexual abuse of children

Dr. Gene Abel: My first sex research was on the rape of adult women. At that time, in the 1970's, the child molester was thought to be a rare bird who was, in most cases, harmless.

But then there came a pivotal event that led me to concentrate on sexual violence against children. I read a little study published in an obscure journal. Some researchers asked the question: What was the age of the woman who was most physically hurt by sexual violence? They simply examined emergency room hospital records and tabulated what the physician wrote in the patient charts. The woman most seriously physically hurt by sexual violence was under 14.

I turned around on a dime and directed my sex research to stopping the sexual abuse of children.

—— WHO IS THE CHILD MOLESTER? ——
WHO CAUSES SO MUCH DAMAGE TO OUR CHILDREN?

Now that you've heard from three victims, we want to introduce you to a molester. Keep in mind that all of these people belong to an old era—before we knew we could stop child molestation. Far more men than women are molesters. In fact, five out of a hundred men, and only one out of 3,300 women are molesters; let's look at a man who has molested children. We'll call him George.

—— George's Story ——

George was a quiet teenager. He kept to himself. Too much, according to his parents. They took him to a therapist because he was so quiet. His mother was afraid he was depressed. Although the family was never told about what happened during George's therapy, he did seem to improve.

In his twenties, George emerged from his shell, got married, and had two sons. His parents were proud of him, of the family he had established, of the values he taught his children.

During his thirties, he was promoted to a new position in his company every two or three years. More money, more responsibility, more travel, more stress.

One day when George was on the road, his wife got a call. Her husband was three states away. He'd been arrested in that state for child molestation. By now George was 43.

His wife remembers smiling into the phone. She had a flash image—her telling the story about this mistake. "Can you imagine? Poor George,—the most conservative man in the world."—and how their friends would laugh. She repeated her husband's name, including middle name. She spelled out the first, middle, and last name. His wife was sure it was somebody else with a similar name. After she was convinced that her husband was the George in custody, her next emotion was fury. Who would falsely accuse a fine man like her husband? Would the lawyer's fees bankrupt them? What would his boss say? After 20 years of marriage she knew George, knew he was the last man in the world who would ever. . . .

But did she know George?

Like most people, George's wife, when she considered child molestation at all—thought about it *only* as a sin or a crime. Her husband was simply not a criminal. He had never even had a traffic ticket. He was a regular hardworking man with a great sense of responsibility. If anything, he was a law-and-order guy. He was, like many husbands, concerned for his family's safety. He was their protector.

His religion was an important part of his life. Their religious beliefs were important to both of them and to their children.

And besides that George couldn't be a child molester, she thought, because they had a vigorous and happy sex life.

Through the months that followed, George's wife and his parents received several shocks. He confessed. Yes, he had sexually molested the 10-year-old girl who accused him, the daughter of a man who'd been his friend since high school. Then she found out there had been other victims. He had molested 23 little girls. The number included two nieces, one the daughter of his wife's sister and, the other the daughter of his own sister. He had also molested several daughters of close friends. His two nieces he had molested in an ongoing relationship over a period of years. Both nieces kept the secret from everybody in the family. In a further shock to his family, he also confessed that when he was 17 and she was in grade school, he had repeatedly molested his stepsister. She also never told.

George's larger family is, of course, destroyed. Neither his sister nor his sister-in-law will ever forgive him for sexually abusing their daughters. They also shun his wife. No matter what she says about her innocence, they believe she knew all along and allowed him to molest. His parents are shocked. Both are devastated by their failure to protect George's young stepsister.

—— AN UNSUCCESSFUL "SUCCESS STORY" ——

Now that you've read about George's 26 years of molesting, what do you think? Is this a success story? His family says yes.

George's wife believes George when he says he's learned his lesson. He's glad he's going to jail. He deserved to be punished. It's as though jail will be his salvation. Now, it's over. He will never touch a little girl again. In her mind, this severe (and deserved) punishment of a flawed man with a good core is all that is needed.

His minister believes George too. He's prayed with him in his jail cell.

The judge hates these cases. Thank goodness the law is clear. He listens to the parade of character witnesses. George is a stellar employee, a person who does good work with the adults in his community, full of remorse, a changed man. The sentence is long—20 years, to serve seven.

In George's case, in that old-era way of doing things, we used every old strategy to stop him.

George was a religious man. He knew that molesting a child was a sin. After his arrest, George's wife found a Bible in his car's glove compartment. Sometimes, when he was fighting his strong desire to sexually touch a child, he would recite certain passages and he would use the power of his deep religious convictions to stop that desire. Religion—in George's case—saved a few little girls from being molested. Still, he molested 23 little girls.

George was arrested and sent to jail. This strategy may have saved more little girls from becoming victims; it did save his nieces from George molesting them again. Still, he molested 23 little girls.

Many of the people around George believe that George's case is a success. After all, George's molesting has been stopped. He's been arrested; he's been put in jail. Many of the little girls have gone into therapy. So we have punished the child molester, we've treated the victims.

At the core, sending molesters to jail will always fail our children. Why? Because in order for a molester to be jailed, the criminal justice strategy *requires* that our children be sexually abused. Without a victim, it can't make a move.

It's the same with treating the victims. As a strategy, it's ineffective until *after* our children are sexually abused.

What we find horrifying in George's case is the waiting. All the adult protectors of those 23 little girls had to wait, powerless. First, they waited while 23 little girls were sexually molested. Then they waited for a little girl to tell an adult. But that wasn't the end of the waiting. They also had to wait for one of the 23 little girls to tell an adult who was willing to report the case. While they waited, they allowed George to go on molesting little girls for 26 years.

George's family did the best they could, given their options in the old era. Today there is no reason why George's story should be repeated.

Why? Because we have new information all of us can use to stop people like George *before* he molests 23 little girls.

—— New Information —— A Typical Child Molester

When George's neighbors heard of the first accusation, they took his side. They didn't know who this 10-year-old girl from another city was, but they knew George. Some of them knew his parents.

When he admitted that he had molested so many little girls, their shock reverberated in their stories: "He was the last person you would imagine." "A very unusual case." "I've known this guy since grade school, it's unbelievable."

Everyone who knows George, is sure of one thing: George is nothing like a typical child molester.

After all, he comes from a good home. His wife comes from a good home. George and his wife, their two children, and both sets of grandparents live near each other and go to the same church. He was baptized in the church and still attends regularly. He pays close attention to the rules. He pays all his bills a week before the due date. He has a college fund for his two sons. He rotates his tires. He drives within the speed limit.

George's wife and his neighbors believe that it's impossible—or *extremely* unusual—for an ordinary man in an ordinary family, a hard working responsible, husband and father of two, a man with high moral standards to be a child molester. They mistakenly believe that his family life, his acts of responsibility, his education, his moral values *all* protect George from becoming a child molester. In fact, they believe that those same things protect his family—and their families' children—from any connection with child molestation.

Is this an unusual case? If you lived in George's community what facts could you tell? You could repeat this fact: George's case is *not* in the least unusual. George *is* the typical child molester. He's married, educated, working, and religious.

Most people will tell you that this couldn't be right.

It is.

We asked the 4,000 admitted child molesters in our Stop Child Molestation Study to answer questions about their lives. These molesters were men aged 18 to 80. They took The Abel Assessment *for sexual interest*™ in 41 states. Some took the test as a requirement of their employer; some were referred from a mental health professional, a caseworker, a lawyer, or a judge. Some sought an evaluation on their own.

How does George compare? George *is* typical.

First of all, he's married, just like 77 percent of the more than 4000 child molesters in our Stop Child Molestation Study. George is religious, like 93 percent of the child molesters. He's educated. More than 46 percent had some college education and another 30 percent were high school graduates. Like 65 percent of child molesters, George was working. Numerous studies of adult victims have sought to link child molestation victims to lower social class and lower family income. All have failed. Child victims and their molesters exist equally in families of all income levels and classes. And, now from our Study, we know that child molesters are as equally married, educated, employed, and religious as any other Americans. (See Table 1-1.)

—— EXAMINING THE FACTS WITH CARE ——

Is it possible that the profile of the child molester is this: a man who is married, educated, working, and religious?

Yes. However, we all have to be careful at this point. We have to ask the next question: What does this mean? To answer that we come to another finding from The Abel and Harlow Stop Child Molestation Study.

This one has to do with cause and effect. Facts. A majority of children who develop cavities brush their teeth. A majority of children who developed polio in the 1950's ate candy. A majority of child molesters are married, educated, working, and religious.

TABLE 1-1

Contrasts: Admitted Molesters vs. All Americans

	Admitted Child Molesters	All Americans
Married or formerly married	77%	73%
Some College	46%	49%
High School Graduate	30%	32%
Working	65%	64%
Religious	93%	93%

Sources: The Abel and Harlow Stop Child Molestation Study and the 1999 U.S. Census Statistical Abstract

Note: All people in both groups were at least 25 years old.

So, does brushing their teeth cause children to develop cavities? No. That's simply what most children do. Did eating candy cause children to develop polio? No. That's simply what most children do.

This may have already occurred to you. Rather than *causing* a person to molest, being married, educated, working, and religious is who we are as Americans.[12] These are the facts. It's crucial that everyone understands them. In order for adult protectors to stand as a barrier between their children and a child molester, the protectors have to know what a child molester looks like. *He looks like George.*

And he looks like a lot of other people you know. In analyzing the reports of the 4,000 admitted child molesters we found this: in their outward characteristics, matching percentages of child molesters to percentages of Americans, *the average child molester closely matched the average American.*

They matched all the outward characteristics listed in Table 1-1.

──── WHICH ETHNIC GROUPS MOLEST CHILDREN? ────

Are there ethnic groups in which child molestation does not occur? Probably not. Results from The Abel and Harlow Stop Child Molestation Study suggest that each ethnic group in America has child molesters among them. Once again, the percentages bear a resemblance to the U.S. Census. (See The Abel and Harlow Stop Child Molestation Study in the appendices for further details about ethnic groups).

TABLE 1-2

Ethnic Groups: Admitted Molesters vs. All Americans

	Admitted Child Molesters	All Americans
Caucasian	79%	72%
Hispanic/Latin-American	9%	11%
African-American	6%	12%
Asian	1%	4%
American Indian	3%	1%

Sources: *The Abel and Harlow Stop Child Molestation Study and the 1999 U.S. Census Statistical Abstract*

Note: *3,952 men who admitted to molesting children were compared to American men of various ethnic groups. Asians were under-represented in the complete sample of 15,508 men. They were 1.2 percent. American Indians were over-represented in the complete sample. They were 3 percent. Both groups had child molesters in proportions equal to their percentages of representation in the complete sample.*

Fact: *In their outward characteristics, child molesters are the mirror image of all Americans.*

That makes the child molesters among us invisible.

While it is frightening to know that we can't protect our children merely by teaching them never to take candy bars from strangers, this fact of the invisible child molester does make sense: Of course child molesters are invisible, if we could see them, we would have put an end to child molestation years ago.

—— WHICH CHILDREN ARE MOLESTED? ——

Children are most at risk from the adults in their own family, *and* from the adults who are in their parents' social circle. Furthermore, our study results suggest that the risk is across the board: Child molesters come from every part of our society, and so children from every part of our society are at risk.

TABLE 1-3

Which Children Do Child Molesters Target?

CHILDREN IN THE FAMILY	
Biological Child	19%
Stepchild, Adopted or Foster Child	30%
Brothers & Sisters	12%
Nieces &Nephews	18%
Grandchild	5%
CHILDREN IN THE NEIGHBORHOOD	
Child Left in My Care	5%
Child of Friend or Neighbor	40%
CHILDREN WHO ARE STRANGERS	
Child Strangers	10%

Source: *The Abel and Harlow Stop Child Molestation Study.*

Note: *Since child molesters often molest children in more than one category, the categories total more than 100 percent. The same child molester may have molested his biological child and his stepchild, therefore, we cannot say that those two categories combined represent 49 percent, but must say that they represent a lower number.*

Notice that only 10 percent of the child molesters report that they molest a child who is a stranger.

Let's put the facts together:

- Child molesters exist in every part of our society.
- They molest children close to them, mainly children in their family or children in their social circle.
- Most child molesters, 90 percent, report that they know their child victims very well.

We want you to look carefully at that last fact on the list. While there are several facts that you will use as part of The Stop Child Molestation Plan's Step Two, this is the most important.

THE STOP CHILD MOLESTATION PLAN

1. Tell others the facts.

2. **Save the greatest number of children in the shortest possible time.**

To save the greatest number of children in the shortest possible time, we must turn the focus of our efforts upside down. Right now, 90 percent of our efforts go toward protecting our children from strangers, when what we need to do is the opposite. We need to focus 90 percent of our efforts on saving children from the molesters who are *not* strangers—the molesters in their families and the molesters who are the friends of their parents.

And we must ask the next important question: What causes the one member of the family who molests to be so different from the rest of his or her family? To end child molestation we also have to use Step Three.

THE STOP CHILD MOLESTATION PLAN

1. Tell others the facts.

2. Save the greatest number of children in the shortest possible time.

3. **Focus on the cause: Start saving children at the beginning — before a child becomes a victim.**

Focus on the cause. To do that, we must *know* the cause. What could possibly cause someone to suddenly molest a child?

—— WHAT CAUSES SOMEONE TO MOLEST? ——

What causes someone like George to become a child molester?

In general, molesters act because they fit into one of four broad categories. They act because:

1. They are children or teenagers who are sexually curious or experimenting.
2. They have a medical or mental problem that needs treatment.
3. They are opportunists, who lack feelings for others and who have an antisocial personality disorder.[13]
4. They have an ongoing sexual interest in children.

Let's look at each category.

1. Children and teenagers are sexually curious. Curiosity is a major trait of humans. Some teens use much younger children to find out about sex because they can convince these children to take their clothes off. Most teenage experimenters, as they get older, stop all sexual interactions with children.

    George is too old to be in this category.

2. A few child molesters will sexually touch a child

because they are profoundly mentally retarded, or they have developed a brain disorder, or they are psychotic. Close supervision and, when appropriate, medications to control the disorder often stop child molesters in this group.

George does not fit here.

3.   Some child molesters will sexually touch a child because they have an antisocial personality disorder. Think "anti-society." People with this disorder may be social, even glib. So why do we call them "antisocial"? Because they believe that the rules of society do not apply to them. They break many of society's rules. Essentially, antisocials lack feelings for others. In the mind of an antisocial, all of the rest of us, including children, exist to be used. The child molesters in this group appear most often in horrific accounts you see on television and in the newspaper.

George, in most of his behavior, sticks to the rules. So he does not belong in this group, either.

When we analyzed the data provided by the 4,000 molesters in our Study, we found this fact. Put all together, these first three categories of child molesters —the sexually curious teens, the adults with medical or mental disorders, and the antisocials —molested only 12 percent of the child victims. The members of the fourth category were responsible for abusing 88 percent of the child victims.

4.   Child molesters who molest because of an ongoing sexual attraction to children. They have a disorder called pedophilia. Pedophilia can be diagnosed early by a sex- specific physician or therapist, and then successfully controlled with medications and sex-specific therapies.

George is part of this group

—— PEDOPHILIA: THE SINGLE GREATEST —— CAUSE OF SEX ACTS AGAINST CHILDREN

The single greatest cause that drives a grown-up to sexually interact with a child is a *sexual desire* for a little girl or boy.

The people in this group are called *pedophiles*. Their problem, a sexual desire directed toward children, is called *pedophilia*.

Pedophiles molest 88 percent of our children who are molested. They commit 95 percent of the acts. This is a serious disorder.

To be a force to protect the children closest to you, you must understand the difference between a pedophile and a child molester.

Pedophilia is a well-known disorder. It's defined by the American Psychiatric Association in the *Diagnostic and Statistical Manual of Mental Disorders, DSM-IV-TR.*

You are familiar with the main features of this disorder, but we want to be sure you understand the importance of some of the details.

Diagnostic criteria for pedophilia

To be diagnosed with pedophilia, a person must:

- be sexually aroused by, have intense, recurring sexual fantasies of, or be involved in sexual behavior with a prepubescent child or children (generally 13 years or younger);

- be aroused by, have sexual fantasies of, or be involved with a child for at least six months.;

- be at least 16 years old, and

- be at least five years older than the child or children he or she is attracted to.[14][15]

George matches the criteria for being a pedophile. He's been doing the "behaviors" (molesting children) for 26 years. That's well over six months.

He's past 16, and he's been at least five years older than all his victims—including his first victim, his 10-year-old stepsister Abby.

The diagnosis of females with the disorder pedophilia is exactly the same. As authors, we decided to concentrate on male pedophiles because they come into either the mental health or criminal justice system in huge numbers. Of the over 16,000 people in the original sample of our study, only 601 were women. Of the 4,000 people who admitted to being a child molester, only 1.4 percent or 55 of them were women. However, female child molesters do present a problem. In reports of daycare workers who are molesters, women account for 40 percent.[16]

How early can a pedophile be stopped?

What was the beginning for George? What *caused* him to molest? What happened *before* he molested his stepsister?

The year he was 13, he began having recurrent sexually arousing fantasies of very young girls. That's when he started fantasizing about sexually interacting with his six-year-old stepsister, who stayed over one weekend a month. These sexual urges toward her remained fantasies until he turned 17, when he molested her. George molested Abby repeatedly that year. Abby was ten.

When the little girl's mother complained to her ex-husband, who by then was George's stepfather, about how the boy seemed to be "mooning over Abby," her former husband told her she'd have to get used to it: "Our daughter is a pretty little girl. This is only the beginning. Get prepared. You're going to see many boys 'mooning' over Miss Abby before she hits 18."

George's mother and stepfather did the best they could. They lived in the old era when families didn't know what to do to protect their children. They failed Abby.

First of all, Abby's father refused to consider the fact that a 13-year-old boy "mooning over" his six-year-old daughter might indicate the boy had a problem. He saw no possible danger. Abby's mother went along.

Take another look at the first diagnostic criterion for pedophilia: "Over a period of at least six months, recurrent, intense, sexually arousing fantasies, sexual urges, *or* behaviors involving sexual activity with a child or children."

Notice that little word "*or.*" It's the most important word you will see in this book. It's the cornerstone of The Stop Child Molestation Plan. What it means is that someone can be diagnosed *before they have done the behaviors.* George could have been stopped before his developing disorder caused him to molest Abby.

Why six months? Because having a fleeting sex fantasy involving a child doesn't mean someone has a disorder. These sexual fantasies, these sexual urges, have to go on for at least six months to be considered a sign of pedophilia.

It's also true that just because someone sexually molests a child doesn't mean they have a *diagnosable disorder.* There is a big difference between a child molester and a pedophile.

A *child molester* is someone who sexually touches a child. What defines a child molester is the fact that a child molester has *molested* a child. A child molester *always* has a child victim.

A pedophile is different. At 16, a full year before he molested Abby, George already had the disorder, pedophilia. He met all the diagnostic criteria for being a pedophile. However, he was not yet a child molester. *Because he had never molested a child.*

The distinction: Child molesters include four categories of people: much older children, mentally or medically disabled, antisocials, and pedophiles. Within that last category—pedophiles—there exists teenagers and adults who are in an early stage of pedophilia. They have thoughts of sexually touching young children, they have urges to sexually touch young children, they have had these thoughts for more than six months, but they have never molested a child. They have pedophilia, but they are *not* child molesters. (See Table 1-4.) It's that early stage of pedophilia—the stage before the pedophile becomes a child molester—that allows all of us to act to stop 95% of the sex acts against our children before they happen.

—— WHAT IS A PARAPHILIA? ——

Paraphilia is a medical term. It refers to a class of disorders recognized by the American Psychiatric Association as sexual disorders. Pedophilia is one of a number of sexual disorders grouped together as paraphilias. Some other examples of paraphilias are **fetishism (sexual obsession with objects), sadism (hurting others), masochism (hurting oneself), exhibitionism (flashing), voyeurism (window-peeping), and making obscene phone calls.** Paraphilic disorders are sexual, ongoing, and can be diagnosed.[17]

Why is it important to know about paraphilias? Because this tells us that pedophilia is not a mystery that leaves all of us helpless. Pedophilia is well known and, in fact, is one of a group or class of sexual disorders that share similarities: All of them respond positively to variations of the same basic therapy approach, and all of them respond to the same type of medicines. All of them are treated by specialists—physicians and therapists—who are trained to alter sex drive using tests, therapies, and medicines.

The specialists who treat teenagers and adults with the disorder, pedophilia, are called *sex-specific therapists.* Sex-*specific* therapists should not be confused with sex therapists. Sex therapists treat problems of sexual dysfunction—impotence, premature ejaculation, anorgasmia (women's failure to orgasm), and lack of desire. Sex-*specific* therapists treat people with paraphilias, such as—fetishism, exhibitionism, voyeurism and pedophilia.

Because people with one paraphilia often also have other, related paraphilias, our efforts to reduce the number of acts of child molestation will, in turn, have a high likelihood of also reducing the number of acts of flashing and window-peeping. Chapter Six gives more details about the sex-specific physicians and therapists who treat patients with paraphilias and about the tests used to help them with the diagnoses. Chapter Seven gives more details about the medications and therapies used to treat paraphilias.

Now you have the big picture. You know the language. You know the basic facts. And, you know the three steps of The Stop Child Molestation Plan.

Do we have any evidence that this plan will work?

Yes.

TABLE 1-4

Contrasts: Child Molester vs. Pedophile

Child Molester	Pedophile
Anyone who sexually touches a child.	Some people with this disorder have sexually touched a child; some are in the early stages and have no victims
The *cause* is one of the following: • an older child's curiosity • a mental or medical condition • an antisocial's lack of feeling for others • a pedophile's ongoing sexual interest in children.	The *cause* is an ongoing or chronic sexual interest in children. The person suffers from a disorder called pedophilia.
When *tested,* his results will show that he has no sexual interest in children, if he sexually touched a child because he was: • a sexually curious older child, • suffering from a mental or medical condition, • an antisocial using people,	When *tested,* because he or she has recurrent sexual fantasies, sexual urges *or* has sexually touched a child because of an ongoing sexual drive toward children, he or she will *test* positive for a sexual interest in children.
A curious child *responds* to family advice about what is sexually appropriate. **A person with a psychotic episode or organic brain syndrome, or stroke *responds*** to medicine for the major condition. **A mentally challenged person or an antisocial *responds* to** increased supervision.	**A pedophile has a paraphilia and *responds* to** tests, medicines, and therapies directed at that disorder.

It will work because it's a well-known and almost always successful plan that medical professionals use to stop any public health problem.

—— CHILD MOLESTATION AND PUBLIC HEALTH ——

Is child molestation a public health problem? It qualifies on two counts: damage to health and numbers of victims. Molesting a child endangers that child's physical and emotional health. And, of course, the number of victims is in the millions.

In the history of the world, only one strategy has worked to conquer a public health problem: Focus on the cause.

That's the Stop Child Molestation Plan's Step Three. What health professionals have always done that worked is to first find out what *causes* the disease or disorder. Then, they work to devise something—a vaccine, a therapy, a medication, a nutritional change—that will stop that cause.

Child molestation has four broad categories of cause, as you have seen. Here again, we follow a well-known and successful strategy: Save the greatest number of victims in the shortest possible time. That's the Stop Child Molestation Plan's Step Two. To do this, we ask the classic medical question: Which one cause, if we could eliminate it tomorrow, would drastically reduce the number of victims? Here we are lucky, because the cause that leads to the molestation of 88 percent of our children has already been discovered: the sexual disorder called pedophilia. If we could stop our older children, the ones who live ordinary lives in ordinary families, from developing that disorder, the number of child victims would plummet.

The Stop Child Molestation Plan's Step One—Telling others the facts—is equally proven and equally important. Once medical professionals know what causes a disease or disorder, once they single out the major cause, the next question is: How do we get people to do what is needed to rid our country of this problem? How will they learn the facts? How can we convince them to act on the facts? And at what speed?

In the 1950s, studies began to appear linking smoking to lung cancer. In 1965, responding to the evidence and to the wishes of great numbers of ordinary people, the U.S. Surgeon General put a warning label on cigarettes. Before that, medical professionals had weighed the numerous causes of lung cancer and determined that the one cause—if they eliminated it tomorrow—that would create the biggest drop in victim numbers was smoking. And, now, because of the knowledge of ordinary people, because of the demands ordinary people made to theater owners, restaurant owners, airline owners, and hospital management—who would not have acted had not ordinary people demanded it—our children can live in a mostly smoke-free world.

We talk easily of our right to a smoke-free environment. And we have the important evidence of our success. Every year the number of lung cancer victims drop.

In the 1970s, medical researchers discovered the link between a pregnant woman drinking alcohol and the birth of neurologically damaged babies. And again, you have been successful in telling others the facts, saving the greatest number of children in the shortest possible time, and keeping your focus on the cause.

While the process is the same, we know that stopping child molestation will be more difficult because it demands that all of us talk about sex between adults and children to relatives who may know none of the facts but may already have their minds set in concrete. Convinced they know all they need to know, they may have decided they don't want to hear anything about child molestation.

To rid our children of the plague of sexual abuse we have to answer one last question: If pedophilia causes 95 percent of the sex acts against our children, what causes pedophilia?

There are three main causes: spontaneous occurrence in childhood development, accidental conditioning, and a molested child's identification with his or her aggressor.

In the next three chapters you'll meet three teenagers who illustrate these three causes of pedophilia. Each is in a different stage of developing the disorder. You'll experience their families' struggles—ultimately successful—in saving each teenager from following George's path.

Where do we start? With a high school football player.

Time is of the essence

Nora Harlow: Twenty-five years ago, as the editor of *Sexual Medicine*, a publication for physicians, I wrote an article on fetal alcohol syndrome. On the cover of our Easter issue were the sad pictures of six babies born with neurological damage caused by their pregnant mothers' drinking.

It was a breaking news story and, because I had a pre-publication copy of the research, I was the first to publish it. Then it hit *The New York Times*. But nothing changed. It became hard for me to go to restaurants or parties and watch pregnant women drinking. I often thought I ought to carry copies of that issue of *Sexual Medicine*, with those sad little baby faces on the cover, and place one delicately between every pregnant woman I saw and her drink.

Two years later, for the first time, I heard a woman refuse a glass of wine because she was pregnant. I was excited that the word was finally getting out. Three years after that, signs began to appear in New York restaurants warning pregnant women to avoid alcohol. Years later, warnings appeared on the labels of alcoholic beverages. I was thrilled! Today, it's one of the first things a woman thinks of as soon as she finds out she's pregnant.

You may feel frustrated, knowing the child molestation facts and seeing others fail to protect their children. But take heart. There will be a year when you'll be surrounded by adult protectors who — with you — will demand and will get for all children — a molester-free environment.

THE STOP CHILD MOLESTATION PLAN IN ACTION
— CHAPTER 1 —

1. **Tell others the facts.**	**Tell your family and friends:**
	• The molesters who cause 95 percent of the sex acts against children are driven by a sexual disorder called pedophilia
	• We can diagnose pedophilia early — during the teenage years.
	• Some pedophiles are not child molesters because they've never acted on their disorder.
	• We can put an end to child molestation by following a three-step plan that's been proven successful in conquering other public health problems.
2. **Save the greatest number of children in the shortest possible time.**	• Of the four general causes of child molestation, the one that leads to the greatest number of victims is a sex drive directed at children.
	• That sex drive, called pedophilia, can be easily diagnosed, and then reduced or extinguished.
3. **Focus on the cause: Start saving children at the beginning — before a child becomes a victim**	• We can place child molesters in four groups separated by what *causes* them to sexually abuse a child.
	• There are remedies appropriate for each cause

2

CHILDHOOD BEGINNINGS OF THE DESIRE TO MOLEST

A FACT

What do parents do that causes their son or daughter to grow up to be a pedophile? Nothing. Some child molesters show a sexual interest in much younger children before they themselves are 12 years old. At puberty, when most older children develop a strong sexual interest in other kids their age, these kids develop a strong sex drive toward much younger children.[18] The eighth-grader develops a crush on a kid in first grade. As he gets older, this sex drive intensifies. At 25, 35, and 45, he will *still* have a sex drive directed toward children of grade-school age.[19] However, early diagnosis of this disorder can stop it at its beginning.

YOUR OPPORTUNITY TO SAVE CHILDREN

If you keep this possibility in mind when someone in your family or at your child's school tells you about a sexual interaction between an older child and a younger child, you could be a voice of reason that saves many children. Instead of joining the conventional wisdom that "he will outgrow it" and "it was just awful of the little kid's mom to make such a fuss," you could suggest that everyone take the incident seriously and that the older boy's parents see that he has an evaluation to find out if he has a sexual interest in much younger children.

2

—— ALEX'S STORY ——

Alex's family trusted him. He was one of those kids who had a knack for going outside his age group to be nice to adults. Every year he climbed on his great-aunt's roof and cleaned her gutters — even during football season. Football was his passion. He played, he watched, he dreamed football. That had been going on since he was five. When it wasn't football season, he was the unofficial babysitter for all his small cousins on both sides of the family. Everyone knew that he put all his babysitting money straight into his savings for college. All his aunts said they would rather give him the money than some girl they didn't know, who was likely to just spend it on lipstick, nail polish, and fast food. Besides, two of the aunts were divorced and were grateful to Alex for playing touch football with their sons and, of course, being a good role model.

When he was sixteen, his Aunt Kathie called his mother. Something had happened. Her two little girls, ages five and seven, had said Alex gave them a bath. This surprised his Aunt Kathie because she had told him he should not give the girls baths. The girls giggled a lot and their faces got red. The seven-year-old ran into her room and hid in the closet. The five-year-old said he touched her "tee tee."

The two mothers decided to handle this on their own. Alex's mother said, "Oh lord, I'm sorry this happened. I guess Alex is finally getting curious about girls. I'll have his dad talk to him. You know how his dad is — he'll put the fear of God in him."

Before she hung up, Aunt Kathie suggested they wait a few days. Aunt Kathie didn't want her nephew to think that she was mad at him or talking behind his back or didn't trust him.

—— IN THIS CHAPTER ——

"Childhood Beginnings of the Desire to Molest" tells you about the first of three causes of pedophilia and how to stop this cause at its beginning.

Chapter 2

It also tells you the most basic facts about pedophilia. In it you will learn:

- what causes good kids to molest; why parents hold the keys to putting an end to child molestation;

- why most people who develop a sexual interest in children are male;

- what role puberty plays in the development of pedophilia;

- how limited thinking can limit our effectiveness;

- what is the *single most important thing* a parent can do to stop a son or daughter from developing a sex drive toward children —and how to do it;

- what Alex's parents did to save their son.

——— WHAT CAUSES A GOOD KID ——— LIKE ALEX TO MOLEST?

Alex's family seems about to take the wrong road. When a boy of 16 sexually touches a child in the family who is at least five years younger, that is a signal the teenager might have a serious problem. Either he has a diagnosable disorder called pedophilia, or he has pedophilic symptoms. To protect Alex *and* the younger children in the family, Alex's mother and her sister should *not* assume they know what to do. As you saw in Chapter One, there are four possible causes of child molestation. In Alex's case, the family has no way of knowing which cause motivated him. The question to answer: Could Alex have pedophilia?

Focus on the cause: The question for Alex's mom and dad at this point is, "What *caused* this good kid to suddenly sexually touch these little girls?"

It's unlikely, given his past history, that Alex is either an antisocial or has a serious medical or mental problem causing him to touch a child. That leaves two possibilities:

1. He did it because — as his mother said — he is "finally getting curious about girls." He is a teenager experimenting.

OR

2.   He did it because he has an ongoing sexual
        interest in little girls five years younger than he is.

Alex's mother and her sister, Aunt Kathie, may be right. The boy may simply be curious. After all, every child has sexual curiosity. Children naturally do find a way to look at each other's naked bodies and to touch.

But there's also the possibility Alex's mother and aunt may be wrong. In that case, they have seriously failed Alex by leaving him adrift to cope with this disorder on his own.

—— WHY PARENTS HOLD THE KEYS —— TO ENDING CHILD MOLESTATION

How can we use the facts we know to protect our children? First and most important, we know that an estimated one out of every twenty boys grows up to be a child molester. So, to stop child molestation, families have to consider that possibility.

We know that the sexual desire for much younger children suddenly emerges in some teenagers when they hit puberty at 13 or 14. And we know that it appears without regard to their home environment. There is one exception, however. If one of their parents is molesting the child, that parent *may* cause the molested child to become a pedophile.

The first cause of pedophilia we simply call "childhood beginnings." Although we don't know everything about it, we know enough to stop this cause at its beginning. How can we stop it? The key to saving children from teenage molesters who develop a sexual interest in children sponta-neously when they hit puberty is—*the teenager's parents*.

Here's the logic: If this starts early—in the sexual development of certain teenagers, independent of the way they are raised—then we have to move to stop its development. The ones who have the most power to do this are the child's parents. How can they do it? Focus on the cause.

So, why should Alex's parents give this sexual incident so much attention? Why should we urge them to be so concerned about their teenage son sexually touching his five-year-old cousin? Because Alex is a boy.

—— Why 99 Percent Of Adults —— Who Have Sex With Kids Are Male: Testosterone

Out of 100 percent of the child molesters in our Stop Child Molestation Study, nearly 99 percent are male and one percent are female. Why?

There's a good reason. Testosterone. Males have high levels of it, females have low levels. It's testosterone that sets the stage for the development of the ongoing sexual interests of a boy like Alex.

Testosterone's effect in the womb

Testosterone is a powerful hormone that begins to act on the boy baby months before he's born.

It works like this: In the beginning, every fetus is female. The fetus that gets an androgen (testosterone) bath develops into a male baby. The sex hormone testosterone changes the entire gender of what would have been a girl baby into a boy baby.

This is a powerful hormone—and it sets off powerful consequences. From the time he is born, the boy is exceedingly sexually reactive. Changing his diapers can cause him to get an erection. At 11, 12, 13, or 14 years of age, the boy gets another huge outpouring of testosterone. This second batch of testosterone makes his voice deepen and hair grow on his face. He also begins to get more numerous erections.

Testosterone's effect on the brain

As boys become teenagers, their testosterone makes them exceedingly responsive to sexual stimuli. High levels of testosterone actually appear to change the way the brain works. They appear to make males more sexually reactive to images. The major sex symbol for heterosexual men is an extremely curvaceous woman. You see this image everywhere. It's the *Playboy* centerfold. It's the women on the TV soaps. It's the 1960s Barbie dolls. It's even the stainless steel images on the mud flaps of many 18-wheel trucks.

Women process sexual information in a different way. They are more sexually reactive to complicated ideas of sex, such as thinking of a man who is caring and concerned.

As a test, draw a picture of a woman who has exaggerated curves. Now draw a picture of a man who is caring and concerned. You see the difference. *The curvy woman is easy to draw. Drawing a picture of a caring and concerned man is difficult—nearly impossible.*[20]

Since their testosterone directly causes their brains to be exceedingly reactive to images, males are much more likely to develop sexual deviations that are rare in females. A few men will develop an obsessive sexual preoccupation with high-heeled shoes, garter belts, or women's feet. In similar fashion, a few boys and men will also develop a sexual interest in watching women through windows, or an interest in flashing their penis at unsuspecting women—or a sexual desire for children.

All of these examples are paraphilias: a *group* of ongoing sexual deviations. They only occur in a small number of males, but they are even more rare in females.[21]

The take-home message is that there will always be a few babies born who, as they get older, will develop a sexual attraction to children. We aren't certain why. Perhaps it is part of their biological make-up from birth. What we do know is that these boys are sexually interested at an early age in much younger children. We also know that their sex interests are fueled by their testosterone.

How can we use these facts to protect our children? We can open our thinking to admit this possibility. Once we admit that a child of ours could have a problem with his sex drive, we will be able to help him.

—— HOW LIMITED THINKING —— LIMITS OUR EFFECTIVENESS

By working to stop child molestation before it starts, we are stopping boys and men from developing into pedophiles. That's why it's important to learn how someone like Alex might develop a sexual desire for children.

Keep in mind that the vast majority of males, nineteen out of twenty, although they are very sexually reactive, never develop a sexual deviation. *Most boys and men are not child molesters and never will be.*

However, if we're going to save the greatest number of children in the shortest possible time, we have to stay open to the possibility that an ordinary boy from an ordinary family might develop pedophilia. Yet, most people believe that since child molestation is a criminal act, we will only find molesters in criminal families.

Alex's mother knows her son should not be sexually touching his five-year-old cousin. What he did was wrong. So her first inclination is to set up the problem as simply good behavior vs. bad behavior. Her job and that of her husband is to bring up Alex to be good; therefore his father is assigned the task to "put the fear of god in him." And off they go in the wrong direction.

Alex's father did have a talk with him. He laid the law down. He said if he heard Alex had laid a hand on any *girl — that was the end of football. He also gave him a copy of* Penthouse *and a copy of* Playboy *and said, "This is between you and me, if you want to look at naked girls, here's plenty to look at. Oh, and hide them and don't you* dare *tell your mother I gave them to you. This is just man-to-man."*

If stopping boys from growing up to be molesters were as simple as that we wouldn't have a national crisis.

Most parents, to this day—when we know we have more than five million child molesters from all walks of life, when we know the overwhelming majority of them are like Alex and molest children in their own families or children of close friends or neighbors—are certain that their teenagers and their adult children could never molest a child because they have raised them to be good.

——Eight Reasons Alex Couldn't Be Developing—— Pedophilia (According To His Family)

1. No child of ours could possibly sexually molest a child. Our family isn't like that.

2. We've taught our son right from wrong.

3. He doesn't even think about sex, he's too busy with football.

4. He cares too much about his cousins to ever do anything to hurt them.

5. Alex has always had a special relationship with his dad. His dad has never had to tell him

anything twice. Once his dad lays down the law, that's it.

6. Alex would never commit a crime. When he was in junior high, a bunch of the kids — on a lark—went on a shoplifting spree. They had a club that you could only join if you stole some little thing like a pack of gum, something costing less than a dollar. Alex didn't. He said he didn't see any fun in that.

7. Alex shows more maturity and a greater sense of responsibility than other boys his age. He has serious goals.

8. We've told him if he keeps his grades up and keeps out of trouble, we'll match the money he's saved for college. His grandparents have also pledged to match that money. Besides that, he's in line for a scholarship. He'd never risk all that.

This idea, that a good teenager could never have a sexual interest in children, goes beyond Alex's parents to everyone who knows him and knows his family.

Only a few months after his father talked to Alex, a mother complained to Mrs. Price, the principal at the grade school about this boy who kept staring at her seven-year-old daughter. He was a big kid — at least 200 pounds. Had to be in high school or maybe even college. Clean cut. Sandy hair.

The principal laughed. "Oh, that's Alex. He's a good kid. All he ever thinks about is football. He's teaching our little boys some of the fundamentals so they'll have a better chance to make the team when they get to junior high. I've known him since he started kindergarten here. Wonderful family. I think his aunt and her girls go to your church."

What none of these grown-ups knew is that when Alex stared at the woman's seven-year-old daughter, he was thinking sex. When he gave all his girl cousins horsy rides, he was thinking sex. On the hard jounces, by concentrating very intensely, he could feel what he thought was their vaginas, against his leg. What his mother and father and aunt and uncle also didn't know was that he would lie awake in bed at night and fantasize about those horsy rides. He would imagine the little girls naked.

Men as the caretakers of young children

Nora Harlow: Testosterone. Are we trying to condemn an entire sex on the basis of testosterone? No. Should we keep boys and men away from children? No. In fact, I have a *strong* belief that we should do the opposite. We need to protect the rights of the nineteen out of twenty men who will never *be* child molesters. Our children need those men.

At the daycare center I founded with several other mothers, one of our goals was to provide adult men as nurturers for our children. *Sharing the Children*, the book I wrote about the center, contained a chapter on this called "Men and their Babies." In the beginning — this was more than twenty-five years ago — we mothers had this sexist idea that since we were caring for several little boys who had no fathers in the home, we had to find men to be role models for them. I say this was sexist because at first we ignored little girls' need for fatherly nurturing.

What we found was that the fatherless little boys needed men, the fatherless little girls needed men, *and* — and this is a big 'and' — the boys and girls, especially ones this young, who had fathers in the home *also* needed men. Their fathers spent little time on their direct care.

In our third year, we had ninety percent of the fathers working directly with the children. I'm still proud of that feat. The children drank up these men like they had just come out of a desert. Seeing those children with their fathers made me a believer. Children need *more* men caring for them and teaching them.

With the availability of tests that can indicate sexual interest in children, concern about any caretaker — male or female — being a pedophile can become a thing of the past.

—— Puberty and Pedophilia ——

If pedophilia starts at puberty, stop it at puberty. It's a gigantic problem to get parents to pay attention to these facts: Pedophilia develops in an estimated one out of twenty boys; it happens regardless of what the parents teach; like all sex interest it's fueled by testosterone; like all sex interest, it starts with puberty.

Child molesters tell us they molest their first child before they are out of their teens.

Table 2-1 shows that a significant number of adult pedophiles report that they have the onset of their pedophilic interest—and molest their first victim—while they are still teenagers.[22]

TABLE 2-1

Ages of Pedophiles When They Start Molesting

Percentages of pedophiles who molest at a young age				
	Under 10	10 – 15	16 – 19	Total who start before age 20
If their victims are boys	20%	43%	13%	76%
If their victims are girls	12%	32%	10%	54%

Source: *The Abel and Harlow Stop Child Molestation Study*

Note: *Pedophiles who were 18 years of age to 83 years of age were asked at what age they molested their first victim (See the Appendix.)*

What does this information tell us?

It tells us that no matter the sex interest—even if it is an interest in little children—when puberty hits, that second batch of testosterone exaggerates that sex interest.

And so, the boy begins to act.

How does that fact help save our children?

Not our son

Dr. Gene Abel: The problem for Alex's parents is that they imagine their son is like them sexually. They refuse to consider the possibility that their son might be developing a sexual interest in children. This refusal is protective for the *parents*. As long as they close their eyes to this possibility, they feel better. However, closing their eyes is *not* protective of the child, and it is the parent's job to protect their child.

Alex's parents can't imagine that anyone sixteen could be having sex fantasies about anyone seven. *They* never did. They don't know anyone like that. Since they don't have a sexual interest in children, they think it's a piece of cake to stop having a sexual interest in children. They approach it as something that their son did wrong once... or even twice.

His parents believe that they have done all that is necessary. Now that he's been punished — grounded for two weeks — and now that he has his father's threat of "no football" hanging over his head, and now that he knows it's wrong — big time — he'll never do it again.

They are treating their son's sexual interactions with little girls as though they're a minor lapse — like taking the car without permission — and as though this minor lapse can be corrected by family punishments. What they fail to understand is that their son's problem is how to control his testosterone-fueled sex drive that is directed toward little girls.

If our older children are sexually interacting with our younger children, in some cases this is because they have a disorder called pedophilia. We must test for this disorder and help them early. Since pedophilia starts early, we need to stop it early.

Why do we believe it's important that Alex's parents give this incident so much attention? First of all because he's a boy. Second, because he's the age when most child molesters start. And, third, because Alex won't be able to come to them for help. Why not? Because even if he has pedophilia, Alex won't know it.

—— WHY YOUR SON WON'T TELL —— YOU HE HAS A PROBLEM

Humans are built to be egocentric. Each one of us believes that all other humans are essentially like us. Alex is sexually interested in five-year-old girls. He doesn't label this as anything special. He believes all boys his age have this interest. He has no idea that he's different. Helping Alex is difficult because he doesn't know he is any different from the other boys, so he sees no reason to say anything to his parents.

His mother had been saying to his father for years, "Oh, Alex is going through another one of his stages." Because of that, the boy believed that this, too, was "another one of his stages." He mistakenly believed that his secret preoccupation was harmless, that it was a stage he would outgrow. He never thought of checking with anyone. Sex was private. His parents taught him that when he was three. They taught him not to touch himself down there. He took this to mean, "Don't touch your penis when anyone can see you."

His mother told him that he could always tell her anything and she'd understand. But he knew this didn't mean anything about sex. Sex — the kind he thought about—was boy stuff. And she wouldn't understand.

Alex, who has been raised with the highest morals, in addition to believing he's like all the other boys also believes that good people control their sex drive. So that's what he'll do.

But he will need a lot more than will power to control his emerging pedophilia.

—— ALEX TRIES TO CONTROL HIS SEX DRIVE ——

Our sex drive is basic to our survival as a human animal. Because the first order of nature is that we survive as a species, at puberty we are equipped with a sex drive that is often stronger than our reason. People with the disorder pedophilia have just as strong a sex drive as all the rest of us. Although all of us repeatedly see examples of people we know acting on their sex drive with seemingly no thought of the disastrous consequences, we tend to ignore the strength of this basic animal force in pedophiles.

On the nightly news, we hear about a few highly intelligent and successful men who, being public personalities, had so much to lose by having sex outside their marriages — and still risked their careers and their families to have sex.

Just because Alex developed a sex drive directed at an inappropriate partner doesn't mean that his sex drive is any less strong *or* any more reasonable. And just because he is good, responsible, and goal-directed in most areas of his life doesn't mean that he will be any more successful at controlling his sex drive than these famous men.

Actually, what no one in his family knows is that he's already tried to control his sex drive and failed.

When he gave his young cousins horsy rides, those rides where he tried to feel their vaginas gave him an erection and that upset him, so he decided to stop giving horsy rides. He thought about those little girls a lot, about how they would look naked, but he never thought he'd actually see them that way.

When he did, that time he gave them the bath, Alex was definitely thinking of them as sexual—and he lost control.

Alex's testosterone-fueled sex drive is just as strong as any other male's, and it will continue to be strong when he is an adult. Unless something is done, he will continue to be sexually aroused to little girls for the next 70 or 80 years.

—— THE PROBLEMS PARENTS FACE ——
AND HOW THEY CAN DEAL WITH THEM

Parents are up against it with this disorder in several ways:

1. It happens in ordinary families, where it's never suspected.

2. It emerges at puberty, a difficult enough time under the best of circumstances.

3. A son who is developing this disorder —even though he fails to control himself —won't know that he has a problem.

4. Other members of the family will defend the boy *and* the family name by saying that no problem exists.

If everyone around Alex holds fast to the old way of thinking about pedophilia, they will fail him. In the first few weeks after the incident, that was exactly what happened.

Alex's parents failed to consider the possibility that their son had a serious problem. They failed to link his actions with his young female cousins to a biology that was deviant. And so, in essence, they failed their son.

And so did all of the adults who could have done something. Aunt Kathie failed him, the grade-school principal failed him, and the mother of the grade-school girl concerned about "the high school boy staring at my daughter" also failed him.

Think of yourself in this situation. We've shown you in Chapter One that child molesters as a group are a mirror image of us. They grow up and go to college, marry, and earn a good income.

This is tough information to face.

What Alex's parents had to do was consider the possibility that a family like theirs or like the next door neighbors or a family in their church or in the PTA might contain a child molester.

Alex was lucky. His parents did some reading and rather quickly Alex's chances for surviving the life-altering calamities that go with this disorder improved.

Although they didn't know whether their son's actions were caused by normal sexual curiosity or the childhood beginnings of pedophilia, they took the incident seriously.

What should Alex's parents do? Take the three actions any concerned parent should take after an incident:

1. Move to protect other children by isolating the person who might have the desire to molest.

2. Talk to their son about the general nature of his sexual thoughts and fantasies

3. Get professional help, including taking their child for a sexual interest evaluation that includes testing.

Consider the possibility

Nora Harlow: Consider the possibility that your child or your neighbor's child is developing pedophilia. *Consider that possibility.* That's a monumental shift. For most people, it's nearly impossible. But that's the shift in thinking we must have. To save the greatest number of children in the shortest possible time, that's what we have to teach everyone to do: *Consider the possibility.*

Let's look at these actions one at a time.

1. Move to protect the other children.

The very first thing that Alex's mother should do, the second she hears from her sister that Alex has given his young cousins a bath and touched one between the legs, is to talk to her sister about protecting these little girls from Alex; or, in this case keep Alex away from children until his parents have him evaluated to see if he has a sexual problem. Isolate the person with the possible sexual desire for children. "For now," Alex's mother must say, "we should separate him from children until we find out if he has a sex problem or is developing a sex problem."

Now, the mother's sister may fight this idea. Typically, family members do not want to admit the possibility that someone in their family could be a child molester. They don't want Alex or his parents to be angry with them.

They also don't want to upset family members by making a fuss. They fear their actions may label Alex as a person with a sexual problem. And they fear they might be wrong. This last — a fear that they are wrong — is very common. That's because, like everyone else, they cannot imagine that a "good kid" could really want to be sexual with a child.

Aunt Kathie did get angry. "If I'd known you would carry on like this," she said to her sister, "I'd never have told you. You are practically calling your son a child molester. You may have no faith in him, but I do. Good lord, if there is anyone in this world who is *not* a child molester, it's Alex. Children are curious about sex. You and I played doctor with the boys next door — do you think we were child molesters?"

But Alex's parents have to be strong on this point. The children around Alex must be protected until the families have an answer.

This is not so different from protecting the children from other health problems. If Aunt Kathie called to tell her sister that Alex had a severe cough and fever, she would expect his parents to keep him away from her girls until they had an answer. Is it a bad cold, bronchitis, pneumonia, tuberculosis?

At this point, the families have no way of knowing if Alex has a serious problem. From their limited information regarding this one incident, he may not. Alex's aunt may be right. This act could be experimentation. Older children often have sexual interactions with younger children out of curiosity and because they can get the younger children to take their clothes off. If that's the case, then the family punishments imposed by Alex's father would probably be effective. Since they don't know, Alex's parents do the right thing, they take the conservative approach. As they would do with other potentially dangerous health problems, they separate Alex from children until they have an answer.

What no family wants is a second incident. Unfortunately, the way some families find out that their son or daughter has an actual sex drive directed at children is when the teenager—despite the family's restrictions and punishments—sexually touches a second child. If Alex sexually touches another child, not only is there another child victim but the disposition of Alex's developing pedophilia will most likely be taken out of the hands of the family. The legal system sees two incidents as profoundly significant — even if the perpetrator is a good teenager like Alex. Should Alex have a second molestation incident, in some states he would be labeled a predator. Then the state would deal with him in a harsh manner. He might receive a mandatory jail sentence. He might be civilly committed to a psychiatric hospital on release. To protect her son, Alex's mother has to insist that her sister "not trust Alex." This protects the little girls and protects Alex from molesting another child.

2. Talk to your child about his sex thoughts.

This is the *single most important thing a parent can do* to help identify pedophilia early so something can be done. Either parent could talk to a teenage son. In the best of all possible worlds, every mother and father — without being a sex-specific therapist — would know enough about the difference between teenage sexual experimentation and an ongoing sexual interest in children to talk to their teenager in a way that would not only reassure the child, but also protect all the children around him. When would you have this talk? Certainly you would have it immediately after there is an incident. How would you have this talk? What would you say? The model conversation between Alex and his Dad later in this chapter offers you some ideas.

3. Get professional help. See a sex-specific therapist for testing and evaluation.

Simple curiosity about sex causes most sexual interactions between older children and younger children. Still, one boy in twenty will grow up to be a pedophile.[23]

So how do you tell the difference? As parents, you can't. Admitting the possibility that your son might be that one out of twenty boys who needs help, you take him to a sex-specific therapist for testing. If he tests positive, you get him treatment. That boy needs help to control or extinguish his sex drive towards children.[24] For an explanation of what is available to your family from a sex-specific therapist, see Chapters Six and Seven.

—— The Single Most Important Thing —— A Parent Can Do: How to Have A Conversation with Your Son

Alex's parents decide that since his father has already "grounded" him and since Alex and his Dad have a special bond, his Dad should be the one who talks to him. His mother admits to herself that there is a possibility Alex has a sex disorder. Since this is a talk to have with a teenage boy in private, she has told her husband that she'll be nearby if Alex wants to talk to her. A mother can be equally effective in having this talk with her teenage son. The important communication is this: I am a strong capable parent who can help you with your problems.

Rather than being a talk about the parent's anger because of the son's bad behavior, this talk is one to reassure the son, it is also a talk in which the parent gathers information. The conversation goes like this:

> **Dad:** You know I've always told you that you could come to me and tell me anything that was bothering you. Anything at all.
>
> **Alex:** Yeah, well, nothing's bothering me.
>
> **Dad:** Maybe something should be bothering you.
>
> **Alex:** I said I was sorry. I swear I'll never ever do *that* again. I don't want to talk about it.
>
> **Dad:** I may have been wrong to ground you.
>
> **Alex:** You mean I'm *not* grounded?!
>
> **Dad:** Alex, you know how much you mean to us. I am so proud of you. I've been proud of you since you could walk. I've watched you all these years, and I've admired how you care about other people. You don't remember, but from the time you could walk you were taking care of others. When your little brother threw his toy out of the playpen and then cried after it, you would run and get it for him. I'm on your side Alex, I'm on your team. Son, I'm ready to move heaven and earth to help you, but . . .
>
> **Alex:** I *said* I'd never do it again. I *know* it's wrong. I told you that.

Dad: I need you to be straight with me . . . Alex, this may be a big problem. I'm your father, so it's my job to help you.

Alex: What are you going to do?

Dad: I'm going to explain to you what might —I'm only saying *might* —be the case. Some regular boys like you in regular families like ours develop a problem. They get sexually aroused to very young girls and stay aroused to them. They think about these little girls a lot. Now this isn't these boys' fault. It just happens to them.

Alex: What's a lot?

Dad: All of us have weird sex thoughts that flash through our minds and are gone. They're so different that most people can't even remember they had them. I'm talking about having sex thoughts about little girls day after day.

Alex: If somebody had those thoughts what would that mean?

Dad: How long have you had sex thoughts about little girls?

Alex: I don't know. I think since seventh grade. But I never did anything. And I never will again. You can believe me, Dad.

Dad: How long did you plan to touch your cousins?

Alex: I thought about them naked, but I never planned anything — it just happened, honest. I don't know. One thing led to another. I bought them ice cream and it dripped on them, so I said I'd better get them cleaned up . . . and I don't know, honest.

Dad: What do you think prevents guys from telling their dads when they start daydreaming about seeing very young girls naked?

Alex: Well, guys don't talk to their parents about that stuff. It makes guys feel weird. My friends, anyway, a lot of them, if they said any sex stuff in front of their parents, their parents would go ballistic.

Dad: You mean their parents would be nervous because they didn't know how to help them. That's too bad.

Alex: Why?

Dad: Because it's a lot to handle all the things that go with sex thoughts and sex activities. Parents need to help their kids —without getting too personal. They need to let their kids know that some sex things can be dangerous for them.

Alex: Like what?

Dad: Some sex thoughts are dangerous. I know I've told you different, that everybody has hateful thoughts. Sometimes they may want to smash somebody else in the face, but they don't do it. Just thinking about *wanting* to do it never hurts anyone —because it's what you *do* that counts. Only with sex it can be different.

Alex: Like what?

Dad: Well, thinking about little girls.

Alex: Like, just thinking? Why?

Dad: Our sex drive is connected to our sex fantasies. For most sex thoughts that's no problem. But it's different when you work yourself up sexually over and over for a non-consenting partner.

Alex: What's that?

Dad: You are a lot more powerful than your young cousins so you are taking advantage of them. That's why people call children non-consenting. You can convince them to take their clothes off or to let you feel them up. But you just told me you know it's wrong. Now, most sex thoughts are okay, it's the ones you have about girls or boys five grades behind you in school that can be dangerous.

Alex: Why?

Dad: Because those sex thoughts you have over and

over about little children can lead you to want to take their clothes off or touch them. Like what happened with you and your cousins. You've been thinking about little girls for a while. I'm surprised something didn't happen before now.

Alex: Are you disappointed in me?

Dad: No, I'm disappointed in *me*. I wish I had talked to you when you were in sixth grade, before you first started having these sex thoughts. Something like this never entered my mind. You are going to need help with this, son. And I'm going to see that you get help.

Alex: Are you going to tell Mom? I mean, about me thinking crazy sex stuff?

Dad: You should tell her. You know your mother loves you. She can handle this.

Alex: What do you think she'll say?

Dad: Oh, you know your mother. She's likely to go into high gear to help you solve this. She'll make lists. She'll find the best doctor. She'll have a list of books for us to read.

There are doctors who specialize in treating kids with your exact problem. You can tell them anything.

Okay, Alex, here's our game plan. I think we should not keep this from your mother. So, first I'm going to ask her to come in here so you can tell her. Your mother will find you the right doctor.

Now, we have to have some rules about when you and I are going to talk about this again. How would it be if we plan to talk — this is Monday — let's plan to talk about this again on Thursday. You have a game on Friday, so what do you say to planning to talk Thursday to see where we are on dealing with this.

Alex: Okay.

Dad: Okay, then you stay here; I'll go find your mother.

——A Closer Look At The Conversation——

Let's look at this conversation again. This time we'll analyze it to see all the things Alex's father did right.

> **Dad:** You know I've always told you that you could come to me and tell my anything that was bothering you. Anything at all.

Avoid an argument

Notice he does not start by asking: "What's wrong with you? Are you so sick you get a charge out of a five-year old?" Questions like that would put Alex on the defensive, so that the boy would most likely give a quick and outraged answer. The conversation would then quickly turn into an argument, depriving the father of the important information he needs to know.

> **Alex:** Yeah, well, nothing's bothering me.
>
> **Dad:** Maybe something should be bothering you.
>
> **Alex:** I said I was sorry. I swear I'll never ever do *that* again. I don't want to talk about it.
>
> **Dad:** I may have been wrong to ground you.
>
> **Alex:** You mean I'm *not* grounded?!

Notice the way that the father talks to his son. First, he reassures his son that Alex can talk to him about anything. He does not react to his son's negative comments or to his son's saying he'll never do it again. If Alex has a pedophilic disorder fueled by testosterone, he'll need more than will power to handle that problem.

> **Dad:** Alex, you know how much you mean to us. I am so proud of you. I've been proud of you since you could walk. I've watched you all these years and I've admired how you care about other people. You don't remember, but from the time you could walk you were taking care of others. When your little brother threw his toy out of the playpen and then cried after it, you would run and get it for him.
>
> I'm on your side Alex, I'm on your team. Son, I'm ready to move heaven and earth to help you, but . . .

The father's job

He reassures his son that he still cares about him and that he still sees him as a good kid. Then the father assures his son that whatever the son's problem, the father is capable of dealing with it. The message to the boy is this: It is the father's job to help his son.

> **Alex:** I *said* I'd never do it again. I *know* it's wrong. I told you that.
>
> **Dad:** I need you to be straight with me . . . Alex, this may be a big problem. I'm your father, so it's my job to help you.
>
> **Alex:** What are you going to do?
>
> **Dad:** I'm going to explain to you what might —I'm only saying *might* —be the case. Some regular boys like you in regular families like ours develop a problem — they get sexually aroused to very young girls and stay aroused to them. They think about these little girls a lot. Now this isn't these boys' fault. It just happens to them.

He is letting his son know that he is a knowledgeable and capable adult who can see that his son's problem gets dealt with.

> **Alex:** What's a lot?
>
> **Dad:** All of us have weird sex thoughts that flash through our minds and are gone. They're so different that most people can't even remember they've had them. I'm talking about having sex thoughts about little girls day after day.
>
> **Alex:** If somebody had those thoughts what would that mean?
>
> **Dad:** How long have you had sex thoughts about little girls?
>
> **Alex:** I don't know. I think since seventh grade. But I never did anything. And I never will again. You can believe me, Dad.
>
> **Dad:** How long had you planned to touch your cousins?

The important questions

Also notice how he phrases the important questions: "How *long* have you been interested in little girls?" "How *long* had you planned to touch the girls?" By asking, "How long have you. . . ?" he is giving his son the message that having such thoughts might be expected, and therefore makes it easier for his son to admit he has them. And, it's often easier for a teenager to talk about how many years or months he's been involved in a sexual activity than to talk about the activity itself.

> **Alex:** I thought about them naked, but I never planned anything—it just happened, honest. I don't know. One thing led to another. I bought them ice cream and it dripped on them, so I said I'd better get them cleaned up . . . and I don't know, honest.

> **Dad:** What do you think stops guys from telling their dads when they start daydreaming about seeing very young girls naked?

Non-sexual, non-embarrassing words

Again, he gives his son space to answer when he asks, "What do you think stops guys from talking to their parents about "sex stuff"? Notice, he avoids the emotionally loaded question: "Why didn't you tell me?"

What do we mean by giving the boy space to answer? Notice there is a pattern to these questions. They are matter-of-fact questions phrased in a way that does not embarrass the teenager. They also have little potentially embarrassing sexual content. This allows the boy to answer easily. In fact, what this parent is doing is giving his son the "non-sexual" words that the son can copy from his father so that he can now use those words to answer his father's questions.

"What do you think stops guys from talking to their parents about sex stuff?" is a question that is far enough removed to give the son space to answer. The boy's answer will, of course, be about why he could not talk to his own father about this problem. Again, the father gets important information from his son.

> **Alex:** Well, guys don't talk to their parents about that

---

stuff. It makes guys feel weird. My friends, anyway, a lot of them, if they said any sex stuff in front of their parents, their parents would go ballistic.

Dad: You mean their parents would be nervous because they didn't know how to help them. That's too bad.

Alex: Why?

Dad: Because it's a lot to handle all the things that go with sex thoughts and sex activities. Parents need to help their kids —without getting too personal. They need to let their kids know that some sex things can be dangerous for them.

Alex: Like what?

A teenager's sexual privacy

Alex's Dad points out that when "parents go ballistic" that often means the parent doesn't know how to respond in a helpful way. He also presents himself as a parent who knows that someone Alex's age needs help. Notice he indicates to his son—"without getting too personal"—that he intends to let Alex maintain his sexual privacy.

Dad: Some sex thoughts are dangerous. I know I've told you different, that everybody has hateful thoughts. Sometimes they want to smash somebody else in the face, but they don't do it. Just thinking about *wanting* to do it never hurts anyone, because it's what you *do* that counts. Only with sex it can be different.

Alex: Like what?

Dad: Well, you've been thinking about little girls.

Alex: Like, just thinking? Why?

Dad: Our sex drive is connected to our sex fantasies. For most sex thoughts that's no problem. But it's different when you work yourself up sexually over and over for a non-consenting partner.

Alex: What's that?

> **Dad:** You are a lot more powerful than your young
> cousins so you are taking advantage of them. That's
> why people call children non-consenting. You can
> convince them to take their clothes off or to let you
> touch them. But you just told me you know it's wrong.

Repetitive sex fantasies of a non-consenting partner

Dad indicates that sex thoughts of little children are a problem when they
are repetitive. He begins to educate his son about the difference between
a consenting and non-consenting partner with the phrase, "you are taking
advantage of them."

> **Dad:** Now, most sex thoughts are okay, it's the ones you
> have about girls or boys five grades behind you in
> school that can be dangerous.

> **Alex:** Why?

Dad is emphasizing the importance of the age difference; he's teaching his
son the distinction of five years difference in age. Having a sexual fantasy
about someone one or two years younger is not an indication of a serious
problem.

> **Dad:** Because those sex thoughts you have over and
> over about little children can lead you to want to take
> their clothes off. Like what happened with you and
> your cousins. You've been thinking about little girls for a
> while. I'm surprised something didn't happen before
> now.

> **Alex:** Are you disappointed in me?

> **Dad:** No, I'm disappointed in *me*. I wish I had talked to
> you when you were in sixth grade, when you first
> started having these sex thoughts. Something like this
> never entered my mind. You are going to need help
> with this, son. And I'm going to see that you get help.

A strong, capable father

Again, Dad reassures Alex that it is the parent's responsibility to help his son with this problem. This relieves some of the pressure and anxiety Alex feels. Alex's Dad has switched some of the focus from Alex to himself: the parent is the one who has to seek answers to this problem. By taking this attitude the father puts sexual interest in little girls in the same framework as the son's other problems. The son isn't responsible for solving this problem because this is a problem beyond what a parent could expect a child to solve. Dad also outlines his role: he is the adult who knows enough to get help for his son.

> **Alex:** Are you going to tell Mom? I mean, about me thinking crazy sex stuff?
>
> **Dad:** I think you should tell her. You know your mother loves you. She can handle this.
>
> **Alex:** What do you think she'll say?
>
> **Dad:** Oh, you know your mother. She's likely to go into high gear to help you solve this. She'll make lists. She'll find the best doctor. She'll have a list of books for us to read.
>
> There are doctors who specialize in treating kids with your exact problem. You can tell them anything.

Dad also assures his son that the boy's mother will join in these efforts. Alex's parents have talked about the situation with each other beforehand, and both have a thorough understanding of what they must do. They will be united in positive efforts to help the boy with this — as they've helped and guided him through other crises. They want Alex to know that he has two parents who understand and who will support him.

> **Dad:** Okay, Alex, here's our game plan. I think we should not keep this from your mother. So, first I'm going to ask her to come in here so you can tell her. Your mother will find you the right doctor.

Another thing the father accomplishes in this talk is to set a game plan for dealing with what may turn out to be his son's developing pedophilia. By using the phrase "*our* game plan," the father lets Alex know that this is a problem the whole family will handle together. Within the week they will have accomplished a certain amount and they will check on their progress.

> **Dad:** Now, we have to have some rules about when you and I are going to talk about this again. How would it be if we plan to talk — this is Monday — let's plan to talk about this again on Thursday. You have a game on Friday, so what do you say to planning to talk on Thursday to see where we are on dealing with this.

> **Alex:** Okay.

> **Dad:** Okay, then you stay here, I'll go find your mother. She's been worried. She'll be glad to hear you are all right and that we have a plan to deal with this.

Conversation essentials

In some families the mother may be the one who should talk to her son. What should she do differently? Nothing. Of course, exactly what you say as a parent will vary depending on your family. However the essentials will stay the same.

The take-home messages to the son:

1. This problem sometimes happens to regular boys in regular families, it's not your fault.

2. Your father already knows about this and can help you. And so will your mother.

3. It's important that we move quickly to deal with your problem.

4. There are professionals who deal with this; we'll take you to one

5. We have a game plan to set in motion and we will monitor the plan in weekly scheduled tasks.

—— WHAT ALEX'S PARENTS DID TO SAVE THEIR SON ——

Alex's mother did find her son a sex-specific therapist. She called her local mental health facility and asked this question: "I'm concerned that my sixteen-year-old son may be developing a sexual interest in first-grade girls, could you refer me to a sex-specific therapist who could do an evaluation?"

In that way, she found a referral to a sex-specific therapist in her city.

Consultation with the sex-specific therapist

In Alex's case, the testing revealed that Alex had some sexual interest in girls his own age, but his major sexual interest was in girls of grade-school age.

In his interview with the sex-specific therapist, he revealed what his father already knew — that he had been having sexual thoughts of girls much younger than himself since he was thirteen.

When he first started having sex fantasies about much younger girls, it didn't bother him. He kept the thoughts to himself. He knew that you didn't talk about that stuff, and he didn't want to be teased.

He didn't know why he gave his cousins a bath or why he touched one of them. The bath just happened. But then when he was so close to them and they were naked, he had an urge. After the incident, he didn't tell his cousins *not* to tell or anything. He wondered if his aunt would find out.

He also worried. Did this test mean his dad wouldn't let him play football? What would he say at school? He didn't want anyone to find out. His therapist reassured him that his test was confidential, identified only by a number. It would help to determine the cause of his behavior with his cousins.

Getting the family involved to protect the children

One of the first things that the sex-specific therapist did was to bring Alex' parents in to talk about protecting the children around Alex. With Alex in the room, he talked about the risks Alex posed to girls of grade-school age. He praised the little girls' parents for having a home in which these little girls had permission to tell their parents when someone touched them in a way that made them uncomfortable. He talked about the potential harm that Alex could have done to these little girls if the family hadn't moved so quickly. He explained that Alex, though he knew it was wrong and though he constantly fought his urges, without treatment was likely to lose control and do it again. He advised Alex's parents to organize the adults in the family — including the aunts — to monitor Alex (and to protect him) during family gatherings by being sure that Alex had an adult with him at all times.

He re-affirmed Alex's mother's message to the aunts, telling both parents that they should *not* trust Alex to be alone with any young children. Alex had already agreed to stop going to the grade school to help the boys develop football skills. The therapist also advised these parents to organize family members to help Alex find jobs to make money for college other than babysitting. He also told them that Alex needed to give up his plan to be a camp counselor next summer. In the months ahead, he wanted Alex to explore career possibilities that would place him in a work situation with adults and adults only.

You can learn much more about Alex's evaluation and treatment in Chapters Six and Seven.

—— LAST WORDS ——

What do mothers and fathers do that turns their sons into child molesters? Nothing. Still, one in twenty develop the disorder pedophilia. The first sexual incidents that offer an opportunity for adults—parents, grandparents, aunts, uncles, teachers, caseworkers, and therapists—to stop the disorder happen early in the child's life. Pedophiles report that more than half of their first acts occur while they are teenagers as we showed you in Table 2-1.

Simple curiosity about sex causes most sexual interactions between older children and younger children. Still, every boy who does develop a pedophilic disorder needs help to control or extinguish his sex drive toward children.[25]

So how do you tell the difference? You can't. Admitting the possibility that your son needs help, you take him to a sex-specific therapist for an evaluation. This relieves all doubt about which boy is experimenting and which boy is developing a serious problem that poses a risk to younger children. Remember that this act—if his total evaluation suggests that he has pedophilic symptoms or has developed the disorder, pedophilia — will save him from terrible tragedy in the future.

Early diagnosis not only saves the boy, it saves our children from being sexually molested. On average, every pedophile molests 12 children. By taking your son for testing and an evaluation, you could save him—and you could save 12 children.[26]

—— WHO ARE THE HEROES —— IN ALEX'S STORY?

If we are going to work together to save children, we have to move forward, take action and turn ourselves into heroes like the heroes in Alex's story.

- **The little girls** who told their mother are the first heroes. This was difficult, but they overcame their embarrassment and talked to her.

- **Aunt Kathie** is a hero twice. First, she created a relationship with her young daughters that gave them permission to tell. Second, she called the boy's mother immediately. Every time one of her daughters asked a sex question she told them the truth in simple language. As for telling her sister, she believed this act was something the boy's mother should know. And she was right.

- **Mom and Dad,** who educated themselves so they were able to consider the possibility that their son could have a problem. This was not easy. They had to overcome the nasty comments of friends and family who felt that by even gaining knowledge in this area, which meant they were considering the possibility that their son might have a sexual problem, Alex's parents were letting the family down.

- **Dad,** who talked to Alex, assuring him that he had parents who could help him. Dad was nervous — especially about talking about sex to a 16-year-old son. Alex was going through a surly, "what are my parents going to do next to embarrass me" stage. So, Dad took deep breaths, talked slowly, and stuck to points he wanted to make and the information he needed to find out to get help for his son.

- **Mom,** who acted to protect all the family's children and held her ground against her sister until the results were in. She followed one step of The Plan by isolating the molester. To do that she had to stand up to her sister and other family members who angrily *refused to consider the possibility* that Alex was sexually attracted to children and who were openly hostile.

She arranged for the evaluation. At the beginning, when she was searching for a therapist, she was very nervous and had doubts. It seemed all so secret. If she had any friends who had ever taken a teenager for an evaluation, they had never told her. She felt like a pioneer, and she didn't like that feeling. But she believed in what she read about pedophilia, and she wasn't about to take any chances that her son would have to grow up with that secret —and all the damage it would do to him. Suicide was the answer some people with this disorder found.

THE STOP CHILD MOLESTATION PLAN IN ACTION
— CHAPTER 2 —

1. Tell others the facts.	**Tell your family and friends:** • It happens in ordinary families where it is never suspected. • No little boy or girl says when they are eight years old, "Gee, I hope I grow up to be a child molester." If they develop the disorder called pedophilia, it happens to them. • The disorder starts early. In most cases, pedophiles have their first victim while they are teenagers. • It's most likely to occur in boys. According to estimates, it occurs in one in twenty boys. • Testosterone plays a major role. • A boy is often unable to go to his parents for help, because he doesn't know he has a problem. • Parents can help their children who may be developing symptoms by talking with them, giving them the facts, reassuring the teenager that there is effective treatment for pedophilia, and seeking testing and an evaluation by a sex-specific therapist.
2. **Save the greatest number of children in the shortest possible time.**	• Concentrate first on boys who are developing the symptoms of pedophilia because males are 99 percent of all child molesters. • Concentrate on teenagers, because most child molesters have their first victims before they are 20.
3. **Focus on the cause: Start saving children at the beginning — before a child becomes a victim**	• Be aware that a sexual interest in children happens to some boys and is fueled by the increased testosterone that occurs at puberty.

　　　　THE STOP CHILD MOLESTATION BOOK

3

CHILD MOLESTERS BY ACCIDENT

A FACT

Childhood sexual experiences are extremely powerful. A teenager's fantasies of sexually touching a child are likely to lead to acts of child molestation. Some boys —because they are unaware of the dangers —actually condition themselves to be sexually attracted to much younger children. Because no one tells them this, some boys develop a sexual interest in much younger children by accident.

YOUR OPPORTUNITY TO SAVE CHILDREN:

To protect a child you love from growing up to be a child molester, you can help him understand this cause of pedophilia —and how to stay clear of sexual fantasies that may endanger his healthy sexual development.

3

—— BRIAN'S STORY ——

Brian is 13. He's with a bunch of kids playing in the churchyard. They've run up the fire escape of the Sunday School building in order to slide down the pole from the second floor. Brian is sliding down the pole, and he's staring up with some anxiety at the six-year-old girl who's jumped on the pole before he got a chance to get all the way down. Will she smash into him? He sees her frilly pink dress and blonde curls. He sees her white panties scrunched to the side and the parts of her genitalia. Before this, he's only seen girls' genitals in pictures. He's staring up— startled and intensely interested. The friction from the pole sliding is giving him an erection. That night in bed he re-creates the same scene while touching his penis.

—— IN THIS CHAPTER ——

In the last chapter you learned that the first cause of pedophilia was it's spontaneous occurrence in childhood. As in the case of Alex, it just happens. "Child Molesters By Accident" tells you about the second cause of pedophilia and how to stop this cause at its beginning. In it you will learn: how children with no interest in molesting younger children sometimes build on an innocent childhood sexual experience to *condition themselves* to have a sex drive directed at much younger children:

- how sexual fantasies have the power to increase the child's drive to molest younger children —before he or she has touched a child;

- how sexual fantasies about categories of people differ in a very important way from sexual fantasies about individual people;

- how to educate your child about the dangerous power of sexual fantasies;

- how to give your children resources to prevent their own victimization.

Gene G. Abel, M.D. and Nora Harlow

——A CLEAR-CUT SUCCESS STORY——

If Brian's story lacks the drama of other cases in this book that's because it is the book's most clear-cut success story.

When pedophilia occurs because of an incident that arouses the boy, and then is reinforced in fantasy, it passes unnoticed by the boy and by his parents. It's invisible. It's also deadly effective as a way of creating pedophiles that molest millions of children. Yet Brian's story is our best success story because there are *no victims*. Brian's parents actually stop the development of pedophilia early, when Brian first starts having symptoms, and *before* he has a victim.

They do this by talking to Brian at an early age—at 13, when he is in seventh grade. They teach him what causes boys to grow up to be child molesters and the ways we have to stop that from happening. They also teach him about the dangers of having sex fantasies of child sex partners.

Brian's parents are successful. That's what we want. Someday, we'd love to write a book with one chapter after another of uneventful case histories—in which families stop the development of pedophilia *before* the teenager acts. Before he has even one victim.

——THE IMPORTANCE OF CHILDHOOD——
SEXUAL FANTASIES

Having sexual fantasies of very young children is a dangerous thing. Some teenagers who would never develop pedophilia in the way Alex did, by having it *happen to them* in childhood, actually condition themselves to have a sexual interest in much younger children.

Brian has a sexual experience that excites his imagination. He doesn't label the experience as good or bad, he only notices that it is exciting. Then he re-creates the experience in his imagination.

Brian, at 13, has just got his second batch of testosterone. He has a new and intense interest in all things sexual. He conditions himself because he doesn't know any better. He does it innocently. He does it by accident.

Children have very few sexual experiences, so each one takes on an importance greater than what we imagine as adults. Brian — until that moment sliding down the pole — had never had a sex thought about a girl that young.

This might be a fantasy a boy might never think of again. Or he might, night after night, use it, and feel the pleasure of his sexual response, expand on it, and keep it with him until he is an adult. When Brian thinks of a six-year-old girl night after night while masturbating, his thoughts are dangerous to the children around him.

—— THE POWER OF SEXUAL FANTASIES ——

Sexual thoughts are powerful. Sexual fantasies linked to orgasm are extremely powerful.[27] [28]

Orgasms drive us to repeat whatever we were doing when we had the last one. Every time Brian has a sexual fantasy of seeing a six-year-old girl's vaginal area, it reinforces his sex drive toward a young girl.

You should know that the orgasm you, the reader, have during fantasies of sex with an adult or during actual sex with that adult makes you have a great desire to use the same erotic fantasies again. Orgasm is a monumental reinforcer. This is yet another one of nature's ways of making sure humans have numerous opportunities to reproduce. And, even though in modern times the overwhelming majority of sex acts between consenting adults are *not* meant to lead to a baby, the original power of the orgasm is just as great as it was in the days we lived in caves.

—— THE MAJOR REASON ——
CHILD MOLESTERS STAY CHILD MOLESTERS

Why is the orgasm linked to sex fantasies of children important? *It's the major reason that child molesters stay child molesters.*

When a teenage boy, like Brian, masturbates to orgasm, if he is using a sexual fantasy of a very young girl or boy, then that orgasm will sustain and intensify his sexual interest in very young children.

It's true for Brian. It's also true for Alex, the football-playing teenager in the previous chapter, whose desire to molest little girls happened to him early in his life. Since little girls sexually excite him, Alex is quite likely to pair orgasm with his sex thoughts about his young female cousins. This pairing of his sex

A groundbreaking discovery

Dr. Gene Abel: Years ago Dr. Ed Blanchard and I did a research project published in the *Archives of General Psychiatry* that turned out to be more important than we expected. We surveyed the extensive world literature on sex fantasies. We found that children's first sexual experiences are critical to their adult sexual development. How do we define "first"? The child's first experience is the first one that the *child identifies* as sexual; the first experience where the child says, "This is sex."

Those experiences or fantasies about possible sexual experiences become exceedingly powerful. The child and teenager pair those first fantasies with arousal. That pairing guides the child to develop his or her adult interests. This is true of all of us — including teenagers and adults who develop paraphilias.

The man with a shoe fetish will recount his arousal to women's shoes starting at an early age. Men with urges to flash their penis, with urges to window peep, or with urges to sexually touch children will recount early sexual fantasies centered on the deviant behavior.

The finding that turned out to be unexpectedly important was this: We can change people's sex fantasies. Scientists used to believe that our sex fantasies just entered the mind from who knows where, that the sex thought simply appeared and there was nothing anyone could do about it.

Now we know the powerful relationship between the child's first sexual experience ("this is sex") and his adult sex interests. We know that sometimes haphazard or accidental happenings in childhood lead to child molesting fantasies that often solidify in the memory bank. At the same time, other more appropriate fantasies of sexual arousal to people of the same age appear, but are mainly ignored.

One of the most effective things we can do to protect children from sexual abuse is to teach teenagers and adults to stop using sex fantasies with children in them and to increase their use of sex fantasies with teenagers or adults in them

99

thoughts of younger children with the pleasurable sensation of masturbation further entrenches his sexual attraction to young children.

The problem is that neither Brian nor Alex can imagine any danger here. And they have no way of knowing that most other boys their age do not have these kinds of sexual thoughts.

Brian also believes that, since he is a good person and he knows its wrong to sexually touch a child, he'll never actually do it. He cannot imagine there is any connection between the sex high he gets in bed at night pretending he's going down a pole looking up at a six-year-old's vaginal area and the real thing. Some older teenagers like Alex take this belief a step further. Alex thinks that if he only *thinks about* children, he'll be less likely to ever *do* anything with a real child.

But he's wrong. With every orgasm paired with the image of a six-year-old girl, he's solidifying his drive to molest a little girl.

In fact, as you saw in the previous chapter, a teenage boy may believe his sex fantasies about little girls are harmless *because of what his parents have told him about other thoughts.* Say, his parents have explained to him that we all have bad thoughts, that having them is natural. "You may hate your sister and think for a second that you want to hit her, but you don't do it. You talk, you negotiate, and the thought goes away. The next hour you love your sister again. Thoughts are harmless."

That's quite true for momentary thoughts about hitting your sister. And it's true for most sex fantasies. But it's not true for thoughts of sexually interacting with a young child. Children—because they are children—have no ability to give consent. That's the issue. Children are off limits sexually. *What becomes especially dangerous then, are sex thoughts of little children linked to orgasm.* And, what makes this a real problem is that the boys have no way of knowing the potential danger of such sex thoughts. A boy would be unlikely to check with his parents—or even with his friends—about the appropriate nature of his private sex fantasies. So he may well go on for years building his sexual desire for much younger children, increasing his risk to molest a very young girl.

He needs to be told this. One of the best things we can do for our children is to teach boys the potential dangers in sexual thoughts featuring child sex partners.

—— Sex Thoughts About Specific People ——
Vs. Sex Thoughts About Categories Of People
An Important Difference

What if the teenager thinks about sexually touching a little kid, but never acts on it?

This is a good question. Do adults sexually touch every person they think about sexually touching? In any discussion about sex thoughts of teenagers leading to the sexual abuse of children, many people will focus on this issue. All of us can say, "Oh, I've had thoughts of a sexual nature that I haven't acted on." Everyone has had sex fantasies or felt sexual interest in someone with whom they have never had sex. Julia Roberts. Tom Cruise. A next-door neighbor. Someone at work. And so, to fantasize but never act seems quite probable. Most of us never have sex with the hundreds of specific people that we have a momentary fantasy about.

People who claim that it is common to have sex thoughts and never act on them are correct. However, we have to make a distinction here. The distinction: fantasies of sex with *specific people* versus fantasies of having sex with *a category of people*. People who claim it is *common* to have sex thoughts and never act on them are talking about a sex fantasy they've had about a specific person with whom they have never acted, and with whom they know they will never act. When you shift that to a large category of people — say, women, men, or children — the picture changes. Nearly all people who think about sexually interacting with women do, at some point in their lives, sexually interact with women. Nearly all people who think about sexually interacting with men do, at some point in their lives, sexually interact with men. And, nearly all people who think about sexually interacting with children do, at some point in their lives, sexually interact with children.

What we know for sure is that molesters who say that half or more of their sex fantasies are about sexually touching children molest many more children than men who say they seldom or never have sex fantasies involving children. When we divided the admitted child molesters in our Stop Child Molestation Study into men *with* sex fantasies of children and men *without* sex fantasies of children, we found a significant difference both in the number of children each group molested and the number of child molestation acts each group committed. Men who fantasized about sexually touching children molested nearly four times as many children as

A search for the man who *only* fantasizes but never touches a child

Dr. Gene Abel: During an extensive research project at Columbia University's Department of Psychiatry, Dr. Judith Becker and I tried to find men who had sexual fantasies of children but never sexually touched a child. During a five-year study for the National Institute of Mental Health, we set out to study three groups: those who had committed child molestation and still were molesting, a second group who had committed child molestation and had stopped, and a third group who had the interest, the desire, and the ongoing sexual fantasies, but had never acted on them.

This last group — the one with sex thoughts of children but no acts — was the group I considered the most important. I wanted to find out how they successfully put limits on themselves to never molest.

Eight men did come forward reporting that they had had the interest, desire, and fantasies, but never acted on them. However, when I talked with these men, I found that all of them were actual child molesters. Instead of being men who only had sexual thoughts of children, they were child molesters in denial. These men had made up their own private definition of child molestation. Some would say they had never molested a child because they only sexually fondled a child. As fantastic as it may seem, a few even claimed that, although they had had vaginal or anal sex with a child, they had never molested the child because they had not used force.

Our failure to find that third group was a big deal. We had grant approval; we already had the research money. We were advertising for these men in a city with a population of over seven million. More than five hundred men volunteered, but we could not find even one for that third group.

Now, it is believed that there are people who have sexual thoughts of children but never act on them. However, researchers have been unable to find them. There has been no systematic study of this group.

Gene G. Abel, M.D. and Nora Harlow

the molesters who said they had no fantasies of sexually touching children. As for acts of molestation, molesters *with* sex fantasies of children averaged more than double the number of child molestation acts.

(See Table 3-1.)

TABLE 3-1

How Sex Fantasies Increase the Molester's Number of Child Victims

	Number of Molesters	Average Number of Victims	Average Number of Acts
Men **WITH** adult-child sex fantasies	1,596	15	73
Men **WITHOUT** adult-child sex fantasies	2,314	4	30

Source: The Abel and Harlow Stop Child Molestation Study

——How To Talk To Your Child About—— His Sexual Fantasies

How can we use these facts to protect our children?

We can tell our children the facts so they can use that knowledge to get help if they need it. We know that the idea of talking to your teenager about child molesters and the dangers of certain sexual fantasies may be difficult, so we are giving you an example of how a conversation with your son might go. Of course you will use your own words. And, knowing your own son, you will have the best idea of how to approach him about this.

The good news is that you don't have to do this well. In fact, you can stutter and sweat and forget what you intended to say. The important thing is to *do* it. Once you open the door, your child has the powerful

THE STOP CHILD MOLESTATION BOOK

advantage of being able not only to bring you his questions but to come to you for help.

Why teach the children?

Nora Harlow: Sex education makes people nervous. Because they don't appreciate the power of the sex drive, they worry about the wrong things. The purpose of sex education is not to teach children and teenagers the facts of sex so they'll run out the door and have sex.

No one needs a book or a teacher. We humans have managed to reproduce ourselves before we had sex books, in fact, before we had words. We don't need sex education to teach us how to do it, we need sex education to teach us how to protect our health when we are overcome with this powerful sexual push of nature. What our children need from us is an education about sex aimed at relieving their fears — a sex education that protects them.

99

But if we talk about sex—won't something bad happen?

No. Having a talk about child molesters, child molesting, and the dangers of sex fantasies centered on very young children is something to do where you get two good things happening for the price of one.

Suppose your son or daughter is sexually healthy. In that case, you are teaching them about child molestation as a way of protecting them. Many children become victims because they are overwhelmed. They have no knowledge, they have no way of thinking about what is happening to them, *and* their parents have never talked with them about sex, which would give the children permission to tell their parents what sexual touch is happening to them.

The child needs to know that his or her parents know about adult-child sexual touch and that the conversation door is open through which the child can run with an assurance of getting help.

Won't talking about molesting children give our children the idea to molest?

Dr. Gene Abel: It's unlikely. I've evaluated thousands of men and women with paraphilias — and I've never heard one person say he or she started doing deviant sex acts because of a talk with another person.

——When To Talk To Your Child—— Earlier Is Better

Talking to your child about his sexual fantasies is easier than you might think, especially if you start at an early age. What's early? When we asked teenagers and then adults how young they were the first time they molested, we got two different answers. Teenagers who admit to sexually touching a much younger child and then go on to sexually interact with many younger children tell us that they have their first victims when they are 11 or 12.[29] Adults who admit to being molesters say they had their first victim at 14 or 15. What we know is that, for people who develop sexual interest in children, the sex thoughts come *before* the act. Often years before.

What you should do is to teach your child about the dangers of having sex thoughts about much younger children in the same way you would teach him about the importance of having safe sex. And you need to do it early. When is the best time? There isn't one special "best" time. We would say "best *times*." We believe parents should have *several* conversations at different times.

There isn't a specific age, either. We would say "good ages." This should be a conversation a parent has with his or her child at different times at different ages. Several conversations are necessary because—as in most things you teach your children—you can't assume that, just because you've talked to them once about a topic, the child fully understands it.

You will want to have this conversation with a child in sixth or seventh grade, at the time he is getting a puberty onslaught of testosterone and, along with that, a greater interest in sex. You will also want to have this conversation immediately following any incident. Go to Chapter Two, "Childhood Beginnings of the Desire to Molest" to read another father-and-son conversation that might take place in response to an incident. And there's a third reason to have this talk with your teenage son or daughter: You will want to educate your children so that they will grow up knowing the facts. That way they can, as adults, be forces of reason to stop child molestation.

—— How Do You Begin? What Do You Say? ——

Because many grown-ups become anxious when they think of talking about sex with their children—and even more anxious when they think of talking about a deviant sex activity—we're giving you examples of how such conversations might go.

These conversations are between Brian and his dad. The first time, Brian's mother pushed his dad to do this; he resisted on the grounds that his son was still too much of a little boy to sit still for a sex talk. He pointed out to his wife that, only two days earlier, Brian filled his nose with toothpaste and then blew it out to entertain his little sister. To Dad's way of thinking, nothing much could come from a serious sex talk with a son who still acted so childish. Although he was reluctant, Brian's dad decided, with continued prodding from his wife, to teach Brian a few facts.

When you do this, you might also think of the conversation as a teaching conversation. You will be teaching your children about child molestation as simply another one of the thousands of things adults in the family teach children about the way the world works. That's what Brian's dad decided to do. In his first conversation, he decided to tell Brian a few simple facts about child molesters: They start early; sex fantasies about very young children lead to acts; child molesters exist in all kinds of families; and medicines and therapy are effective.

The subject might come up quite naturally, from a comment about a child molester made in your son's presence. (Remember, we're most concerned about boys because millions develop pedophilia.) Or it might come up after a television show featuring a character who is a child molester. That's what happened at Brian's house.

—— CONVERSATION #1: ——
SEX EDUCATION ABOUT CHILD MOLESTERS

Notice that, while giving the facts, the father's conversation is also protective of his son's sexual privacy.

> **Dad**: You know how I've always told you that you could tell me anything that's upsetting you. And I would help you.
>
> **Brian**: Yeah. Do you think I'm upset?

Ignoring the negative

Dad starts by giving his son permission to talk to him. He ignores his son's response that would end the conversation. Every time the son becomes nervous and says something negative Dad simply ignores that comment and continues.

> **Dad**: No, I didn't want you to believe what you saw on that TV show. They're telling lies, sort of, the way they show it. It's not real.
>
> **Brian**: Dad, I *know* it's not real. It's a TV show. And anyway, we don't know anyone like that.
>
> **Dad**: Well, we might.
>
> **Brian**: We do not! Who?

Dad anchors the conversation to real-life happenings—first the TV show and then later to the child molester, who used to live in the neighborhood. Real life examples help the child learn and remember what he's learned. These also give the parent and child TV characters and real people to discuss and so shifts the conversation to a space removed from the two of them.

> **Dad**: There's something they never mention on TV.

Some guys get crushes — like 13-year-old boys get crushes on 4-year-old girls.

Brian: Gross-out!

Dad accepts his son's negative comments and continues.

> **Dad:** That is strange, isn't it? Most guys your age wouldn't have an interest in a little girl that young. They'd be interested in girls their own age or older girls —girls more developed. But there are a few guys your age who think just the opposite. They get sexually hot when they think about kids who are way too young for them. And they keep it a secret from their parents. They don't know that most of the other boys never have these thoughts. They think they're just like everyone else. So, when he's alone, some guy your age just thinks about little girls or little boys five grades behind him and keeps having these fantasies till he gets himself sexually worked up.
>
> **Brian:** No boys I know.

Easy-to-understand words

Dad, by correcting the television show's vision of a pedophile, gives his son new information. He talks about boys similar to Brian. And he uses easy-to-understand phrases like "getting a crush" and "girls and boys five grades behind." By using these non-sexual phrases he is giving his son words and phrases to use that will help Brian feel comfortable coming to his Dad for more information.

> **Dad:** If you were getting sexually turned on by little girls, would you tell the guys in your class?
>
> **Brian:** No way. Dad, are you trying to tell me I'm a pervert?
>
> **Dad:** No. I just want you to realize that none of us knows what sex thoughts others are having. You wouldn't tell them and they wouldn't tell you.

Sex thoughts are secret

Dad gives the important information that sex thoughts *are* secret—that Brian's friends would *not* tell him or anybody else. So nobody would know if his friends were doing dangerous things.

> **Dad:** Do you think if any of your friends were getting sexed up over little girls, they'd tell their dads?
>
> **Brian:** Geez, no! Their dads would kill them.
>
> **Dad:** You mean their dads wouldn't know what to do to help them stop?
>
> **Brian:** I guess . . . Do you know . . .

A strong and capable father

Dad lets his son know that something exists that will help the teenager with this problem—something a parent can do besides just yelling at the boy or as Brian says, "Their dads would kill them."

> **Dad:** I know enough that if any kid of mine had a big problem — like some older person was messing around with them or if they started getting sexed up over little kids — I could help them sort it out.
>
> **Brian:** You could?

Dad presents himself as a knowledgeable, strong parent who can take care of his son's problems—even if the problem is a sexual one.

> **Dad:** You know, we had a child molester in this neighborhood. So when you were younger, you knew a child molester.
>
> **Brian:** Here? Who was it?
>
> **Dad:** Do you remember Mr. West? The family with the two little girls? They used to live in the McClelland's house. They moved when you were in third grade.
>
> **Brian:** They had that great dog named Seagrams. And the pool. That one girl was older than me and she held me under the water. I remember that. I remember their

dad — he came home from work in the afternoon. I think I remember that. Their mom was nice.

Dad: Their Dad was a child molester.

Brian: Did he do it to the sisters?

Dad: I don't know. Your mother heard that he molested another little girl, a daughter of a friend of his. He moved soon after we heard about it. If he was like other child molesters, though, when he was your age he was thinking sex stuff to do with little kids, even then. He was telling nobody. And he was building up to do bad sex stuff to kids.

A child's perspective

Dad is showing his son that there are pedophiles in ordinary families and that the disorder begins at Brian's age.

Brian: What bad sex stuff?

Dad: Sometimes kids who are your age and a little older do things that hurt little kids. They don't mean to hurt the kid.

Brian: Like what? What sex things?

In answer to "What sex things?" Dad avoids taking on the adult perspective of sex either being oral or involving penetration. Instead, he takes on the more generalized idea of sexual touching that might occur to a child of 11, 12, or 13. The message of sex touching is appropriate to his son's age.

Dad: Well, like if a teenager gets a crush on a first-grade girl. And if he started holding her hand like she was his girlfriend or, kissing her, or trying to feel her between the legs — that would be bad. He'd be hurting her. Even if she didn't cry or anything.

Without embarrassment

Here the father avoids explicit sex language that would upset both the father and the son. He is educating his child without embarrassing either himself or his child. He also explains to Brian the important fact that sexually touching such a young girl hurts her—even if she doesn't appear to be hurt.

> **Brian:** Would one of my friends do that to my little sister?
>
> **Dad:** It's not too likely, but it could happen. You understand what I'm talking about. The little girl is seven. And I'm not talking about someone her age, another second grader. I'm talking about a boy who is much older—like a boy in seventh grade, one of your friends.

> **Brian:** If anybody hurt my sister, I'd beat him up bad.
>
> **Dad:** Hitting him won't solve the problem. It would probably keep him away from your little sister, but it wouldn't stop him from molesting other kids. What most people don't know is that we can help those boys get rid of those sex thoughts. That's what upset me about that TV show. They never talked about getting help for that young man or giving him medicine. And nobody talked about his parents, why they didn't take him to a doctor when he was your age before he molested a bunch of children.

A medical alternative

Again, Dad is teaching his son that there is a medical alternative; there is something more that can be of help besides getting angry. Dad also teaches the idea that we need to protect *all* children, not just Brian's little sister.

> **Brian:** Does my doctor give medicine to child molesters?
>
> **Dad:** No. You wouldn't go to your pediatrician. You'd go to a different kind of doctor who treats patients for sex problems. I just wanted you to know that if you ever have thoughts of kissing girls in first grade . . .

> **Brian:** Oh, yucky! I would never . . .

Dad: . . . or if any of your friends do, I know how to get you to a doctor who can take care of you.

Dad emphasizes that help is available, opening the door for the son to feel free to talk with his father in the future about molesters.

Brian: I don't understand. What's wrong with kissing six-year-old girls?

Dad: There's nothing wrong with a brotherly kiss. I'm talking about a long kiss on the mouth and thinking about the little girl as a girlfriend.

Dad helps his son understand the difference between good touch and bad touch.

—— CONVERSATION #2: ——
SEX EDUCATION ABOUT THE DANGERS OF FANTASY

Notice that near the end of the first father-son talk Brian says, "I don't understand. What's wrong with kissing six-year-old girls?" Just because you talk to your child once does not mean your child gets the picture. This is a conversation you would have several times at different ages. As you establish this as a regular discussion, you take away the mystery of child molestation. Most important, you give your child permission to come to you for help with his sexual fears or problems.

A son's confusion

Let's look at a more sexually explicit conversation that Brian's father had with his son a few days later. This is how he answered a question from Brian.

Brian: "Dad . . . what's wrong with a guy daydreaming about a first-grade girl? Uncle Brent is ten years older than Aunt Mary."

Dad: Good question. The family teased Uncle Brent about it. They said he was "robbing the cradle" when he fell in love with your Aunt Mary. But it's not the same thing as a seventh-grade guy and a first-grade girl. Mary was a grown-up. She was 23 when Uncle Brent got a crush on her. She was an adult, and so was

Uncle Brent. They were both adults when he kissed her for the first time.

Now, I see there's something I forgot to tell you about the danger of a seventh-grade guy thinking sex thoughts about a first-grade girl.

Brian: His friends would make fun of him — for being a . . . baby robber.

Dad: Okay, probably, but the trouble is a lot worse than getting teased. You see, when a boy your age gets a crush on a first grader — if he keeps working himself up over her or if he uses thoughts of her to get sexed up — then the trouble is he will most probably still like six-year-old girls. He will still get sexually turned on by little girls when he's all grown up — when he's 25 or 30 years old.

Brian: But she'd be all grown-up by then, too.

Dad: It seems like that's the way it would be. But that isn't what happens. The seventh-grader who thinks about this first grader to get turned on keeps liking first-graders when he is in eighth grade, ninth grade, tenth grade, even after he gets out of college. He just keeps getting sexually turned on by first-grade girls even after he gets married.

Brian: Gross!

His son's question gives Dad another opportunity to teach him. He's able to straighten out his son's natural confusion.

Dad: There's another sex thing I've never told you.

Brian: What sex thing?

Dad: It's about touching your penis.

Brian: Yeah.

Dad: Remember how your Mom and I used to tell you not to touch your penis in front of other people?

Brian: No. You never told me that.

Dad: Okay, you don't remember, do you? You were three years old. We taught you that it was all right to touch your penis when you were alone. You do that in private. You don't do that where others can see you.

Brian: So?

Dad: What you think about when you touch your penis is just as important.

Brian: Really weird. Like what?

Dad: Like what I said a couple of days ago. There are hundreds and hundreds of people it's fine to think about. People about your own age. And adults. Whatever you think about to get turned on *becomes* what turns you on. So, if you think sexy thoughts about girls your age or about older girls, then those girls are the ones you'll want to kiss. But, if you think sexy thoughts about first-grade girls — while you're touching your penis — then first-grade girls are also the ones you'll want to do sex things with.

Brian: Weird. Are you sure about this?

Giving your son the words to ask you questions

Dad has told his son about the danger of masturbating to fantasies focused on little kids using a language a seventh grader can understand. In the process, he's giving his son language the son can use to ask his father questions.

Dad: Yes. I know you would never *want* to hurt a little girl your sister's age. So, please promise me, if you ever — and I'm not saying you would — but if you are working yourself up with thoughts about girls much younger than you, promise you will tell me so I can find a doctor to help you stop.

Brian: How does it hurt these little girls when a guy just thinks about them? Do they know what you're thinking?

Dad: No, the problem, Brian, is that the sex thoughts come first. Thinking about very young girls to get sexually turned on comes first. After you have those sex thoughts a bunch of times, it makes you want to do it! The sex thoughts lead to *doing* the sex things.

Brian: Are you sure?

Dad: It isn't like the guy is going to run out in the street and grab a first-grader after the first time he thinks about it. It's that every time he touches his penis thinking sex thoughts about such a young girl, he increases his chances that he'll do sex things with someone that young — maybe even a year later or two years later. Then, he'd be a child molester. Your mom and I want you to know this, so you can help other boys who might be getting on the wrong track. Some of them do this by accident. And we wouldn't want you to just accidentally start thinking sex thoughts that could get you in trouble.

Brian: Does Mom know about this?

Dad: Your Mom is the one who asked me to talk to you.

The important message

The father lets his son know that he has two parents who are strong, informed, and can help him. In the earlier conversation he's given Brian two messages: You can tell me; I can help you. His reply in this conversation is consistent with those two messages.

Dad: Remember when I told you when you were little that getting really mad in your head, just thinking about how you hate someone, was okay. It was just in your head. And it wouldn't actually hurt anyone.

Brian: Yeah!

Dad: Well, that wasn't the complete truth.

Brian: What wasn't?

Dad: Some sex thoughts that teenagers have become a problem for them.

Brian: What sex thoughts?

Dad: The ones that might cause you to become sexually focused on young children.

Brian: Dad, you talk about the weirdest stuff.

Dad ignores his son's negative comment.

Dad: Becoming sexually interested in young children is serious. It probably seems strange to you because this is *not* stuff we explain to kids. I'm talking to you about it because I think you're growing up and can understand these things. I see you as more grown-up than a lot of boys your age

Dad tells his son that some sex thoughts can become dangerous. He also lets him know that he's telling him about this because he thinks Brian is old enough to handle this information that is grown-up information.

Dad: Most guys your age don't have thoughts about a girl so young being their girlfriend. But the ones who *do* sit around thinking and getting themselves turned on to thoughts about very young girls, those boys could be starting to have serious problems that need attention from a doctor.

Again, Dad lets his son know that his father can solve this problem.

Dad: If nobody helps them they could grow up to be child molesters like on that TV show. Or the father of those little girls who lived down the street. So, we would want to do something to help that boy so that didn't happen to him. It's important to do something when he's still young, before he hurts a bunch of little kids.

—— WHAT THE TWO CONVERSATIONS ACCOMPLISH ——

Brian's father gives his son permission to come to him for help. That's the most important thing he does in these two conversations. Beyond that, Brian's father put several important family possibilities in place:

1. This is a family that can talk about the fact that child molestation exists and that it hurts children.

2. This is a family open to the possibility that a child

molester is an ordinary person who may be living among their relatives, their friends, or in their neighborhood.

3. This is a family who knows some of the causes that lead to acts of molestation.

4. This is a family whose adults are strong enough to offer protection and help to a child who is a victim (20 percent of all girls and 10 percent of all boys).

5. This is a family whose adults are strong enough to help a teenage boy whose childhood experiences —fueled by his testosterone —are leading him toward possible acts of child molestation (1 in 20 boys).

—— WHAT BRIAN REVEALS ——

In the next few weeks, Brian started several similar conversations with his Dad. Finally, he told his Dad what had been worrying him.

Brian: Well, I've been wondering about something and maybe I should tell you.

Dad: What is it, son?

Brian: Once or twice I had . . . in the shower, sometimes I imagined this little girl, one I saw while we were playing in the churchyard. And last week when Cheryl had her friend over, I did something bad.

Dad: Her friend from kindergarten?

Brian: I don't know how to tell you. . . .

Dad: Any way you want to say it is fine with me. I am so proud of you for talking to me about what is worrying you.

Brian: Well they were giggling, almost screaming with giggles. When I went to tell them to pipe down, I saw them bouncing on Cheryl's bed. They were supposed to put on their nightgowns when they finished their bath, but there they were, naked. Anyway, I spied on them. Are you mad?

Dad: You must have been really interested.

Brian: I guess.

Dad: Is that what's bothering you?

Brian: No, I'm doing like you were saying. I'm thinking about what I saw a lot. I tried to stop thinking about those girls and the one in the churchyard. But no matter what I do, they're in my daydream again. Dad, they get me feeling . . . like sexy. Is that going to happen to me — like on the TV show?

Dad: (He doesn't get upset, he doesn't get angry.) Well, we aren't going to let it happen. What I want you to do, son, is think about something else. Think about a girl your age or a woman. It's easy to change your thoughts at your age. I'll take you to a doctor who can help you. She helps lots of boys like you. She'll know what you can do. She'll be able to help you a lot more than I can.

—— WHO ARE THE HEROES —— IN BRIAN'S STORY?

If we are going to work together to save children, we have to move forward, take action and turn ourselves into heroes like the heroes in Brian's story.

- **Dad** is the hero here, because he talked to his son about a serious problem that affects a lot of boys. He was reluctant and nervous about starting that first conversation. After all, this was the son who recently filled his nose with toothpaste. But this was also the son who had recently posted a big sign on his bedroom door that said, "Keep Out! This Means You!"

  He could have pretended that child molestation didn't exist, or only existed on TV. Instead, he treated the dangers of child molestation just as seriously as he treated drug abuse. Although child molestation is a major public health problem, it would have been far easier to remain silent.

  However, a dad's silence doesn't make the fact of molested children go away. As a matter of fact, if we all keep silent we increase the number of victims. Fathers and mothers are in a unique position. They have the freedom to tell their children the facts, to talk to them about the dangers. Those conversations that make some parents so anxious are instrumental in the future safety of their children.

Brian's dad won't get a trophy for discussing such a serious issue with his son. However, he should get a trophy — a hero's trophy — for stopping a cause of pedophilia right at it's beginning.

- **Mom** is a hero because she urged her husband to go ahead, to push through his misgivings and teach his son some facts about sex that would protect him.

- **Brian** was also a hero in this story. He knew that something was possibly wrong. Although he had no idea that his first sexual experience had had such a profound effect on him, he trusted his dad to help him sort out this new experience. He risked his sexual privacy; he risked being embarrassed. By revealing that he was having sex thoughts about little girls six grades behind him in school, he was taking a chance. Luckily, his dad paved the way for him to take that chance. The use of those inappropriate sexual fantasies, if ignored, could have a devastating effect on Brian's life. This child was in trouble. His first sexual experience was —by accident — filling his mind and arousing his body to the kinds of sexual interactions that seriously hurt little children.

Brian trusted his father, and therefore revealed this secret. This revelation may bring a stop to Brian's developing pedophilia. In that case, Dad and Brian are two real heroes.

THE STOP CHILD MOLESTATION PLAN IN ACTION
— CHAPTER 3 —

1. Tell others the facts.	**Tell your family and friends:**
	• Since some boys develop a sexual interest in much younger children at 11, 12, or 13, talk to your son about this problem when he's in sixth grade.
	• Teach your son the dangers of thinking about much younger girls to get sexually aroused and set a time to revisit the issue.
	• Establish yourself as a strong, calm parent capable of helping your child.
	• Correct what's missing from media depictions.
	• Tell your friends and family, "Here is a serious problem, here's what causes it, and here's what we can do to solve it."
2. Save the greatest number of children in the shortest possible time.	• Understand the one factor that builds and sustains the sexual drive to molest young children: the pairing of sex thoughts of young children with orgasm.
	• Create a home atmosphere that allows your child to come to you with any of his sexual concerns. Give your children permission to come to you for help both if someone older is molesting them *and* if they are having sex thoughts about much younger children.
3. Focus on the cause: Start saving children at the beginning — before a child becomes a victim	• Pedophilia may be caused by a boy accidentally conditioning himself to have an ongoing sexual interest in much younger children. He does this when he pairs sex thoughts of little girls and boys with sexual arousal or orgasms.

4

VICTIMS OF MOLESTATION WHO BECOME MOLESTERS:

WHY IT HAPPENS AND HOW WE CAN STOP IT

A FACT

Little boys who are molested frequently find much younger children to molest. Overwhelmed and extremely upset by their own sexual abuse, they often overcome their shame and fear of being molested by doing what the adult or older child did to them: They become the aggressor. Now they are the powerful ones. This is one of the many ways humans survive trauma. It's called "identification with the aggressor."

YOUR OPPORTUNITY TO SAVE CHILDREN

You can help save many generations of children from sexual abuse by telling others about this fact. If you hear that a friend's son has been molested, you can suggest that for his healing to be complete it must have two parts: therapy for his experience as a victim *and* therapy and testing to stop his possible identification with the aggressor.

THE STOP CHILD MOLESTATION BOOK

4

—— JAKE'S STORY ——
PART 1

Jake was seven when his three-year-old sister, Jennifer, was molested. Their mother, Sara, a special education teacher, had chosen the daycare center very carefully. It was small, with an adult teacher or volunteer for every four children. The owners, Michael Jones and his wife, were in the adult Sunday school class Sara taught at a local church. Jake had started at the daycare center when he was three and at seven was in their after-school program. Jennifer also started at three. She had only been there a few months when she told her mother what Michael Jones had done to her that day. As Sara listened, she realized her little girl was describing an oral sex act. She couldn't believe that Michael Jones had molested her daughter. He and his wife had been to their house for dinner. Still, Sara knew that a three-year-old could hardly make up a story like the one Jennifer had told.

She immediately checked in with Jake. Did he know anything about what happened to his baby sister? At first he said, "No." Then he coughed. Then he hung his head and started crying. He said he thought funny things happened when Mr. Jones took the girls into the bathroom. Why? Because "Mr. Jones takes a long time and they act funny when they come out."

Sara called other mothers. Three families charged the daycare owner. After Mr. Jones' arrest, as lawyers and therapists got involved, Jake grew more and more distressed. Sara thought it was because of his worry over his baby sister. Jake was always a super big brother, very protective of her. She reassured him that Jennifer was going to be fine. But he acted strange, as though he didn't believe her.

Then months later, on the night after Michael Jones finally confessed, waived his right to a trial, and was taken to prison, Sara got a shock. "I had put Jake to bed," she said, "and I was standing at the kitchen sink washing dishes, when I heard Jake's little footsteps coming up behind me. Then I heard him say in his sweet little voice, 'Mommy, is it okay for me to tell you now what Mr. Jones did to me?'

"He told me how Michael Jones had made him put his mouth on Jones's penis and how he threatened Jake by telling him he'd kill me if Jake ever told anyone. I was flabbergasted. I never once thought that my son could be molested. I only worried about my daughter. Then Jake told me this had been going on for years! I didn't know I had so much adrenaline in my body. My heart started beating so hard I felt I couldn't keep it in my chest."

Sara said that even though both her son and her daughter were molested, she felt her son suffered more. "I think that's because Jake was molested more often. My daughter, who was barely touched and was only three at the time, recovered almost immediately. She went on being her usual, sociable self; she was a happy little girl going on with her life. But even after three or four years had gone by, Jake had not recovered.

"At first, Jake withdrew," Sara said. "He didn't want to be around any of his friends. Even today he is very selective. And although he is very bright, his grades fell. He stayed away from all men except his dad. And he clung to me. When he was ten and eleven, he still didn't want me out of his sight.

"For years, he was afraid that someone would find out what happened to him. When he was seven, when it was time for him to tell his story to the case-worker, he curled up behind the pillows on my bed and screamed, 'No! No! This is bad! I don't want anyone to know! This is bad!'"

Sara had so many worries about her son after his molestation that she once joked to a friend—as a bit of dark humor—"Well, at least I don't have to worry about him becoming a child molester."

But she was wrong. When Jake was fourteen, she got a call from her next door neighbor: Jake had sexually molested the neighbor's seven-year-old son. The neighbor boy's mother was sympathetic; the neighbor boy's father called the police.

—— IN THIS CHAPTER ——

"Victims Who Become Molesters" tells you about the third cause of pedophilia and how to stop that cause at its beginning. In it you will learn:

- what causes boy victims to become molesters;
- the difference in number of victims between child molesters who were molested as children and those who weren't;

- why most men who molest boys are not gay;
- the six reasons molesters choose boys over girls;
- why boys won't tell you that they are being molested;
- how to talk to your son so you are more powerful than his molester;
- the biggest mistake parents make when they think of their son being molested.

——— WHY BOY VICTIMS BECOME MOLESTERS ———
IDENTIFYING WITH THE AGGRESSOR

From the moment he is molested, a little boy like Jake has an increased risk to become a child molester. Two experiences make him different from other little boys: He's experienced sex between someone much older and someone much younger. And he is likely to be overwhelmed not only by fear but also by shame.

Like other little boys his age, Jake had had very few sexual experiences. This made his experience with Mr. Jones loom huge in his mind. He was scared continually that Mr. Jones would make good on his threat to kill his mother. He had nightmares for years. He told his parents that they were "bad bear" dreams. The bad bear was Michael Jones.

When a boy like Jake is molested, if it is a traumatic enough event, even after the adults around him move to protect him he may continue to fear he'll be molested again.

The child's mind, however, has a powerful ability to protect the child. If his terror becomes too great, his mind spins the fear (of being molested by someone much bigger and stronger) into its opposite. The child imagines himself as the aggressor. Now he's the bigger and stronger one. Now he has nothing to fear, since it is he who molests younger children. This is called "identification with the aggressor."

A boy like Jake—at puberty—has high levels of testosterone, which lead him to be very sexually reactive. It was this combination of identifying with his aggressor and getting his adolescent testosterone hike that pushed Jake toward developing a sexual interest in much younger children.

Jake was scared that Mr. Jones was going to kill his mother. He was deeply ashamed, because even when he was very little he knew that what he and Mr. Jones were doing was wrong. The fear and shame were intensified because he was scared to death to tell anyone.

What Jake's mother didn't know was that it was boys like her son, boys who were repeatedly sexually abused over a long period of time, who were more likely to grow up to molest the most children.

—— SEXUALLY ABUSED MOLESTERS MOLEST —— THE MOST CHILDREN

When we look at a group of nearly 4,000 admitted male child molesters in our Stop Child Molestation Study we can see radical differences between the 53 percent of molesters who were never molested as children and the 47 percent of molesters who were sexually abused children. As a group, the sexually abused molesters start molesting at a younger age, they molest more children, and they commit more child sexual abuse acts.

Within that category were molesters who—as children—were sexually abused more than fifty times. Those boys who become molesters after being sexually molested more than 50 times have an astounding number of victims. They molest more than triple the number of children as the other child molesters. It's boys like Jake who—after identifying with the aggressor—are more likely to commit the most sex acts against children and have the most victims. (See Table 4-1.)

How can we use this fact to protect our children? Now that we know that sexually abused boys are at risk to become child molesters, what action should we take? Your part is essential: as you go about your everyday life, as you hear about a molested boy, tell the adults around him that he is at risk to become a child molester and will need to be evaluated by a sex-specific therapist.

We have to interrupt the path of little boys like Jake while they are young—before they have the chance to molest nearly five times as many children as the other child molesters. To do that, we have to save them twice—the first time from being victims and the second time from developing pedophilia.

TABLE 4-1

Contrasts: Average Number of Victims of Adult Molesters Who Were Sexually Abused as Children

	Number of Molesters	Average Number of Victims	Average Number of Acts
Not Molested as a child	*2,066*	*7*	*37*
Molested 1–50 times as a child	*1,674*	*10*	*51*
Molested more than 50 times as a child	*158*	*25*	*142*

Source: The Abel and Harlow Stop Child Molestation Study

What about girl victims? There are also cases of girl victims who identify with the aggressor and go on to molest many children. And, large numbers of girls never report their sexual abuse because they have the same fears and they are overwhelmed by the same lies told to them by their molesters. You can use these same basic techniques we're describing here to help your daughter reveal sexual abuse. For more information on the problems of the sexually abused girl, read Chapter Five, "Child Molester In the Family."

We've chosen to focus on the sexually abused boy, because we want to save the greatest number of children in the shortest possible time. Testosterone puts boys at a disadvantage, especially when they are sexually abused. Compared to girl victims, they become pedophiles in far higher numbers. They commit more acts. And they molest more children. On top of that, they molest little boys, some of whom then become molesters, and so on, and so on.

The biggest obstacle we face in saving these little boys is this: they never tell us they are being molested. Little boys are tough. They keep their secrets—and being molested is a terrible secret. How do you get tough little boys to tell?

——— CONSIDER THE POSSIBILITY THAT YOUR ——— SON HAS BEEN MOLESTED

First, you need to consider the possibility that your son has been molested. That possibility is stronger than most of us think. Look at these facts, which you already know from reading this book:

- One in ten boys are molested. That's one in ten boys brought up in all kinds of families, including ordinary families.

- Family and friends molest 90 percent of the children.

- Pedophiles come from all kinds of families —including ordinary ones. They don't decide to become pedophiles. It happens to them. It occurs accidentally by chance conditioning. And it happens early in their lives.

- The majority of men molesting children closely match U.S. demographics. They are heterosexual, married, educated, working and religious.

Jake did try to tell his mother or tried to make her guess, when he was very young. But Sara—who didn't know the things you know from reading this book—like most parents refused to let the possibility register.

Jake's major tactic was to try to avoid Mr. Jones. He made up silly excuses about why he didn't want to go to daycare and later to after-school daycare.

Sara: "I missed the signals. When he was four, I thought he was jealous of his baby sister's time alone with me. Then when he was six or seven, I thought Jake just didn't want to be around so many little kids. There were only two other kids his age at the daycare center after school and they were both girls."

But that changed with her daughter's announcement.

Now, Sara knows that Michael Jones is a child molester. She knows that someone close to her family, someone she trusts with her children can molest her child. Michael Jones fits the profile perfectly: He's married, educated, working, and religious. So why doesn't she immediately consider the possibility that Michael Jones molested her son?

Because of two new facts from The Abel and Harlow Stop Child Molestation Study she doesn't know:

- More than 20 percent of men who molest little girls also molest little boys.

- More than 70 percent of men who sexually abuse little boys are heterosexual, most are married, and have children of their own.

Sara knew Michael Jones and his wife and children well enough to know he was heterosexual. So, when her three-year-old daughter told her what Mr. Jones had done to her, she was in shock that this nice, religious, happily married, and financially reliable man could have committed such an act. The possibility that he might have also molested her son never entered her mind, because she was like most parents: She was, in general, far less protective of her son than her daughter.

Even if she were to consider the possibility that her son might be sexually abused, she would never consider a man who was known to molest little girls. Sara mistakenly believed that some molesters targeted girls and others targeted boys. On top of that belief she added another belief that seemed to make sense: Heterosexual men targeted girls; homosexual men targeted boys. Seen from an adult's view, that would seem to be the case.

Like nearly everyone else, Sara never considered the possibility that an obviously heterosexual man—even one she knew to be a molester of little girls—would molest her son. She expected the molester of little boys to be gay.

—— REALIZE THAT MOST MEN WHO MOLEST —— LITTLE BOYS ARE *NOT* GAY

In the Abel and Harlow Stop Child Molestation Study when we asked the male molesters who sexually abused boys about their preferences in adult sex partners—men or women, the majority said they preferred women. The majority said they were heterosexual. The majority said they were married. These were the reports of the 1,047 male molesters who said they molested boys. Only 8 percent said they were exclusively homosexual. More than 70 percent said they were heterosexual. Another 9 percent said they were equally heterosexual and homosexual in their adult sexual preferences. (See The Abel and Harlow Stop Child Molestation Study in the Appendices.)[30]

In most cases, sexual interest in children runs on a different track than sexual interest in adults. One has nothing to do with the other. For most molesters, it is the sexual desire for a *child* that is important. Note the emphasis on the word "child." Many molesters, like Mr. Jones, molest girls *and* boys.[31] The sex of the child is far less important than the simple fact that the child is a child. These molesters are sexually attracted to *small bodies.*

—— WHY DO MOLESTERS CHOOSE BOYS? ——

Consider this fact: some molesters of boys, when they are tested, have a higher sexual interest in girls. [32] They say they molest boys because:

- Boys are more accessible; their parents don't protect them as much as they protect little girls.

- Parents rarely suspect their sons are being molested.

- Boys try to be "tough"; they'll keep the secret longer.

- Boys are afraid of being called gay because of having a sexual experience with a male, so they'll keep the secret.

- Boys take more responsibility for sex acts; it's easier to convince a boy that whatever happens when he's molested is the boy's own fault.

- Boys offer molesters the biggest advantage: They can molest hundreds of boys without getting caught.

—— WHY YOUR SON WON'T TELL YOU ——

There are several reasons why a boy who has been molested won't tell even the one person he's closest to in the world—his own mother.

Tough boys don't cry

Jake, at seven, felt deep shame. Boys know at a very early age that they are expected to be tough and to be brave when they are hurt. Because they know that they are expected to handle bad situations without crying or acting like a "sissy," it is often, ironically, the toughest boys who keep the secret longest—tough little boys like Jake. Believing that he had to handle this terrifying situation like a strong male, believing even at three, that it was his job to protect his mother, the little boy kept his silence.

The boy's family approves of the molester

It's far easier for a child to report a molester that the family doesn't like or doesn't even know than one they do. Sara said she was overcome with horror remembering what she said to Jake every morning as she dropped him off: "You be a good boy and do whatever Mr. Jones tells you."

Molested boys feel guilty

Rather than talk with the caseworker, Jake hid behind the pillows, crying, "No! No! This is bad!" What Sara didn't know is that Mr. Jones also convinced Jake that Jake *wanted* to do it. His evidence: The little boy had many sexual experiences with Mr. Jones, but didn't tell, therefore, he wanted it. Even a boy of three or four can feel severe guilt. He's already absorbed the idea that he should keep his clothes on and that there should be no touching of genitals in public. The child, if he takes his clothes off or lets someone else do it, often feels that he's been bad.

Molested boys worry that they are gay

Boys like Jake, who are molested at six or seven, and certainly boys molested at 10, 11, and 12, often worry that they are gay. They worry because they sometimes *do* get erections while they are being molested. They also worry because they think that the molester picked them out because he knew that—deep down—the little boy wanted to sexually interact with another male. Unfortunately, the adult protectors of these boys often believe the same things.

Sara had a run-in with her brother-in-law after she asked him why he always left the room when she or her husband talked about Jake. His answer: "Look, every man gets approached by some homo. Jake should have told the man no."

We've heard lawyers defend an accused child molester by explaining the fact that the molested boy got an erection at the time of the encounter. He says this as though it has great significance. The lawyer sees this from his own experience as an adult. Adult males get erections because they are sexually attracted to another adult. A boy gets an erection for an infinite number of reasons. When his mother changes his diaper. When he's thinking about baseball cards. When he's playing hopscotch. When he's asleep. The fact that a little boy has an erection is irrelevant. The relevant fact is that a child, whether or not he gets an erection, has no ability—because he is a child—to give consent to sexual interactions with an adult. Read the next chapter, "Child Molester in the Family" for more information about consent.

Molested boys protect their families

Jake was a super-tough kid who kept the secret for five years. He told Mr. Jones he would never tell on him. In return, Mr. Jones promised to let Jake's mother live. For five years Jake told no one. He also refused to tell through five months of therapists and lawyers. No matter what happened or who asked, Jake was keeping his promise.

—— THE BIG LIE: WHAT MOLESTERS TELL BOYS —— TO KEEP THEIR SILENCE

The molester tells the boy one major lie: If you tell anybody about what we're doing, very bad things will happen to you and your family. The message is always the same, but what they actually say comes in many forms.

A molester may—like Mr. Jones—threaten to kill a boy's parent or his pets. In Chapter One, Steve, an adult survivor, told the story of the church activities director who simply carried a briefcase that he left open occasionally so the boy could see the gun inside it.

There is another threat the molester makes that will keep an older boy from telling his parents: He may convince the boy that this sexual interaction means the boy is gay.[33]

As we said before, a molested boy worries that being molested *means* he is gay. The reason he worries is because his molester uses this possibility as a threat. The molester's threat might be that he, the molester, will tell the boy's parents exactly what the boy has done: "If you don't keep doing this with me, I'm going to tell your mom and dad, and they'll be really upset."

Now, the molester (who is usually heterosexual, married, and a father) does not think of himself as gay. Typically, he will have no interest in sexual interactions with consenting adult male partners. What he knows is that boys of this age get messages from other boys and from the adults around them that they are expected to never engage in male-to-male sexual activities.

There are a number of other threats molesters commonly use that sound silly to adults, but which terrify children like Jake. One molester threatened a six-year-old boy that if he told his parents, the molester would call the police and the police would grab the boy and put the little boy in jail and he'd never see his mother again. Young children don't know the way the world works. They believe what adults tell them. Molested boys are especially vulnerable, because they are stopped from going to their parents to check on whether or not what the molester says is true.

Jake's molester had convinced him that he was to blame—that because he sometimes got an erection, he was responsible. Because of this, Jake was living with a second of his molester's threats. The man had warned Jake that if he ever told, he would tell the boy's mother *exactly* what Jake had done and then his mother wouldn't love him anymore.

To adults this sounds silly—the molester's big threat is that he'll tell a parent that he's been molesting their child. But to a child this can cause extreme anxiety.

——Three Obstacles A Mother Must Overcome —— Before Talking To Her Molested Son

Very young boys, who do tell, like Jake, go to their mothers.[34] A mother has a serious challenge in talking to her son. She must overcome the boy's *fear of telling*.

Before she begins, a mother has to overcome three obstacles.

1. Giving the boy permission to talk about his sexual experiences.
2. Dealing with her own strong emotions.
3. Overcoming the molester's lies to the child

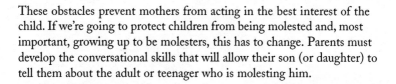

A double tragedy

Nora Harlow: I feel such sympathy for these molested little boys. Theirs is a double tragedy. First, they have to deal with the pain of being sexually abused. Then they are at high risk to *become* molesters. A large number of molested boys are hit with a second tragedy — dealing with their own sexual drive toward children. By the time they've molested other children and gotten away with it, by the time they are in their twenties or thirties, the fact that *they* were molested as children carries no weight. And it shouldn't. As responsible adults, our job is to stop molesters. What's most important is to protect the children who might become the victims of a child molester. No matter what caused the molester to do it.

These obstacles prevent mothers from acting in the best interest of the child. If we're going to protect children from being molested and, most important, growing up to be molesters, this has to change. Parents must develop the conversational skills that will allow their son (or daughter) to tell them about the adult or teenager who is molesting him.

1. Giving the child permission to tell you

It's much easier for a molested child to tell his mother if he lives in a house with parents who have already told him what bad touch is (touching or rubbing you on the parts of your body that are covered by your bathing suit) *and* a few facts about child molesters. (They lie to kids and tell them their mom and dad will be mad at them; sometimes they are grown-ups in your own family or who take care of you.) Knowing these facts makes the child feel less anxious about talking to his parents. The child feels he has their permission to tell them about this bad thing that has happened to him. In the last chapter, Brian's father had a conversation with his son that might serve as a model.

Unfortunately, many good parents, without realizing what they're doing, unconsciously forbid their children to tell them if they have been molested. They do this by becoming violently emotional about the child molester and the act of child molestation. "If anyone dared to molest a child of mine, I'd kill them," they say, ignorant of the fact that their child *is* being molested by their best friend, by Uncle Sean, by a loved cousin—or even by Daddy.

Or they say, "That's so disgusting, it makes me want to puke. How could anybody do *that?*"

What's hard for parents to understand is when they say, "How could anybody do *that?*", their child may have been doing *that* and feeling great shame. Children are not like us. They are not short adults. What these parents are teaching their child is that he must never tell them that he has been molested. Never in his whole life.

2. Keeping emotions in check: How to become more powerful than the molester

Violent emotions keep parents from helping their children heal. The first thing most parents have to deal with before they can help their molested child is their own strong emotions.

Sara felt her heart beating so hard she was afraid it would split her chest open. Some of this emotion comes from Sara's own feelings of guilt. She was the one who chose the setting where her children were molested. She was the one who invited her son's molester to dinner. For years after the discovery, she would break into tears.

That's why you must not give in to your emotions. *You will frighten your child.* Remember, the molester has held something over the boy's head that the boy believes will happen and will be a catastrophe for him if he tells. When a mother falls to pieces in front of a child, the child will believe that his molester told him the truth. He will believe that being molested is the worst thing that can happen to him—or his mother. He will also believe that he has to handle this alone, that his mother will be of no help.

The mother's attention to her own feelings in front of the child creates a situation that makes him feel *more* protective of her, and quite likely increases the boy's reluctance to tell. And so, the mother won't know that he was molested. She will be unable to get the help for her son that he needs.

The child molester has very likely already convinced your child that he is more powerful than you are. Your child is overwhelmed, but believes he cannot go to you for help. Your job is to become more powerful in your child's mind than the molester. Your job is to restore yourself as your child's protector.

If you suspect your son has been molested and you feel too emotional to talk to him, there are a couple of things you can do. Practice your conversation in front of a mirror. Keep practicing until you look like a calm and helpful parent. Practice in front of another adult. Keep practicing until your partner assures you that you look like a calm and powerful parent. Keep in mind, your ability to talk calmly to your son allows you to be the most helpful to him.

3. Overcoming the molester's lies

If Jake's mother had suspected something earlier and had asked Jake point blank if he was molested, he would have said "No." For many little boys, simply asking them isn't enough. Sara needed to give Jake permission to tell by dealing with Mr. Jones's threats. First, she needed to assure him that she and his dad were fully able to protect him from the molester—no matter what the molester said. She also needed to reassure him that, if he did tell, no one would kill his parents or his pets, he wouldn't go to jail, and no matter what happened, his mom and dad would still love him.

—— A MOTHER'S CONVERSATION WITH HER —— MOLESTED SON

Here is the conversation Sara had with Jake after he told. Because she was overcome with emotion, all she said at first was that it wasn't Jake's fault. While she finished the dishes, she went over in her mind what she would say. Knowing that the mother must convince her child that she is stronger than the molester, Sara began the conversation like this:

> **Sara:** Jake, you don't know how glad I am that your
> sister told me about what Mr. Jones did to her. It makes

me feel so good to know about this so I can take care of her.

Notice that Sara starts by telling Jake that it's a good thing for children to tell mothers about bad touching. She says it was a good thing for his little sister to tell. She follows this with a second positive statement: " . . . so I can take care of her." Here she's letting her son know that she is strong and can take care of him.

> **Jake:** How do you. . . ?
>
> **Sara:** Take care of your little sister?
>
> **Jake:** Is she going to get a spanking?
>
> **Sara:** Absolutely not. Children *never* get spanked for telling about bad touch. Mommies want them to tell so the mommy can take care of them.

Sara assures her son nothing bad will happen to him if he tells.

> **Jake:** Why?
>
> **Sara:** Mothers are supposed to know when people like Mr. Jones touch little kids. My job is to take care of you kids, take care of your sister —and you. It's all right for boys to tell, too.

You are supposed to tell your mother

Sara lets Jake know that mothers are supposed to know. She repeats that it's all right for him to tell her.

> **Jake:** Do boys get spankings?
>
> **Sara:** I *want* you to tell me about the bad touch. No spankings. Sometimes a grown-up who's doing bad things to kids will lie and say that if the kid says no, he'll tell the mom and she'll be mad —so mad she'll punish her own kid. That's a big lie. I'm not mad at your little sister and I'd never be mad at you. I want you to tell me so I can help you.
>
> **Jake:** No spankings?
>
> **Sara:** No. Only kisses.
>
> **Jake:** What's bad touch?
>
> **Sara:** Remember, I told you it's when someone touches the parts of your body that are under your bathing suit.

Jake: Did he touch my sister there?

Sara: Yes.

Jake: What lies does he tell kids?

Sara: One lie is: I'll hurt your mom. Or I'll hurt your dad. Or I'll hurt your dog.

Jake: What happens if he does that?

Sara: Your dad and I would never let him hurt us. We are stronger than any man who does bad touch. He just says he's going to hurt your mom or dad to trick you. If a man ever says that to you, you run and tell me and I'll take care of it.

Becoming stronger than the child's molester

What she's just done is enormously important. When parents talk to children, they not only have to give them permission to tell, they also *must* deal with the lies the molester has told them to keep them silent. So Sara starts from the premise that Mr. Jones has told her son lies so he'll keep the secret. She assures Jake that she knows all about this — that molesters tell children lies. She gives some examples, then she asks her son, what lie did he tell you?

Sara: What did Mr. Jones tell you would happen if you told me about what he did to you?

Jake: Nothing.

The way Sara talks to her son — asking *what lie* the molester told him — allows the boy to talk first about the molester's lies. This is easier than being asked first about the sexual touching that may have left him feeling ashamed and guilty.

Sara: I need to know, honey, so I can stop Mr. Jones from hurting you and your sister again or from hurting any other kids. Did he say I'd spank you or I'd be mad and never love you? That's a lie. I'll always love you.

No matter what happened, I love you

Sara continually reassures Jake that she loves him. The fear that a parent won't love them anymore keeps many children from telling.

Jake: I'm sorry Mommy. I didn't mean to do it.

Sara: You didn't *do* anything bad.

Jake: He said I had to or he'd kill you and then I wouldn't have any mommy.

Jake starts crying. Sara takes him in her lap and hugs him.

Sara: That's a mean lie. You must have been really scared when he told you that lie. When I was your age, I would have been very, very scared. What a brave little boy you were to try to take care of me like that.

Being seven years old and scared

Sara keeps her emotions under visible control, even though it is very difficult for her. She praises her son for trying to take care of her. While she hugs him, she lets him know that she understands about being seven years old and being scared. Notice that everything she says to Jake about himself is positive. She avoids her strong desire to ask him why he didn't tell her when he was three, because that would suggest that he was at fault. Besides, she knows why he didn't tell her: Mr. Jones scared him to keep him quiet.

Jake: He can't run out of jail, can he?

Sara: No, he can't get out. Now that Daddy and I know about the bad touch we can keep you safe. We love you very much.

Sara reassures her son that he is safe from his molester. She tells him again that she loves him.

Sara: Those are bad things he did. Telling lies and touching you and your sister. Grown-ups should never do bad things like that to kids. I'm so glad you told me. Now, I can help you. How old were you when Mr. Jones first started touching you and telling you lies?

Mommy and Daddy can keep you safe

Once her son tells her the lies, she can assure him that they *are* lies. Next she asks him, "How old were you. . . ?" Again, this question gives the child an easy way to tell her he's been molested. At the point that the child tells the mother that he was molested when he was three, she assures him once again that she loves him, that it's good to tell her, and that she and his dad are strong parents who can help him and protect him even when this grown-up has done this bad thing to him.

> **Jake:** It was after Christmas, when I started going there.
>
> **Sara:** That year you were three. Jake, I love you so much. I'm so glad you're telling me this. Now, I can help you just like I'm going to help your sister. OK, will you tell me all about it?

At this point, Sara says no more. She just listens. This is hard for parents. It's painful information to hear. And it's difficult to wait silently for the time it takes a young child to tell.

When Jake has finished and leaves the room, Sara writes down what he said. Then she calls Child Protective Services to report her son's molestation.

Sara might also say: "Tell me what you remember. If you remember more later, you can tell me later."

The way she listens to her son is important. She listens quietly. She does this without acting nervous or upset. What a parent does *not* want to do is give in to her feelings *before* she helps her child.

—— THREE ESSENTIAL STEPS WHEN TALKING —— TO A MOLESTED CHILD

When she talks to Jake, Sara takes these three steps that are essential for any mother in such a situation:

1. Mother listens, giving her child her full attention until he has completely finished.

2. Mother writes down what the child has just told her.

3. Mother calls the authorities.

—LAST WORDS ABOUT THE QUESTIONS—

You will notice that Sara asks her seven-year-old son several questions that prompt the child to say he was molested. Questions like, "What *lies* did Mr. Jones tell you?" or "How *old* were you when Mr. Jones did bad touch to you?" Questions that assume that the child had been molested.

It's true that molestation cases have been damaged in court because the therapists or lawyers or police investigators repeatedly asked the children questions like these. Those adults should *not* question children in these ways. That would potentially contaminate investigative evidence.

Should a mother ask her child such questions? Yes. Why? For all the reasons the child molester keeps her child from going to her for help. What's at stake is something much bigger than a court case, what's at stake is the healing of her child. A mother's job is *not* to prepare a court case, or to stand up to a defense lawyer who is cross-examining her. A mother's job is to be an advocate for her child. Questions such as these allow you to protect your child.

Family adults caring for children should never try to be independent evaluators. That's not their job. This is in marked contrast to the independent evaluations expected of criminal justice or child advocate professionals who do formal investigative interviews of a child.

As a mother, your job is to protect your child from harm, to give your child the feeling that he is secure in your care. What stops us from saving three million children is *not* that mothers ask their children incorrect questions. What stops us is this: Three million children are being molested and their parents have never asked them anything.

—— JAKE'S STORY ——
PART 2

—— THE SEVERELY MOLESTED BOY BECOMES ——
THE MOLESTER

Sara took her son and daughter to a family therapist to help them heal. The family therapist helped Jake a great deal. The boy was full of shame for his participation in sex acts with Mr. Jones. Jake—one of the toughest, most responsible boys of seven you ever want to meet—took on the full responsibility and blame for his molestation and his sister's. Simply telling him it wasn't his fault made no impression. Helping him let go of that burden took years.

Jones served three years in prison and then was back in the neighborhood and back at church. Jake, who had been doing better, suddenly began having nightmares again. Jake's parents moved their family to a different church.

Then when Jake was twelve, his mother found an odd thing in his room. Jake had been collecting pictures of very young children. He cut them from magazines and pasted them in a special scrapbook he kept in his closet. Sara admired his artistry in placing the pictures on the page. She mentioned it to her husband, and with neither parent questioning Jake, his scrapbook work became an accepted addition to the boy's other hobbies—collecting baseball cards and building model battleships.

What Jake was doing was looking at the pictures of these very young children while imagining touching them sexually. He would kiss them and stroke them.

He had turned the fear of his sexual experience with Jones inside out. Now, the terror he experienced in an adult-child sexual interaction was gone. Instead, as he imagined the same interaction, this time with himself as the bigger and stronger person controlling the sexual touching of a smaller and weaker child, he found a source of pleasure.

What Jake's parents didn't know was that he had begun to masturbate while looking at these pictures. He was pairing his orgasm with fantasies of sexually touching much younger children. As he got older, Jake began to extend this practice beyond his scrapbook pictures. At the swimming pool, standing chest deep in the water, he would masturbate while watching real children run around in their bathing suits. Sometime before his fourteenth birthday, Jake got that second batch of testosterone that comes with adolescence. His sexual activity accelerated. He was building his sexual interest in little kids by pairing his fantasies of them with orgasms.

Next, he began window peeping on the little boy next door. Then he offered to play "summer rain" with this seven-year-old boy. He would prompt the boy to put on his bathing suit, then he would spray the boy with the hose, concentrating much of the spraying on the boy's crotch. While Jake was spraying, he masturbated. Rapidly, Jake's involvement in the "summer rain" activity intensified. First, he pasted a picture of the neighbor boy in his scrapbook. Then, he kissed the picture so often during masturbation that he kissed the face off the picture. He watched the boy through a window every day. Finally, he took the boy into his bedroom, "to show him his battle ships," and molested him.

—— HOW JAKE, A MOLESTER'S VICTIM, BECAME —— A MOLESTER HIMSELF

What happened with Jake demonstrates how a molested boy can turn the traumatic event inside out. First, the boy is afraid, ashamed, and feels he has lost all control of his life. Then he identifies with his aggressor. As if a magic cloak had been thrown over his trauma, he is at peace. Through his sex fantasies of a younger child, he gains control of his frightening experience. He pairs orgasm with thoughts of sexually touching little kids, which builds his drive to sexually touch little kids. And finally, when his testosterone level increases at puberty, he moves to act on his fantasies of fondling, caressing, molesting young boys.

Jake's parents had been pleased by his new confidence. They never considered that their son's trauma might have returned in a new form. They knew nothing of his use of scrapbook pictures in masturbation. That was a private activity.

—— A FAMILY OUTLAWS SEX TALK ——

Jake had a good reason for not telling his mom and dad anything about his thoughts of sexually touching a much younger child. He now lived in a home where sex talk was outlawed.

After two years of family therapy, Sara's sense of logic told her that Jake, rescued at seven, was so upset that, of course, he would never do anything like that to another child. Jake believed that, too. Father and son agreed with Sara when she said, "I think we need to put this behind us." After Mr. Jones' release, in an effort to never see Jake's molester again, Jake's parents had even moved their family to a different church. After they stopped therapy, the family entered a period where they pretended nothing had ever happened. Their idea: If nobody talks about it, then none of us will think about it, and then there won't be any problem.

So there was no help for the little boy. Jake was back in the same place he had been in when he was seven. He felt he had no one to go to for help. He had to deal with his sexuality on his own. Dealing with it on his own, he had conditioned himself to develop a sex drive to an event he feared—

---

a much bigger and stronger person sexually interacting with a much smaller and weaker person.

By the time Jake molested the neighbor boy, he had collected nearly a hundred pictures of little kids and had paired them with masturbation and orgasm numerous times, so that his sexual interest in children was ingrained.

After the neighbor's report to the police and their 14-year-old son's arrest, Jake's parents felt so emotionally keyed up and harassed that all they could do at their first meeting with the sex-specific therapist was vent their anger. Especially Sara. The neighbors were making their life a nightmare. Although the neighbor boy's mother had been understanding, the father had called the police. How could anyone have arrested Jake? He had been through so much. The judge, pending adjudication, had ordered Jake to the sex-specific therapist for an evaluation.

Molested molesters: What the statistics mean, and what they *don't* mean

Dr. Gene Abel: Forty-seven percent of the male child molesters in our Study were sexually molested themselves when they were children. Although we do know that being molested as a child increases the risk to the boy victim that he will become a child molester, please remember that *the majority of men who were molested as children never have any sexual urges toward children.* Slightly more than half of male child molesters were never molested as children, but they became child molesters anyway.

And, although Jake admitted he did the molestation, Sara still refused to believe it. "That little boy next door is confused. Something might have happened, but it wasn't child molestation. Jake would never hurt a kid that way. He couldn't—not after what he's been through."

—— THREE REASONS VICTIMS MAY MOLEST ——

The sex-specific therapist explained that they would go about finding what was causing Jake's behavior in an orderly fashion. There were many possibilities—but three rose to the top as the most likely causes:

1. Experimentation,
2. Modeling,
3. Identifying with the aggressor.

Jake could be going through a period of sexual curiosity and have interacted with the neighbor boy as part of the sexual experimentation that most kids his age do. Jake's having been molested may have had nothing to do with this recent incident. However, the therapist explained, for a boy who's been molested there are two more possibilities. The experience may have served as a model. "Children model: They do the things they see others do. So, a molested boy may copy behavior he's seen in a grown-up. The boy may model his own molestation by molesting younger children."

Another possibility was that Jake—because he had a severe reaction to his repeated molestations—may have a more serious psychological problem. A molested boy often feels an extreme loss of control. The boy is doing things he doesn't want to be doing, he feels it is bad, he knows he is not supposed to be doing this, and yet he is helpless to do anything to stop it and it keeps going on and on. The way some boys "put their arms around" this impossible dilemma is to identify with the aggressor. This act binds their anxiety. They no longer have to worry about being molested, since they are now the molesters.

Of the three possibilities, a parent of a molested boy should expect that it's more likely sexual curiosity or modeling that leads to an incident. We emphasize "identifying with the aggressor" here, because this possibility leads to the greatest number of children being molested.

—— WHY JAKE WAS NOT FULLY HEALED —— THE FIRST TIME

Jake's mother was also angry at the family therapist who had worked with them—particularly Jake—for two years following the discovery of Jake's molestation. Why had she let this happen?

While identifying with the aggressor is important, it often lays dormant and only emerges in the molested boy when he hits puberty.

To be fair to Sara and the family therapist, since Jake was severely victimized at seven, they had both concentrated on healing his victim trauma. While, like most people, they had read that many molesters had been sexually abused, their minds went no further.

But *our* minds *must* go further. If we're going to save the greatest number of children in the shortest possible time, we have to make a major shift in the way everyone thinks about molested children—particularly boys. Now, nearly everyone talks about the suffering of the child victim as though there were no other consequences, except the child's immediate suffering. Most people assume that good, decent kids raised in good homes would *never* do such a thing. And of course this includes good, decent kids who had the misfortune to be molested.

Such closed thinking leaves out early childhood development, testosterone, the pairing of orgasm with child sex fantasies, and the power of the human mind to protect itself from terror. And when we do that, we cripple our ability to stop child molestation.

Instead, we must go back to that all-important question: How does this fact — 47 percent of male child molesters were sexually abused as boys — help us to protect our children?

We can let this fact lead us to consider the possibility that the molested boy may develop a sexual interest in children, secretly build this sexual interest, and then molest a child.

Sara was so overwhelmed with her children's victimizations and the painful aftermath that appeared as though it would affect her son forever that she wouldn't have been able to tolerate such a suggestion. Child molesters were the bad guys; child victims were the good guys. Any idea that someone would mention Jake in the same breath as Mr. Jones would have driven her crazy. And now, seven years later, Mr. Jones and her son Jake were in the same group. They were both child molesters.

—— WHAT WE CAN DO TO SAVE MOLESTED BOYS —— JAKE'S SECOND HEALING

What can we do to save molested boys?

We can heal the child so he becomes a survivor. That's first. Then, we can complete that healing by making sure he never becomes a molester. The greatest tragedy occurs when we fail with the second half of the healing process. Once we ignore this part of his struggle, we truly fail him. Once he has molested a number of children, then we have not only failed our molested child, we've also failed the children who become his victims.

How families fail their children

Nora Harlow: Where my heart aches is thinking of the monstrous tragedy that the well-meaning adults around these molested children so often fail them. Either they fail to consider the possibility that their son might need to be rescued from a molester in the first place or, once he is rescued, they fail him by ignoring the risk that he might have a second, related struggle ahead. The knowledge to save him from that struggle has been available for fifteen years. It's time to use it.

During his talks with 14-year-old Jake, the sex-specific therapist was able to follow up on the family therapist's work and reassure Jake that he was never to blame for anything that happened with his molester.

He also was able to convince Jake that Mr. Jones sought him out because he was a child—not because he was a male. Sex-specific therapists are used to this concern about homosexuality. A number of fathers of molested boys ask for a private meeting during which the father's first question is: "Tell me the truth, Doc, is my boy gay?"

—— IDENTIFYING WITH THE AGGRESSOR ——

It is not so unusual that a boy like Jake would show no signs of sexual interest in little children for five years after he was molested. Jake was twelve when he started his scrapbook.

In many cases, the seven-year-old child who is traumatized by being molested — who is very emotionally upset, so much so that he withdraws from every man except his father and doesn't want to go to school —

shows no signs of sexual interest in children until he reaches puberty. The identification with the aggressor lies dormant until that second batch of testosterone comes flooding over the child. Dealing with his more intensified sexuality prompts him to get control of everything to do with sex by molesting younger children.

When a child becomes a molester, it isn't molestation full-blown. Initially, it's just parts of it, because the child is still experimenting with his own sexuality. Children of 10, 11, 12, 13, or 14 do not become highly sophisticated child molesters. They just do more acts of a sexual nature. As we said about all victims, the boy who's been molested at age five or seven, often acts out sexually by doing far more sexual acts than other children or teens his age. Because no adults are thinking of this as a possibility, such a child, one with a jumpstart on sexual experience, can commit act after act of molestation.

What we found in our Stop Child Molestation Study: Being a child victim sharply lowers the age the pedophile has his first victim. (See Table 4-2.) Boys like Jake who've suffered more than 50 molestations, when they become molesters, start molesting very early in their lives, 25 percent before they are 10 years old, and another 40 percent before they are 16. Jake's test results showed that he did have an ongoing sexual interest in seven-year-old boys. Luckily, Jake did not molest a child until he was 14. What was also in his favor was the neighbor boy's father, who took the incident seriously.

—— How Jake Got Healed ——

The judge put Jake on probation—not because he was severely abused as a child, but because he had only one victim and was charged with only one act. The therapist assured Jake and his parents that treating a 14-year-old boy's sexual interest in children was an easier task than treating an adult's. As a teenager, Jake had an advantage: His sexual interest was still somewhat in flux.

See Chapter Seven, "Treatment: The Medicines and The Therapies," for details of Jake's treatment.

When Jake was 16, his father was transferred to another city. And, just as Sara found her son a new general doctor, she also found a sex-specific therapist who would monitor and protect the boy's newly found sexual well-being.

TABLE 4-2

Boy Victims Who Become Pedophiles: Their Ages When They First Molest

	Age at which they first molest			
	Under 10	10 – 15	16 – 19	Total under 20
Not molested as a child	*9%*	*28%*	*12%*	*49%*
Molested 1–50 times as a child	*15%*	*36%*	*10%*	*61%*
Molested more than 50 times as a child	*25%*	*40%*	*11%*	*76%*

Source: The Abel and Harlow Stop Child Molestation Study

—— WHO ARE THE HEROES —— IN JAKE'S STORY?

If we are going to work together to save children, we have to move forward, take action, and turn ourselves into heroes like the heroes in Jake's story.

> **Jake's little sister** is a hero for telling her mother. Sara, of course, helped her daughter by teaching her about sexual privacy without attaching fear or shame. The child understood about modesty, while feeling free to tell her mother about sexual happenings at school. Because of this three-year-old girl, Michael Jones never touched another child — including her brother —at daycare.
>
> **Sara** is four times a hero. She not only protected her daughter, but she took action to protect all the children in the daycare center. She let her son tell her what happened without putting her emotions

before his needs. And she sought professional help for her molested children.

To protect all of these children, Sara had to overcome her intense emotions. She even had a moment of denial when she thought that perhaps her little girl was playing make-believe or copying something she heard and then repeating it back in a jumbled fashion. She wished for this explanation. She wanted to tell her child that this was impossible or grill her on where she heard this —but she kept quiet. She allowed herself to analyze the possibilities. Her conclusion: Yes, her little girl was only three, but she trusted her. This story was way beyond anything her daughter would know about or could make up.

Sara also spent a half-hour wanting to yank her children out of that daycare center, get as far away as possible, and never think about the incident again. She's a special hero because she moved forward to protect all the children. She did this with great anxiety. All the parents *loved* Mr. Jones. Would they think she was a crazy woman carrying some sort of personal vendetta against him? Her entire charge rested on her belief in the words of a three-year-old. She started easy. Her first phone call was to her best friend, whose five-year-old daughter was in the program. When her friend called back in tears about what Mr. Jones had also done to *her* daughter, Sara had a confirmation of what she had trusted all along.

Taking that vital step to protect other people's children, that makes Sara a special hero. In the months that followed, parents called, parents stopped her at church; some parents she didn't even know stopped her in the grocery store to thank her. They would go on and on about how grateful they were to her. "Without you," they said, "this man would still be molesting my daughter."

When Jake came to her with his molestation, Sara was shocked. Rage flooded her body. How had she let this happen to her precious little boy? All she could do at first was hug him and say over and over, "I'm sorry," and "It's going to be OK." What she wanted to do was let go, break down, cry, run away and let someone else take care of it. But she didn't. She put her son first. She was strong for him. She was slow and gentle with her questions. She comforted him, when she wanted more then anything to rush away to someone who would comfort her. Patiently, she collected the information she needed to know. She wrote it down. She made copies for the authorities and for the therapist she knew he would need. She waited till Jake was sound asleep and she was alone with her husband to give in to her feelings. Guilt. Sorrow. Rage at Michael Jones.

The neighbor boy's father, when Jake was 14, stopped Jake from perhaps becoming one of those fellows who commit on average more than 140 acts.[35] That took a different kind of heroism.

The temptation to protect your own child and say nothing to anybody else is great. This father could have told his wife and son that they were never to allow Jake in the yard and that their boy was *never* to go to Jake's house. After all, the boy's mother had called Jake's mother to tell her there had been a sexual incident. They needn't have told her any-thing. The father didn't pick up the phone to call the authorities easily. As he told his wife, "No one wants to narc on the neighbor." He also called Jake's parents. They would be able to figure out that he called, but he wanted them to know up front. He made the call. He wasn't angry, he wasn't upset, he wanted them to know that this sort of happening was something more than could be settled between neighbors. He wished their son well, but this thing that had happened was serious and it had to be stopped.

Jake's mother wouldn't look at the neighbor boy's father for nearly six months. Then one day she walked boldly up to him and thanked him. "My Jake was in serious trouble. I would never have believed it —except for you. You made the difference. Now, my boy is getting the help he needs. You may not believe this," she said, "but I do know what you have been going through because of what Jake did to your boy. I know saying I'm sorry isn't nearly enough, but from the bottom of my heart, I am truly sorry."

The judge is a hero for ordering Jake, at 14, to have a sex-specific evaluation.

The sex-specific therapist who evaluated Jake is a hero. He calmed Jake's parents, and used tests, medicines, and therapies to evaluate and control Jake's disorder.

THE STOP CHILD MOLESTATION PLAN IN ACTION
— CHAPTER 4 —

1. Tell others the facts.	**Tell your family and friends:** • About the danger of a molested boy becoming a molester; say this to your friend whose son has been molested. • That there is a second step of healing that many molested children need. • That 47 percent of molesters were once sexually abused boys. • Those severely sexually abused boys start molesting at puberty. • That severely sexually abused boys molest five times as many children as molesters who were never sexually abused
2. Save the greatest number of children in the shortest possible time.	• Consider the possibility that a boy is being molested. • Have the molested boy evaluated for sexual interest in children. • Have the boys who have the interest treated. • Keep the molested boy who has "identified with the aggressor" from being alone with other children.
3. Focus on the cause: Start saving children at the beginning — before a child becomes a victim	**Pedophilia may be caused when a molested boy identifies with the aggressor.** • Identify the molested boy. • Take him through a two-part healing process: first, healing for being a victim, *and* second, healing to prevent his becoming a molester.

5

A Child Molester in the Family: Father Molests Daughter

—The Mother's Story —

A FACT

Most men who commit incest do so because they have a long-standing sexual interest in children. Often they commit their first act of incest as teenagers by molesting a younger brother or sister.[36]

YOUR OPPORTUNITY TO SAVE CHILDREN

Since 68 percent of child molesters molest children in the family, you can be a strong force to protect your family's children by considering the possibility that children you are close to may be victims who are protecting someone they love.

5

—— AMANDA'S STORY ——

Amanda was happily married to John. They had met during their first year of college. They decided when the first of their two children was born that she would be a stay-at-home mother. She quit her job as a nurse, with the idea that she would return to nursing when the youngest entered seventh grade. John, who had been a college athlete, coached both basketball and track and field at the local high school. Several seasons of winning teams had made him a local hero. To make extra money, he also worked summers building houses with his brother who was a contractor. John was known for being an excellent family man. Amanda was admired for her mothering skills.

After twelve years of marriage, when her daughter Kerrie was nine and her son Mike was seven, she got a phone call. That was the beginning of the day Amanda's world fell apart.

The phone call was from a Child Protective Services caseworker. She told Amanda that she had already called John at the high school and that Amanda and John were to come to her office immediately and bring their children.

In the car on the way over to the caseworker's office, Amanda asked her children if they knew what this was about. Kerrie started crying. Amanda pried out of her that "Grandmother said she was calling them." Her daughter cried, "I told her not to, I did Mommy, I did."

Amanda was baffled. John's mother was, as she often told friends, "a piece of work." Still, she couldn't imagine what she, Amanda, could have done wrong or even what John's mother could have imagined she'd done wrong.

The caseworker talked to each child separately and then to John and Amanda. To Amanda's shock, the caseworker said there had been a report that John had molested Kerrie.

—— IN THIS CHAPTER ——

"Child Molester in the Family" is meant to serve as a family guide on how to deal with the family child molester and how to heal the child.

- In it you will learn: why the caseworker investigates both parents;

- what crucial decisions the victim's mother must make immediately;

- the one simple act that every family member can do to advance our ability to protect children;

- ways to provide the child with physical safety and emotional safety;

- why everyone blames the mother and many blame the child;

- why "yes" from a child is *not* consent;

- what causes a man to commit incest and how the molester can swear that he is innocent when all the evidence is against him;

- why the child often suffers pain that stays with them forever.

——— FACTS ABOUT CHILD MOLESTERS IN THE FAMILY ———

In a case of incest, for the future health of the child, what the mother does is crucial. However, a mother like Amanda arrives at this moment naïve, with no preparation, and usually in shock because she has always assumed this kind of accusation could never happen in her family.

What facts might have helped Amanda? How likely is it that a child in your family may become a victim of a brother, a father or stepfather, an uncle or an older cousin? Quite likely.

The facts speak for themselves.

- One out of 20 boys becomes a child molester.
- Teenagers in ordinary families, as well as, dysfunctional families can develop a disorder called pedophilia.
- When we look at the reports of 4,000 admitted child molesters, we find that 68 percent of them molested children in their own families.

How can we use these facts to protect our children?

We can *act* based on the facts. We can open our eyes to the child molestation that happens in families just like ours and prepare ourselves to stop it right there. In the process, we can learn what to do for the child or children who are molested in our families.

With that in mind we've chosen to focus this chapter on Amanda. Since 90 percent of molesters of children in the family molest girls, we've chosen a case with a girl victim.

—— A *FAMILY* CRISIS: WHY THE CASEWORKER ——
INVESTIGATES BOTH PARENTS

Like Amanda, most women, as they sit in front of the caseworker, mistakenly believe that the caseworker's only job is to investigate the accused father. The caseworker's job is to investigate *both parents*. Why? Because the accusation is that the child is being sexually abused in her own home. The caseworker's job is to protect the child—whose father and mother are not protecting her.

To protect the child, the caseworker in this situation has to find the answers to several questions.

- Is the father sexually abusing his daughter?
- Is the mother participating?
- If the mother is innocent, is she capable of standing up to the accused father and providing a safe place for her child to live?
- Where should the child be placed?

While the investigation into the father's alleged sexual abuse may take some time, the caseworker must make an *immediate* decision about where to place the child.

If Amanda sides with John—or appears to be protecting John—the caseworker is likely to see Amanda as an unfit mother and remove her children from her care. This is a fact.

Amanda is numbed by the caseworker's explanation. Amanda can't take in most of what she says, but she does hear one phrase that pierces her body like a bolt of lightening: " . . . seeking a placement for your daughter."

Evidently John heard the same phrase because he is saying, "You will, over my dead body," and, "If we *ever* talk again, it will be in my lawyer's office." Amanda has never seen John so angry. He's standing and yelling.

Amanda feels as though she's Alice-in-Wonderland gone down the rabbit hole into an upside down world. This woman across the desk has been hostile to John since they came in the door, but everyone always likes John. John is talking about his lawyer, actually yelling about his lawyer, but John doesn't have a lawyer. Besides that, John doesn't yell. John does really well with bureaucrats, he jokes and smiles, talks about sports, and sort of jollies his way around them.

Amanda wants to make peace. She hates conflict. What she wants most of all is to get John and the children out of this place. Once they're home she and John will immediately sort this out. They'll go home and talk it through, make some sound decisions. And, as always, they'll do what is best for their children.

Amanda is still thinking about that one phrase, "seeking a placement for your daughter." Amanda's voice seems disembodied from her when she asks the caseworker what she meant by that.

The caseworker explains slowly, as if Amanda does not quite understand English: "I know this may be difficult for you. Kerrie must be in a safe living situation while we conduct a thorough investigation. Now that your husband has been accused, we have taken Kerrie into the custody of the state. Let me be clear. We will not allow Kerrie to live in the same place with the person who is accused of molesting her. Now, I've asked your husband to move out of the home so Kerrie can continue living there. As you've just heard, he refuses to move."

The caseworker takes a deep breath and continues. "In cases where the accused father refuses to move, the state has the authority to protect the child by finding another place for her to live while the investigation goes on. Do you understand?" Amanda nods yes. The caseworker resumes. "We may place Kerrie in a shelter for a few days until we can find a foster home for her."

John has the arms of his chair in a death grip, his hands are red, his knuckles are white. "I said *I'm innocent*. You have no right to force an *innocent man* out of his home. You are obviously new in town. I've lived here all my life. People here know me. You will never find one person who's lived here awhile who'll agree with you. They'll all tell you I could never have done . . . never . . . it's too disgusting to talk about."

The caseworker ignores John. She stares at Amanda. "This is your decision. You are free to go home with your husband now. This investigation will continue. While the investigation continues, unless your husband agrees to vacate the home, the state will keep custody of Kerrie."

While the caseworker is waiting for Amanda's response to the accusation, Amanda sits quite still, stunned.

"I'll give you some privacy to discuss this with your husband. I know this may be difficult for you."

To Amanda, the caseworker seems determined to ruin John, make Amanda choose between her husband and child, tear their family apart, and destroy them individually and collectively. She hates this woman and all of her repeated catch phrases.

"Difficult for you" hardly describes what Amanda feels. A caseworker, in effect, has kidnapped her daughter and now holds her hostage. All she has to do to get Kerrie back is to, in effect, denounce her husband.

—— HUSBAND OR DAUGHTER: THE MOTHER'S CHOICE ——

Before the phone call, Amanda was like most mothers: She believed she knew exactly what she would do. In cases of father-daughter incest, she saw the mother's response as easy. Since it's obvious the father is an evil monster, the mother quickly takes the side of her daughter, divorces her husband, then plots to send him to jail and keep him there for the rest of his days—along with moving heaven and earth to make sure he never lays eyes on *her* children ever again.

Like most mothers, she also was absolutely certain she would never be in that position. Imagining what she would do when she believed it could never happen in her family was no help now when the accused was the man she loved.

—— NO LONGER A TEAM ——

First of all, Amanda feels she has known John forever. They are a team. Every major decision either of them has made since their senior year in college, they've made together. Since the children came and Amanda quit her job as a nurse, John has often worked 60-hour weeks to support them. For the past nine years, they've made sacrifice after sacrifice in favor of their children. They are proud of their family life.

Amanda has never once thought of her John as an evil child-molesting monster. In fact, no matter what the caseworker said about an investigation, she doesn't even think of this as a problem with John, she thinks of this as a *family* crisis. Her family is being attacked. She can't change everything she's ever thought about John or stop raising the children with him just because the woman sitting across the desk from them delivered some frightening news.

When they are alone John says, "At least *you* know I didn't do this."

—— A PRIVATE TALK ——

Of course, he didn't do it. But Amanda is puzzled. Why in the world would his own mother report him? Did something happen that was misunderstood? Amanda wants to resolve this. She wants to know what happened.

She wants John to guide her in this. In their team decisions, he's always been so reasonable. Now, she's surprised because he has all this rage and everything he says is about his being falsely accused. What about their daughter? They have to get their daughter back.

This private talk that Amanda has so desperately wanted to have with John—as is typical in cases like these—doesn't go the way she imagined.

Although she pats his arm in support, it's not enough for John. He wants *more* assurance from Amanda that she *believes him*.

She wants to talk about Kerrie. She knows it's not right, but he is going to have to move out for a while.

The question about whom she would choose is answered. She's had to answer the question herself—no longer as one of two parents raising children, but as a mother alone. Amanda has chosen Kerrie.

What's difficult is telling John.

He must know what she's going to say because he keeps talking to keep her from saying anything. Every point he brings up makes her feel guilty.

He tells her that if she were the one accused, he would stand by her. "I'd never let some rules-and-regulation witch push you out of your home." What upsets Amanda is that she knows this is true. In the car on the way over, she had a comforting thought: No matter what her mother-in-law's accusations were, she knew John would take her side. She knew they'd face this crisis together.

He also tells her that he's the same man she woke up with this morning. He's worked himself nearly to death for her and the kids. That ought to stand for something. If she doesn't know by now that he'd never do anything to hurt his family, then she's the loser.

What Amanda decides is crucial. What she needs is a cool head.

—— Making A Safe Place For The Child ——

In fact, she's tired of John's complaints. These Child Protective Services people have their child. He *has* to move out. They have to get their little girl back. *After* she gets Kerrie safely back at home, *then* she can work on proving John is innocent, and she tells him this.

John, as she feared, is against this. He's done nothing wrong. If he moves, he explains, people will think he did the horrible things he's accused of. Moving is an admission of guilt. "Everyone will believe that this silly nonsense conjured up in some aberration of my mother's is actually true."

Amanda doesn't bite. "We can't control what other people believe. John, I know this is hard for you. But there will be an investigation. . . ."

John interrupts, "Pretty easy, huh, when no one's accusing you. I guess my own wife has made her decision."

Amanda stays cool. "Our *family* is being investigated. That's the truth here today. Whatever the outcome of this investigation, I want your support and your word that you'll work with me to do whatever we need to do to take the best care of our children. That's what you and I have always done. And it's not going to change."

Amanda is firm. "Until everyone can sort this out, you must understand that you will have to live somewhere else. I *need* you to understand this, John. If you stay in the house, they will take Kerrie away from us. We can't let that happen. You will have to move out."

John reluctantly agrees. He says it'll take him a couple days. What Amanda has to tell him next is hard. "I'm sorry, John, you can't come home with us. They'll keep Kerrie until you are out. Do this for her. She's probably scared she's going to be taken away. When you're ready to pick up what you need from the house, call me and you can come by when the children are at school. You take the car, I'll take the children home in a cab."

Amanda's trip home was not the easiest. She felt uncomfortable in a cab. Mike was whining, "Where's Daddy? I want my Daddy." Kerrie was crying.

—— Forced To Leave Home: Is This —— Fair To Fathers?

Does forcing a father to leave his home signify that the state believes he's guilty? No. All it says is that he is the adult. We expect that children are less able to take care of themselves than adults. The father can handle a move to a new place. The child cannot. John is far more capable than his nine-year-old daughter of adjusting to a new living environment away from his family.

Should a father who is innocent leave his home? Yes. If he's innocent then *something unknown* has provoked this crisis. In that case, John would want to find himself another place to live for two reasons:

1. He can find a new place to live and adjust to it easier than his nine-year-old daughter can.

2. Perhaps Kerrie is lying and needs help; perhaps she is telling half-lies and she has been molested by another man and needs help. By moving, he helps the investigation proceed quickly so he can do everything in his power to help his daughter.

Everyone wants to know if Amanda thinks John did it—including John. That's the first thing John demands of her, that she *believe him*.

In the next few days, that's what everyone wants to know. Does *she* think he did it? Even if they don't ask, they pause as if they are waiting to see if she will defend John.

Kerrie wants to know the same thing: "Do you believe me, Mommy?"

This is tough. As far as Amanda knows, John has never lied to her. Kerrie has always been one of those children who didn't appear to know how to lie. It's simply unimaginable. Who's lying? Before this happened, Amanda was sure she knew both of them. She searches for a truth she can use to answer her daughter's question. "You always tell the truth. You've been that way all your life."

Kerrie is happy to hear this. And Amanda is glad she says no more. What she's thinking is, *Kerrie always tells the truth, but this time she's making a mistake. Something happened. John's too embarrassed to tell me. Whatever it was, whatever Kerrie told her grandmother, it's been blown way out of proportion.*

To friends, she says, "Of course he didn't do it," and when asked about Kerrie, she says, "Kerrie never lies." And immediately she laughs and adds, "Of course, she's young and has a wild imagination." She's said this to three different people. That's three times she's felt she betrayed Kerrie.

—— Do You Believe Me, Mommy? ——

Kerrie never lies. John is not a criminal. No matter whose side she takes, Amanda feels guilty. What can she do?

There's an old saying: "The truth shall set you free." But what's the truth? Sometimes the truth is so obvious, people in Amanda's shoes can't see it.

The truth: *Amanda doesn't know.*

To answer every question from friends, from John, from Kerrie, all she has to say is, "I don't know."

People who know nothing about pedophilia may see this admission—I don't know—as a breach of loyalty or as a sure sign the father did it. That's because they are looking for guilt or innocence. Determining guilt or innocence has no power in it to stop child molestation.

To stop child molestation we have to go beyond that. We have to focus on the cause. Once we know the cause, then we treat that cause. After we treat, we test for treatment effectiveness. If that treatment is effective, we monitor for the recurrence of the cause. That's how we will stop child molestation.

Pedophilia is a serious disorder with a complex etiology. John may have the disorder; or he may not. Like Alex, John may have had the sexual interest in children *happen to him* when he was a teenager. Or like Brian, when

John was a teenager he may have developed a sexual interest in children through chance conditioning. Or like Jake, John may have been sexually abused and, as a teenager, developed a sexual interest in children by identifying with his aggressor. Determining whether or not John has a sexual interest in children is way beyond Amanda's powers.

One in twenty boys in ordinary families do develop that interest, so John could have it. It starts in their teenage years *before* they get married, so John could have it. After marriage, molesters often have fine sex lives with their adult partners, so John could have it.

John wants Amanda to judge him because she slept in the same bed with him for 12 years. But that doesn't tell her anything about his possible sexual interest in children. No matter how many nights she slept in the same bed with him, she still does not know her husband's childhood sexual experiences, or all the targets of his sex thoughts or fantasies, or which sex urges he suppresses. So John could have pedophilia.

His plea that he is the same man she woke up with this morning also implies that she knows everything about his life-long sexual experiences. But she does not. No wife does. And no other member of his family does either.

So to John's plea, Amanda's best position is the truth: She couldn't possibly know. She has to wait for the professionals to sort this out.

—— A SIMPLE ACT THAT PROTECTS —— YOUR FAMILY'S CHILDREN

Just that simple act—admitting you don't know—advances our ability to protect children. How? By admitting you don't know, you also admit the possibility that a sexual disorder might have caused child-molesting behavior in an otherwise law-abiding person in your family.

Pedophiles molest 88 percent of our children who are molested. They commit 95 percent of the acts. This is a serious disorder. To stop child molestation, all of us have to stop playing amateur sleuth. When someone is accused of molesting a child, we have to accept the possibility of their having a serious sexual disorder—one that is far beyond any family member or friend to judge.

We have to accept the fact that this disorder exists, that we can test for it, and most important, that not only are medicines available, but that treatment is effective.

—— LEARNING THE TRUTH ——

Before the week is out, Amanda reels as piece after piece of evidence against John piles up.

John's mother phones. She opens up the conversation by saying, "I didn't know if you'd still be speaking to me." She goes on to say that John's brother forbid her to call John or him again. Her two sons were now refusing to see her or talk to her. "Please don't hang up," she says, before she explains that the reason she called the authorities without saying anything to Amanda was that she was afraid she'd lose her nerve or John would talk her out of it.

What John's mother reveals

Then she reveals that now she thinks what John's little sister told her was true: When John was 18 and a senior in high school, and his sister was ten, he sexually molested her. John's sister told her mother years after the fact. By that time, his little sister had grown up, moved out of the house, and was living on her own. John's mother, given the fact that the victim was grown up, didn't know what to do with that information. Strangely enough, John's sister had asked her mother if she should tell Amanda. The two decided to leave Amanda alone; she looked so happy with John. Before John's mother hangs up, she is crying. "I'm sorry if I upset you, but I let my own daughter down— and then when Kerrie told me . . . she's still a baby . . . and I had to . . . you understand."

After she hangs up, Amanda is crestfallen, but she still has some reason to believe John didn't do it. John and his sister were children back then, she tells herself, children do that sort of thing. It could mean nothing. Maybe it wasn't serious. These days everybody and their mother says somebody molested them. Maybe he told a dirty joke in front of his sister, and now she feels she was molested.

What the caseworker finds

The caseworker phones. She says Kerrie had been molested about 50 times over the last two years. The agency is satisfied that there is a foundation to the case.

"Where was I?" screamed through Amanda's brain. I was with my children every day. If John did this to Kerrie, when did he do it, where did he do it? Amanda now has serious doubts. Still, she isn't going to necessarily believe this woman who is so set on destroying their lives.

At the sex-specific therapist's office

John is given a sexual interest test. The therapist tells Amanda, in front of John, that his test results show that he has two definite categories of sexual interest—an interest in adult women *and* an interest in girls of grade-school age.

When he goes on to tell her that besides Kerrie, John has also sexually touched another child, Amanda, thinking about John's sister, says, "I know." John looks startled. When the therapist says it was the ten-year-old daughter of the woman John lived with when he was 19, Amanda flinches.

Amanda knew that John had a crazy period after high school. He'd told her he'd lived with a woman in her thirties when he was 19. He'd spent a lengthy period around that time in Christian counseling. He felt forever indebted to this particular counselor who helped him pull himself together and get back on track. He left the relationship with the older woman, moved back in with his parents, and began to make plans to go to college. John entered college the same year Amanda did, but he was two years older. What Amanda didn't know was that John's live-in partner was in her thirties, suffered from alcoholism, and had two daughters—ages ten and seven.

Amanda feels as though she's been run over by a truck. She isn't sure she can stand. What has John done to Kerrie? Where was I? she wondered.

While she is trying to absorb what the therapist is telling her, John reaches over and takes her hand. "You are the one person who knows me best," he says, "so you know I'd never hurt anybody. I am not a child molester."

Outside the therapist's office, she can't look at John. The therapist has rocked Amanda's whole concept of her husband. She keeps her head down, but he follows her to the car. "Don't cry," he says. "You shouldn't worry." He tells her he is working on getting their family back together and he feels sure they'll all be back together again real soon.

Although Amanda is a person who, all her life, has offered her opinion on anything and everything, she is completely quiet now. All she can think is that John has gone crazy.

—— BLAMING THE MOTHER ——

Amanda was baffled by John. He was such a liar. John, who she thought always told the truth, always told her everything. She and John, she had believed for 12 years, never kept secrets from each other. She was heartsick over her failure to protect her daughter. And she suddenly had no one to talk to, her neighbors avoided her, but she heard the rumors.

"Do you think she knew?" This became the most asked question in Amanda's neighborhood. Several of her neighbors answered with certainty, "My god, she had to have known, she's hovering over those kids every minute of the day." Linked tightly to that belief was, "She's just as guilty as he is; she knew all along. She was in the same house wasn't she? And didn't lift a finger to protect that poor child."

Two mistaken beliefs stand out in relation to the wife whose husband has molested their child.

Mistaken belief number one:
The mother always knows

Some mothers do know. In the last chapter, Michael Jones' wife, who was co-owner of the daycare center where Jake was molested, knew. A criminal record search during the investigation turned up two arrests in another state. Jones' own daughter had reported her father for sexually abusing her. The authorities dropped the case for lack of evidence. Later, Jones was arrested for the sexual abuse of another child; but again, he escaped conviction. And, at no time did he seek a medical evaluation or treatment. Mrs. Jones knew enough about the accusations against her husband to know that he should be isolated from children.

Amanda, however, was one of the many mothers who did *not* know.

How can that be if she lived in the same house with her husband and daughter? Since most child molesting is fondling, it's easy for the molester to fondle a child without getting caught. Some of the fondling is with clothes on, some under the clothes. When molestations do *not* involve nudity or penetration, it's less likely that the mother will know. Even when there is nudity or penetration she may not know. Why? Because child molestation is a private and secret activity.

Even though Kerrie's molestations happened in the house with Amanda there, Amanda didn't know.

—— A FATHER SETS THE STAGE ——

When Kerrie was seven, John took on more childcare responsibilities. He would put his son to bed first, then bathe Kerrie and put her to bed. While he read her a story he would lie beside her in her bed, then he would sexually fondle her genitals. Some of these molestations were two minutes long, some longer.

Amanda was grateful to her husband for taking on the job of putting the kids to bed. By the time he got home from work, she was tired from being with their baby son all day and caring for Kerrie before and after school, taking her, picking her up, and being a volunteer for class projects.

John accepted his wife's praise for taking on this extra childcare responsibility when he was really just setting the stage for being able to molest Kerrie.

Like many incest fathers, John got so good at masking the sexual part of what he was doing that he could molest Kerrie with her mother in the house rather easily.

—— WHY CHILDREN KEEP DADDY'S SECRET ——

As we've said in previous chapters, children, because they are children, do not have an adult's understanding of sexuality. A father can bounce a daughter on his knee and stimulate the child genitally without the child even being aware that the intent of this behavior is to touch them genitally. Or, he can rub the child's genitals during the course of bathing the child. At seven, Kerrie, like many victims was too young to understand that she was a victim. It requires a fairly sophisticated understanding of behavior before you can label yourself as a victim. That's why many children fail to tell at the time of the molestation. It's not until they are older that they realize that they have been used sexually.

This is further complicated by the child's view of the father. Since the parents decide what is right and wrong, the young child sees whatever the father does as right.

For Kerrie, like most child victims, who agree to "not tell mother," this pact with her father was a strong and sacred commitment. That agreement was so strong for so many years that even when she told an adult, she kept her word to "not tell mother."

In addition, incest fathers often threaten their child: "if you tell . . . you'll get spanked, you won't get your allowance, your mother and I will divorce and you'll have to live in someone else's home."

What's often most troubling for the child is their sexual reaction. Incest fathers can be masters at using the natural pleasurable reaction of the child's body to sexual fondling to make the child feel responsible for their father's act: "I'm only doing this because you want me to do it." The child then doesn't tell because she feels responsible for her own molestation.

Mistaken belief number two:
The mother caused the father to molest his daughter

Amanda's brother called her. "Gee, kiddo," he said, "if you were having problems in the sack, you should have called your big brother. I told you before, I would have given you the name of this great sex therapist and marriage counselor."

What big brother is doing is shifting the blame to Amanda. Amanda's brother believes that incest is usually the wife's fault. John did it because Amanda was frigid. Another mistaken belief.

Twenty years ago, there was a belief among therapists that fathers had sexual interactions with daughters because their wives were cold and distant, so they turned to their daughters for love and sexual gratification. The thinking was: Straighten out the family dynamics and the incest disappears. In other words, the therapists believed that the mother's sexual inadequacies caused the father to do it.

There is a big problem with this idea. The family dynamics may be terrible, but they *don't cause* a man to sexually abuse his daughter.

During the research phase of Dr. Abel's N.I.M.H. grant in the early 1980s, he and his colleagues Dr. Judith V. Becker and Dr. William Murphy, discovered something interesting about the majority of men who commit incest: They had a definite sexual interest in *children*. Not only that, this sexual interest in children was evident early in their lives. Many of these men—when they were teenagers—had molested much younger children in their family, usually their little brothers or sisters. Sometimes their cousins.[37]

Data from The Abel and Harlow Stop Child Molestation Study reconfirmed this finding.

What causes a father to sexually abuse his daughter? *He has a sexual interest in children.* Not only that, in many cases, he had that sexual interest years before he met his wife.[38]

Based on two mistaken beliefs, some people heap blame on the mother: The mother failed because she knew all along and didn't protect her child, *and* the mother failed because she wasn't good enough sexually or good enough in the marriage, or she was debilitated by an illness and so she *caused* her husband to molest her daughter.

New findings show us this is false. Pedophilia doesn't work this way.

How can we use this fact to protect our children?

1. Create a family environment that allows children to understand bad touch *and* to know that they can get help from the adults around them, even if the person doing the bad touch is also in *their* family.

2. Take any incident seriously.

Today, neither of these preventive measures are in place.

You might have already asked yourself the obvious question: Ok, if 68 percent of child molesters are molesting children in their own families *and*

33 percent of them are molesting children related to them by blood, why do mothers like Amanda so seldom face a caseworker?

Because family children rarely tell. Because family members who know, rarely report. John's little sister didn't tell until she was 23—and then neither she nor her mother confronted John or demanded that he get an evaluation. The daughter of John's live-in partner never told.

When children do tell a parent, an uncle or aunt, or a grandparent, the incidents involving family members *are often ignored* or the family members who know *decide not to tell.* For one reason or another, family members rarely report another family member.

—— WHO DOES —AND WHO DOESN'T —— GET REPORTED

The stranger gets reported. The ten percent of child molesters who target children they don't know get reported—by the child or by the child's family. The family's fury at the stranger who sexually abuses one of their children knows no bounds. But, for the 68 percent of child molesters who molest children in their own families, the reaction is different. The family covers for the molester. In fact, the closer the victim is to the molester, the less likely the child is to tell. Rather than seeing child molestation in the family as a symptom that suggests the molester may have a major disorder, the adults in the family are likely to see the act as a family disgrace that must be kept a secret. Or they deny it with a fanciful re-interpretation. "Sixteen-year-old boys are like that. So she's eight. Not important. At sixteen, a boy will try to have sex with a venetian blind. No car for a month. That'll teach him. He'll never try that again."

And, too, there is love between family members.

The child covers for the molester

The closer the family tie the child has to the molester, the less likely she is to tell. She may, like Cyndy in Chapter One, be protecting her mother. Or, like Helen's sister or the boy, Steve, be protecting another child from the same abuse. Notice that the two victims of incest never told anyone—except another family member or a therapist sought out as an adult. Steve's molester, although a family friend, had no family tie.

The adults cover for the molester

The adults in the family search for excuses and they find them.

- It was a mistake
- It wasn't so serious
- He'll never do it again.
- The wife caused it.
- The child caused it.

It's the 68 percent of molesters who sexually abuse children in their own families who frequently remain unevaluated, untreated and free to molest the family's children again.

Much of the blame heaped on the mother comes as a reaction to the great astonishment adults feel when they are presented with a sexual abuse accusation against a man whose interactions with the adults in the family are excellent. They can't believe he *could* do such a thing. And if he did, what was the reason? They look around desperately for a justification for this man doing something so awful.

What is troubling is that, while many adults are busy shifting the blame, they forget that it makes no difference what Amanda did or didn't do— John is *not* supposed to sexually abuse his child. It's the same when adults think of the child. It makes no difference what Kerrie did or didn't do—her father is *not* supposed to sexually abuse her. Again, it's so hard to see the obvious. He did it because he's sexually attracted to *children*.

—— ENSURING THE CHILD'S EMOTIONAL SAFETY ——

Amanda's role in the family shifted the minute she sat down in the caseworker's office. She was no longer part of a husband-and-wife team caring for two children. She was a woman alone whose major job during this crisis was to be the best mother possible.

Amanda accomplished her first task, to provide a home for Kerrie that was *physically safe*. But then, in the midst of dealing with John, a John she no longer knew, she faced a bigger challenge: providing for her daughter's *emotional safety*. [39] [40]

The mother's crucial task during the investigation

On the day they came home from Child Protective Services—without knowing John's guilt or innocence—Amanda comforted her crying daughter. No matter what was discovered, even if Kerrie made a mistake, Amanda wanted Kerrie to know that she was proud of her. Amanda reassured her daughter that she was proud of her for telling her grandmother: "That's exactly what I told you to do. If you think a grown-up—*any* grown-up—is doing bad touch to you, you tell another grown-up. I'm glad you remembered."

What she does is important. She re-assures both of her children that they live in a home in which nothing bad will happen to them if they tell. At this time Amanda also says to herself, *Kerrie is only nine, she can make a mistake, and it's still a good thing that she goes to a grown-up for help.* But to Kerrie she says, "Now, you don't have to worry about this anymore. The adults can take over and do what they have to do." And she points out to her son that that's also what he should do if he feels that a grown-up did bad touch to him. She praises her daughter a second time for telling, "Because now we can get help to sort this out."

Family accusations

A week later, when she hears her son tearfully yelling at his big sister: "You made Daddy go away!" Amanda corrects him. "No," she says to her seven-year-old, "your Daddy and I decided that he should live somewhere else while the grown-ups are doing what the grown-ups need to do.

"Kerrie didn't make your Daddy go away," Amanda continues. "She did what I told her to do. She told a grown-up about bad touch. And that's what I want you to do, also. And that's what your Daddy wants you to do. Now this can be taken care of as quickly as possible. This is what Daddy and I decided would be best for our family. I love you both very much. So does Daddy."

Soon after that, Kerrie runs to her mother in tears. Her eleven-year-old cousin told the other cousins not to play with her: "Kerrie tells lies on Uncle John. Liar, liar, pants on fire."

John has told the family he is not a child molester. In some cases, a family member has called him—and before he could say one word—has assured him they *know* he could never do anything like that. They believe his daughter has a *serious* problem. One family member went on to ask, "Do you think Amanda put her up to it?" John replied, "Gee, I'd hate to believe anything like that."

Amanda talks to the cousin's parents. She tells them a few facts about pedophilia. She tells them they cannot possibly know whether or not John has a sexual interest in children. When she sees that they are unconvinced, Amanda says she will no longer allow Kerrie to play with their daughter.

One simple act every family member can do

When an accusation happens, many family members feel pulled in two directions—they are asked to choose sides and so they feel they *must* choose sides. They are asked to believe one person in the family and to freeze out the other person. Is there a healthier way to go? Yes. Tell the truth. *Say you don't know.* This is the one simple act every family member can do to advance our ability to protect children. Tell the truth; say this is above your skill level. Every family member can do this.

This dilemma is even more common in families in which adult children reveal their childhood sexual abuse. This often happens with no evaluation by a sex-specific therapist, no report to the authorities, and no investigation. Sometimes the expectation that the family must choose to believe the accuser or choose to believe the accused tears the family apart.

Here again, the true answer is: "I don't know. There is no way I could know. It could be true, I know that pedophilia happens to people in ordinary families like ours, I know some adults have a sex drive toward children. However, I don't have the professional skills to find out about this man's sex drive, or about what may have happened sexually to him when he was a child or a teenager."

—— WHY FAMILY MEMBERS BLAME THE CHILD ——

When a child molester in the family is found out, it can turn the family upside down. In the three months since Amanda was at the caseworker's office, nearly everything about her life has changed. Instead of being married to a local sports hero, she is married to a child molester. John has been arrested and charged. He's out on bail, but forbidden to have any communication with Kerrie. Amanda and John are losing their house. She's had to take the kids and move in with her parents. Amanda now works. She chose the hospital's night shift—11 to 7—so she could spend the most time with her children. She gets them off to school in the morning and sleeps most of the day, so she can be up when they come home. She supervises their homework, has dinner with them, and goes to work after they're in bed asleep.

A mother's loss

Amanda has lost a functioning husband, is losing a house, has lost the joint savings account, and lost the emotional health of her daughter. Daily, it seems, she has to shoulder yet another new burden. And she did nothing wrong.

In this situation, some mothers either directly or indirectly blame their abused daughter. If only she hadn't told. If only she had come to her mother first, this devastation would have been avoided.

Kerrie walks in on her mother, when her mother is in tears. The little girl falls apart, but Amanda is clear. Her tears are not because of Kerrie. "I'm crying because of what Daddy did to this family. He's the one making me cry."

The damage anger can do

In contrast to some mothers in the same situation, Amanda is not only clear in what she says, she is clear about how she feels and who she's mad at. Some little girls have to *also* shoulder their mother's anger, direct or indirect. Some mothers, even though they know it's illogical, see the child as the reason they have lost so much and picked up twice the responsibility.

When a mother expresses direct or indirect anger at the victim; her anger blocks the child's healing.

Why? Because most child victims already feel guilt about what happened. They feel that the mother's anger at them is justified. They feel they were in some way responsible for all the family's misfortunes.

Blaming the victim

Blaming the victim is a phenomenon that many women understand from its frequent occurrence in cases of rape. The idea of sexual assault is so upsetting—especially when men they know do it—that some people want to find a justification to wish it away. So they assume that the woman who was raped did something to provoke it: she wore suggestive clothing, she was out late at night, she went into a dark parking lot alone.

It seems impossible that an adult would blame a child for being sexually abused, but some adults do. Sometimes consciously, sometimes unconsciously.

If the child just hadn't told . . .

The idea of child molestation upsets many people. They don't want to hear about it. They don't even want to hear about it from abused children. If only the child had never let this happen. What they really resent is that, because the child told, they, the adults, are forced to think about a very emotionally upsetting occurrence—an adult sexually abusing a child.

If the child had only handled this by herself, they would be free from having such a disgusting thing brought to their attention. Blaming the child is a frequent reaction of adults, which comes straight out of their own emotional discomfort. It isn't that they are saying the child was the aggressor, they are saying that they don't want to know—especially if the molester is in the family.

In such cases, the adults often, even if they don't say it, see the child as causing trouble for the family: Our family was doing fine before this child started talking about being molested.

The child as an unpleasant reminder

Every time the family sees the child, this child victim is an unpleasant reminder of what they don't want to think about.

In the last chapter, the uncle of Jake, the seven-year-old molested by Michael Jones, a respected member of the family's church, told Jake's mother that he was disgusted with talk about Jake: "Every man's been approached by some homo. You just say no." Notice he says, "every *man*."

Jake is seven years old. Mr. Jones started being sexual with him when Jake was three!

Adults, wishing child molestation to just go away, sometimes want the children, the three-year-olds, and the seven-year-olds, and the nine-year-olds, to take care of it for everybody. We've heard a high-ranking member of a large religious denomination in a radio interview hiding behind the children by saying that the church was not to blame for the latest child molestation incidents—that it all happened because the children didn't tell anybody, that it was the children's own fault.

A lawyer defending an accused man asks a child, "Well, if you didn't like it, why did you let it go on for so long?"

In such an atmosphere Amanda has a formidable task in keeping her daughter safe from the hostility of adults.

—— HOW ADULT-CHILD SEX IN THE FAMILY —— IS DIFFERENT FROM ADULT SEX

What Jake's uncle and the lawyer are really saying is that they expect children to handle sexual interactions just like adults do. And we come back to an idea we want to emphasize once again: Children are *not* short adults.

Why didn't Kerrie run to her mother the first time her father touched her genital area? Certainly an adult faced with unwanted sex with another adult would have immediately said, "No!" in no uncertain terms.

Adult-child sex, however, doesn't happen the way sex happens between two adults.

John, like most child molesters, slowly groomed his daughter. Passive touching, introducing sex talk that was private, just between them, then sexually fondling, touching her genital area with all her clothes on.

Kerrie was at a decided disadvantage when her father first sexually fondled her. She was seven. She nearly always did whatever her parents wanted her to do. That included going along with their leadership, following their direction by accepting what they were doing without the adult actually having to say, "Kerrie, do this."

The child sees that the father—or the big brother, or the uncle, or the older cousin—really likes this; so at first, she may want to do it with him, especially if she is very young. Their secret thing. But rather quickly, the father puts the child into a troubling position when he tells her: "Don't tell mommy. And don't tell your brother." So, now she has conflicted loyalties. Still, she does what Daddy says. And continues to do it even after she hates doing it.

—— WHY "YES" FROM A CHILD IS NOT CONSENT ——

Since most adults worry about the 10 percent of child molesters who target the children of strangers, they also teach their children to define bad touch as something that's done by strangers. So the parent warns: "Don't talk to strangers, don't take candy from strangers, don't get into a car with a stranger."

If Daddy does it, Kerrie doesn't expect that it's anything that will hurt her. Children, because they are inexperienced in the world, have no idea how to handle an adult in the family who sexually touches them. Even if they say yes, even if they fail to protest, they are *not* consenting.[41]

For adults, both saying 'yes' to sex and failing to protest is seen as giving consent. Why isn't a child like Jake or Kerrie held to the same standard? Because in order to give a *meaningful yes*, in order to give a yes that will stand up to our laws, both parties have to be on an equal power base. A child is *never* equal in power to an adult.

This is easy to understand in terms of two adults unequal in power. If your adult sister doesn't protest when a man jabs a gun in her back and demands to have sex, no one would ever say that because she had sex with the man, it meant she gave her consent. Whatever anyone does with a gun in one's back—signing over the deed to the house, withdrawing one's life savings from the bank—does *not* mean he or she consented. If a mentally-challenged person signs a contract agreeing to pay 50 percent interest on a loan, that's not consensual— because the mentally-challenged person is not on an equal power base with the other person.

For a child it's the same. No child is either as powerful or as mentally capable as an adult, or as another child who is five years older. And so, no child has the ability to consent to sex; the adult, who is expected to keep the child safe from sexual interactions with adults, is completely to blame.

Jake's uncle's expectation that Jake should be a man and say no is wrong. Why? Because Jake is a *child*.

The lawyer's question can be answered by anybody, even a person with no knowledge of the case. All children, including Jake and Kerrie, let their sexual abuse go on for so long—*not* because they liked it—they let it go on for so long because they were children.

—— Lying To Ourselves —— The Mechanics Of Denial

How could John have possibly said to Amanda, "I am not a child molester?" Did he forget the 50 acts of molestation? Does he have selective amnesia? *Or* is he the most brazen liar who ever lived?

When John says, "I am not a child molester," he believes it. Why? Because he's in denial.

The child has no power to *give* consent to sexual touching with an adult. So, why does John report to the sex-specific therapist that his sexual interactions with his daughter were "by mutual consent?"

Surprisingly, John's report is typical of child molesters. In The Abel and Harlow Stop Child Molestation Study, 15 percent of the admitted child molesters reported that their sexual touching of a child was *initiated by the child* and another 50 percent reported that the child was a *mutually consenting partner*. That means 65 percent of these child molesters held the child responsible.

How can they say this? The same way John can say he is not a child molester—even though he meets all the diagnostic criteria for being a pedophile.

—— John's Diagnosis: Pedophilia ——

John is a pedophile. That is the reason he molested his daughter. He meets seven criteria for diagnosis as a pedophile.

1. He has an ongoing (longer than six months) sexual interest in girls 13 years of age or younger.

    John has had this interest since he was 19.

2. He has recurrent, intense, and sexually arousing fantasies and sexual urges towards girls 13 and younger.

   John has had intense sexual fantasies of young girls since he was 15.

3. He has acted on these sexual urges towards girls.

   He molested his little sister about 20 times. He molested his live-in partner's daughter about 20 times. He molested his daughter about 50 times.

4. He is at least five years older than his victims.

5. He is sexually interested specifically in girl children.

6. He is a non-exclusive type of pedophile, having sexual interest in children and also in adult women.

   John has a good sex life with his wife.

7. He is limited to incest.

   John only molests girls who he lives with, as either brother, in the role of stepfather or as father.

So how can John possibly say to everyone—including Amanda: "I am not a child molester?"

He can do it because he uses cognitive distortions.

—— USING COGNITIVE DISTORTIONS —— TO JUSTIFY WRONG ACTS

What are cognitive distortions? All those things that everyone tells themselves to justify or rationalize the actions they do that are wrong.

All of us use cognitive distortions. We use them when we know something we are about to do is wrong. They're what we say to convince ourselves that this wrong act is really okay when *we* do it because. . . . And we fill in the rest by making up a lie.

One of the most widely used cognitive distortions occurs while driving. You are driving on a heavily traveled highway, the speed limit is 55 miles per hour, and you are driving 65 miles per hour. You are speeding.

However, you tell yourself you are not actually doing anything wrong. You say driving 65 miles per hour is really okay when *you* do it because:

1. Everyone else is going at least 65.

2. You aren't going as fast as that crazy guy doing 80.

3. You aren't a danger to anyone.

4. It's not you going 65 who's doing wrong, it's people doing 50 and 55. It's the people driving too slow that cause all the accidents.

5. You are staying in your lane and the police never ticket anyone who stays in their own lane.

6. The police never tickett anyone as long as they stay at 65 or under.

7. You've been driving 10 miles over the speed limit for years and have never been stopped.

8. If driving 10 miles over the speed limit was wrong, certainly by now a policeman would have pulled you over and given you a ticket.

The truth is you *are* breaking the law. However, you make up lies to justify driving 65 miles per hour and still feel you are a good person and not a lawbreaker. The longer you tell yourself these lies, the more you believe them.

That's the process. We use cognitive distortions (lies) to deny that what we are doing is wrong. We are in denial. At the center of denial is this: Everyone—including people who speed, including people who lie on their tax forms, including child molesters—uses the same process of making up denial stories because they desperately want to see themselves as basically good and basically law-abiding.

Like John, some child molesters are people known for their good works with adults, as physicians, teachers, coaches, members of the clergy. Since others tell John he is good, and John has evidence of his good acts, he makes up lies to allow himself to touch Kerrie for his own sexual gratification. He believes that what he does with Kerrie is actually okay because. . . . And here pedophiles fill in with their cognitive distortions.

—— The Molester In Denial ——

John had created a fragile world of denial, built carefully piece by piece. Like many adults who sexually abuse children in the family, when he built this private world John followed a definite pattern. From the time he was a teenager, his sexual interest in grade school girls was at extreme odds with the way he saw himself as a good person. John, when he told Amanda he was "not a child molester" was a pedophile in denial. The pedophile's core denial: I am a good person; child molesters are bad people; therefore I am not a child molester.[42]

Like most pedophiles, John had a sex drive directed at children. John wanted to sexually touch children. To John, that interaction felt good; it was sexually pleasurable. He wanted to do it. He wanted to do this sex act that he knew was bad and against the law. Since he was basically a good person, John had to, consciously or unconsciously, make up reasons why when he, John, sexually touched a child it was OK. When he did this act, he was still a good person and not a lawbreaker. Whatever you call them, reasons, lies, or cognitive distortions, these statements John made to himself allowed him to molest. They protected his image of himself as a good person.

How John developed pedophilia — and denied it

Here is how John developed into a pedophile and the cognitive distortions that paved the way.

- When he was 18, he molested his 10-year-old sister. He labeled this as incidental kid stuff that he'd grow out of and *therefore he was not a child molester*.

- John masturbated to sex fantasies of 10-year-old girls, which increased his sexual interest in 10-year-old girls. This pairing of sex fantasies with orgasm *caused* him to have the disorder —pedophilia. He refused to recognize what his body was telling him —that he had a sex drive directed at girls of grade-school-age. Instead, he told himself that all boys his age were sexually attracted to 10-year-old girls and *therefore, he was not a child molester.*

- When he was 19, John moved in with an alcoholic 36-year-old waitress with two daughters aged 10 and seven.

He told himself that the presence of the daughters in the house was *not* important; that his reason to move into this household had to do solely with the waitress. When he sexually molested her 10-year-old daughter, he told himself what he did was actually OK because the girl was neglected, she needed affection, she needed sex education, she needed a man's influence, *and* he took her to church, *therefore he was not a child molester.*

When Kerrie was seven, John started to sexually fondle her. For the two years after that, he told himself reason after reason that this was OK when he did it. He told himself it was OK because:

- I'm never going to do it again; *therefore I am not a child molester.*

- Child molestation is bad and I am good; *therefore I am not a child molester.*

- She goes to school and plays with friends and watches TV like other girls her age, so nothing I am doing hurts her; *therefore I am not a child molester.*

- She enjoyed it, or she would have told her mother; *therefore I am not a child molester.*

- She loved going to the circus with me; she would have stayed home if there were anything really wrong with what I did; *therefore, I am not a child molester.*

- I only fondled her, it felt really good, but I've decided to never do anything like actually having intercourse; *therefore I am not a child molester.*

- She wanted to do it, otherwise she would have run out of the room screaming; *therefore I am not a child molester.*

- She's going to be eight next month, she's really maturing, therefore she's perfectly capable of making her own decisions about sex; *therefore I am not a child molester.*

- I've been doing this for years, nothing bad has happened; *therefore, I am not a child molester.*

- If there were anything really wrong with what I did, some bad thing would have happened to me; but

there is no wife raising the roof, no police at the door;
therefore I am not a child molester.

By the time John sees Amanda, in the therapist's office, he is a believer. He knows he is good. What he did to his daughter is nothing serious. In fact, it's okay when he does it because he knows *he is not a child molester.*

So while to Amanda he seems quite crazy, having built his world of denial, John can say to Amanda what he truly believes: "I am not a child molester."

—— Planning To Stop ——

What most people don't realize is that pedophiles like John make many plans to never do it again. So they are doing two things at once—trying to stop *and* protecting themselves with an ever-thicker armor of denial.

Everything comes from the very first problem: When John was a teenager he truly didn't realize that his bodily response to little girls was vastly different from the responses of most teenage boys. Once he paired his orgasms with sex thoughts of 10-year-old girls, his sexual interest in little girls solidified. He refused to believe what his body was telling him.

He masturbated to his fantasies of little girls. This built his drive. He acknowledged that his masturbatory fantasy felt good, but he decided to never do it again. Then he lost control and did it again. Then he lost control and sexually touched a child; this felt good (and nothing bad happened to him) but he decided he wouldn't ever do it again. Then he sexually touched a child again; this felt good (and again nothing bad happened to him), so he made up another denial story.

- *"I only fondled the child; that's not child molestation."*

Since about 75 percent of the acts against children *are* fondling, this denial story is widely used. But even when the act involves penetration, the pedophile redefines the term "child molester" to *exclude* himself.

- *"I only had oral sex (or I penetrated but without the use of force), therefore, I am not a child molester."*

In subsequent instances of loss of control, John experienced "this feels good and nothing bad happens to me." He told himself another denial story: that this was not actually a bad thing for the child.

- *My sister didn't tell, so what I did was okay.*
- *The waitress's daughter didn't tell, so what I did was okay.*
- *"Children aren't really harmed by being sexually touched."*
- *"The child started it; I just did what the child wanted."*
- *"What I did with the child was by mutual consent."*
- *"Children are perfectly capable of making their own sexual choices."*
- *Someday the child will look back on this with warm memories.*

Finally, some pedophiles reach the global denial:

- *"Society is wrong to be against adult-child sex. I am right — adult-child sex is a good thing and someday our society will be supportive of sex between adults and children."*

—— DEPRESSION AND SUICIDE —— TWIN DANGERS IN OVERCOMING DENIAL

What happens when treatment reduces or extinguishes a pedophile's sexual interest in children? What happens when therapy challenges the cognitive distortions that he's used to build his fragile world of denial?

If he's like John, it's as though a mask is ripped away. Now, he sees himself the way the rest of the world sees him. He is a child molester.

Men who fit the profile of the pedophile (married, educated, financially responsible family men who are religious and have good relationships with adults) cannot tolerate seeing themselves as people who do bad acts— acts that, once treatment forces them to give up their denial, they view with the same horror as everyone else in their society.

Men who molest children because they are opportunists and antisocials who see all people as existing simply to be used are rarely bothered by a concern for what they've done. For the man with an antisocial personality, molesting a child is just one more bad act to add to the long list of his bad acts.

On denial

Dr. Gene Abel: Your knowledge will probably be greater about child molestation after reading this book than the average child molester's. As part of his denial, the average child molester avoids trying to understand child molestation or reading about it. Instead, he relies on his own rationalizations and justifications.

The power of a pedophile's denial can be truly amazing. I once had a patient tell me, 'My daughter opened the bathroom door just as I was coming out of the shower. I slipped on the soap and my penis accidentally went into her vagina.' Another patient, had convinced himself he was fondling his daughter's breasts because she needed 'sex education.' I asked him when he was doing this 'teaching.' His answer: 'At night, while she was *asleep.*'

Those family members who deal with family teenagers or adults who have pedophilia become frustrated because they want the molester to come clean, be honest, and stop lying.

Some therapists who are asked to treat molesters feel the same way. They want them to give up their denial *before* the therapist gives advice or recommendations to the molester or his family. That presents a risk. If a therapist waits for the child molester to break through all of his denial before the therapist does something to stop him, while he's waiting he risks the child molester molesting other children. The solution is for the therapist to act."

THE STOP CHILD MOLESTATION BOOK

For pedophiles like John, however, the knowledge that they have sexually molested their child is sometimes too much to bear. They sink into a dark despair. Among pedophiles, there is a high incidence of depression accompanied by suicidal thoughts. Some kill themselves.

——— KEEPING JOHN ALIVE ———

John buys the hose to put on the car. He plans to use his mother's garage. This is what Amanda faces. While she is struggling to be Kerrie's physical and emotional support, she begins to work with the sex-specific therapist to keep John alive. She will not allow him to give his daughter additional pain—and lifelong guilt—by choosing to kill himself.

John's depression came in stages. First, it came as a reaction to his immediate losses. Before the investigation was over, John, the revered football coach, had lost his job at the high school, he had to give a lawyer $5,000 as a retainer, he had to continue to support his wife and children and pay the mortgage *and* the rent on his separate living quarters. Add that to the cost of the therapy—a victim therapist for his daughter and a sex-specific therapist for himself, court ordered, to evaluate and treat his sexual interest. Without a job, John is soon unable to keep up the house payments.

Although John is beset with losses—daughter, son, wife, mother, his financial assets, his job, his good name in his community and soon, his personal freedom—what brings him to the point of suicide is his realization that he is a child molester. He is a man who committed sex acts against his own daughter.

——— SEEING THE MOLESTER IN THE FAMILY ——— AS AN EVIL MONSTER

Once John admits that he sexually molested his daughter, once he takes complete responsibility for his actions, Amanda's family and her friends go from initially seeing the investigation as "something terrible that happened to that poor man" to seeing John as an evil monster. They pressure Amanda to dump him.

Suddenly, instead of having to protect Kerrie from adults blaming the child, Amanda has to protect her daughter from adults who are determined to say—in front of Kerrie—that her father is an evil monster. And, of course, they want Amanda to join in. Surely she should let her daughter know just what an evil monster the little girl has for a father. In many cases, and as Amanda realizes is true for her own family, this harms the child. Amanda chooses to take the high road, saying, "John is Kerrie's father. He will always be her father."

What Amanda does is send clear messages to her daughter:

- I will not live with a man who does bad touch to his little girl.
- You did the right thing to tell.
- What happened was your father's fault.
- Your dad made a mistake, like all people make mistakes. He was wrong.
- You —Kerrie —must make up your own mind about what you think of your father.

Amanda adamantly refuses to turn Kerrie's father into a complete villain in front of his children. When Kerrie remembers good things about her dad—family jokes, how he built the tree house, the day he took everyone to pick out a puppy—her mother agrees with her that those were good times. Her mother helps the little girl. She preserves her daughter's right to see her father as a whole person—a mixture of good and bad.

—— WHY THE VICTIM BLAMES HERSELF ——

John writes Kerrie a letter and sends it to Kerrie's therapist to read to his daughter if the therapist thinks it is okay. In the letter, John says everything that happened was all his fault. He has given up the idea—one part of his denial—that they were equals in these sexual interactions. He takes the responsibility. He assures Kerrie she is a lovely little girl. He tells her he hopes she will go on being her wonderful true self. He hopes that what he has done to her won't make her mistrust the whole world.

Still, the little girl blames herself—though she is only nine. She has collected lots of evidence to prove she's the bad one. Why? Because her father set her up to feel she was to blame for what he did.

It's important to the family molester that the child believes she's the one that wanted this to happen. It's a vital part of denial.

Kerrie, like other child victims, is vulnerable here. As her Daddy pointed out to her when he wanted her sexual co-operation:

- She did keep the secret from her mother.
- She did accept his presents and the special privileges he gave her: late TV nights, trips to the circus, the zoo and the amusement park, overnight camping trips.
- She never told him not to.
- I could tell you liked it from the way your body reacted.

This last is perhaps the cruelest manipulation. Make no mistake—sexual fondling is sexual. What's unpleasant to think about is this: Sexual fondling is *not* the same as hugging and cuddling. The molester's goal is to sexually arouse the child. If the child fails to get aroused, then that puts the complete blame for the act on the father. He can no longer lie to himself that "the child wanted it."

The child's vulnerability is extreme here because, like any little girl in any family, Kerrie finds it is pleasant to be so important to her father.

Amanda is clear about who is at fault. She knows that John manipulated Kerrie and lied to her. She worries about what will happen to Kerrie when it's time for her to form her own family. How severely damaged sexually will she be?

Will sexual arousal be something to run from because it reminds her of a traumatic childhood experience? Or will she take the opposite route, sometimes taken by adult survivors, and become promiscuous? Will she distance herself from sex, see it as meaningless except as a way to get things, and rush to have frequent and inappropriate sexual relations?

Amanda has sworn to herself that no matter what crises appear in front of her or her family, she will put her children first. Which is why she works so hard with the therapist to keep John alive. Every day she fights Kerrie's feelings of guilt and Kerrie's feelings of having brought ruin to the family. She is determined that she will *not* allow John's suicidal urges to be yet another trauma added to the crushing sense of responsibility her nine-year-old daughter carries with her all the time.

How does Kerrie feel? She feels like Cyndy from Chapter One, who says of her molesting stepfather, "I hate him, no, I love him." What this little girl wants is for her Daddy to come home. She wants everything to be like it used to be—except that she wants John to be a good Daddy and not molest her.

For adults who have never been in this situation, it seems so easy: Child molesters are the worst of the worst. They can't understand how the child can possibly be devastated by the sudden loss of a father who did such bad things to her.

—— TELL THEM I LIED, SO DADDY —— CAN COME HOME

When Kerrie learns that her Dad may go to jail, she wants to recant, she wants to tell everyone she lied. If she knows anything about her mother, she knows her mother does not tolerate lies. And that's another thing she feels guilty about: She lied to her mother, she kept Daddy's secret. Now she goes crying to her mother with a fanciful story. The little girl says, "I'm sorry Mommy, I lied about Daddy. He told the truth when he said he never touched me. I got mad at him because I wanted a Barbie dollhouse and Daddy wouldn't let me have one. I told a big lie, Mommy. Tell them I lied, so Daddy can come home."

Amanda sees through her daughter's childish attempt to save her Daddy from jail and put the family back together. After saying she understands that Kerrie doesn't want to get her father into trouble, but that her father is an adult and he made the wrong decisions as many people in life do, she simply tells Kerrie, "No."

Every day Kerrie has the fantasy that everything would have been fine if she just hadn't said a word to her grandmother. When she told, she didn't want all of this to happen, she just wanted Daddy to stop.

Just like some adults, Kerrie had the fantasy that her Dad would have stopped on his own and everything would have been okay. What she imagined would happen is that her Dad's own mother would have scolded him, maybe even have smacked him, and he would stop. Many families have a similar fantasy. They imagine they can handle incidents of child molestation themselves.

But of course, John would not have stopped his behavior. As a matter of fact, without treatment when he is in a state of denial, he would see the child's not reporting as a validation that she really enjoys their sexual encounters. He would also see his mother's failure to report as a sign that what he was doing was not really child molestation.

The caseworker has no such illusions. That's why she immediately separates John from Kerrie. That's why she questions the mother. She knows that some fathers will swear to the high heavens they'll never sexually touch their child again and then, if allowed in the same house with the child, will molest her again.

Unfortunately, too many families don't understand about the intensity of the child molester's sexual interest in children or about the child molester's denial, or about the intensity of his manipulations or lies. They also fail to understand the child's vulnerability. Because they are no longer children, they imagine the molested child can easily handle the adult's advances. They also imagine it's easy for the molester to stop.

Luckily for Kerrie, her mother was a strong woman who quickly educated herself on the dynamics of child molestation. That meant she not only understood the problems of the child victim, but also gained insight into how John developed the disorder, the likelihood of his developing thoughts of committing suicide, and the possibilities available for treatment and change.

—— For Children Molested By Someone In —— The Family The Pain May Never Go Away

When families choose to handle incidents themselves—without reporting or treatment—they put the victim in a bad place. Her molester may molest other children in the family. Some family members may take sides—and choose the molester's story over hers. Family members may see the child as the person who makes them remember something they don't want to think about. The molester keeps all his " . . . therefore I am not a child molester" beliefs. And so, the child may not truly heal.

For children who are victims of fathers, stepfathers, of older brothers and sisters, of uncles, of cousins, *their molester is always there in the family*.

And so the child is never free. Since the molestation happened within a close, sustained family relationship, her molester—at all the events that pull families together—confronts her again. Thanksgiving, Christmas,

Chanukah, Fourth of July, Easter, Memorial Day, family reunions, family weddings, graduations, children's recitals, and so on, are all occasions that may bring her molester into the same room with her.

As the victim gets older, events of importance in her life bring this painful childhood trauma forward again and again—her own wedding, the birth of her children, events in her children's lives as they grow up, the birth of her grandchildren.

When the child molester is in the family, the pain of the molestation never goes away.

For Kerrie, the pain is resolved another way.

—— AMANDA REUNITES HER FAMILY ——

John goes to jail. Four years later he is released and as part of his parole conditions, he returns to treatment. The former coach and schoolteacher gives up any idea of taking another job with children. He works full-time with his brother building houses, lives on little, and gives the bulk of his paychecks to Amanda.

Every situation is different. Every family is different. In some cases, the mother's best and only option is divorce. In a few cases, the family can re-unite.

By the time they see their father again Mike is 10 and Kerrie is 12. John redeems himself in the eyes of Amanda and Kerrie in several ways. At the center of every act is his admission that he was responsible for the family's misfortunes and his daughter's suffering.

John wants to spend time with his wife and children, but does *not* insist. He recognizes this should be a slow process containing many safeguards for Kerrie.

—— VISITATION WITH THE VICTIM ——

Any visitation with Kerrie has to begin after agreement by the family and many professionals. In the order of importance:

1. *Kerrie*. Kerrie has to be willing. She has to feel comfortable. If visitation with her Dad makes

Kerrie feel uncomfortable, then it shouldn't happen.

2. *Kerrie's therapist.* The child's therapist may have a greater understanding of the child's vulnerability than the child. Visitation should not occur until the child's therapist agrees.

3. *Kerrie's mother* (Amanda). The mother has the full responsibility for the family. Whatever problems occur for the child following the incest father's visitation, the mother is left to suffer these repercussions. If Amanda is uncomfortable about visitation, then no visitation should occur.

4. *The sex-specific therapist* who treats John has to report that he is no longer a danger to the child. In addition, the sex-specific therapist must design a method of close supervision for their initial visits.

5. *John's parole officer.* As the representative of the court, the parole officer has the legal responsibility to see that the incest father abides by the legal decisions. For example, the court decree may state that there shall be no visitation until the child is 18.

—— MOLESTER AND VICTIM AT FAMILY GATHERINGS ——

Amanda and Kerrie were lucky that they had the firm support of John's mother and his sister. In many situations, the incest father's side of the family creates trouble by being in denial. Either they want to minimize the seriousness of the molestation or they completely deny it ever happened. Once again, the mother must protect the child.

In circumstances, especially with loving grandparents who may act irresponsibly by assuming their son can come to any family gathering, even ones in which his molested child is present, the mother must talk to them directly to explain the rules. It's best if she does this early, as soon as the molestation is verified. Why? Because this is the time that his family will be listening the closest.

Before John's visits to family gatherings at his mother's or brother's homes, the sex-specific therapist designs a series of checks and balances to prevent John from being alone with children. The therapist will also establish a procedure for the family to follow should anything go awry.

What the family should *not* do is put themselves in the position of having to trust John with children. Typically, an adult family member stays by John's side at family gatherings. If it makes Kerrie uncomfortable to be in a family gathering with her father she should not have to go. Her mother accepts this from the first. Amanda then has to be firm with John's family; they must also accept this.

John also gains Amanda's respect because he does what his sex-specific therapist tells him to do; he finishes treatment, continues to attend relapse prevention sessions, and has sexual interest or sexual arousal tests twice a year forever. John's treatment experience appears in Chapters Six, and Seven.

What John did that perhaps helped his daughter the most was to make her understand that she was courageous when she told her grandmother. It was right for her to tell.

—— WHO ARE THE HEROES —— IN THIS FAMILY'S STORY?

Heroes seem hard to find these days, but sometimes they are hiding in plain sight. This family's story has a number of heroes.

- **John's mother** didn't know what to do. Years ago, when her grown-up daughter told her about the then teenage John molesting her when she was ten, she did nothing. She didn't even let John know that she knew. That information rested inside her like lead. Years later, when her granddaughter asked her to "tell Daddy to stop," her first inclination was to tell Kerrie to keep her mouth shut about this. She didn't know if she could make the call to Child Protective Services. Two hours later she did. Her hands shook so much she thought she might be having a stroke.

  For years —after she saw all the things that happened —she wondered if she had done the right thing. Her son screamed at her. Amanda and John's sister were the only family members who didn't get mad at her. At first, even Kerrie was upset with her. It wasn't until John had been in treatment for almost a year that he stopped seeing his mother's phone call as the cause of everything bad happening to him. He apologized. He also got his house-building brother to stop avoiding her —to understand that their mother did the only thing she could do to protect him from an ever-greater catastrophe.

Like many heroes, John's mother did not always act heroic. However, when Kerrie revealed that John was molesting her she stepped forward. She found making the call very tough. In spite of the terrible things she knew would immediately befall her family, she told the truth. She was determined, no matter what, to stop child molestation in her family. She saved her granddaughter and her son. She is a hero.

• **Kerrie** stepped forward to put an end to her father's life as a child molester. Telling was *not* easy for her. For years she was sorry she told. And no matter what her therapist or her mother said, she hated herself for telling when it caused her father to go to jail. She was mad at her mother for *not* letting her tell her Barbie dollhouse story. She was in high school before she began to see that her Dad was right —when she told, she saved him. Kerrie did marry. She had her Dad walk her down the aisle. When she had her two girls, she made sure they were never alone with grandpa. In this way, Kerrie protected her Dad and her children. There was no fuss about this. It's what everyone in the family did —made sure the family's children were never alone with John.

Kerrie revealed a truth about one of the most significant people in her life and then endured and overcame the harsh consequences that followed that truth. Not all heroes are powerful muscular men fighting hundreds of adversaries. Kerrie came in a small package, but she's a big hero in this story.

- **Amanda** was the one who was most responsible for her daughter's healing. She walked a tightrope. She condemned her husband's molesting behavior, yet she allowed Kerrie to treasure memories of John, when he was being the good father. She was quick to lift the blame from her daughter's shoulders and move all the blame to her husband. She knew who she was angry with —John. She kept the grandparents, aunts, uncles, and cousins on both sides of the family straight. She would *not* tolerate *anyone* blaming her daughter —even unconsciously. John was solely to blame, yet she would not tolerate anyone turning John into an evil monster in front of his children. But when he returned to family gatherings after his prison sentence, she insisted on family rules:

- She must be informed of family invitations to John, so Kerrie could choose to see her father or not.

- No one should allow the family to get in the position of trusting John. The family children were to be protected. An adult chaperone was to be near John at all gatherings.

  Amanda was her daughter's rock. The family was reunited on her daughter's timetable—when Kerrie felt comfortable having her Dad so close at hand.

  Amanda had many days when she felt crushed by the weight of her new circumstances. Many people blamed her. Some of her friends stopped being friends. They didn't feel the same about her, falsely believing that she let her husband molest her child. Kerrie, too, was often angry at her mother. It was only after her daughter was happy in her new family life with her own children that Kerrie understood the enormity of what her mother had done for her.

  Some heroes, like Amanda, have to fight battles alone with little support. Amanda stabilized Kerrie's life by being her steadfast supporter. With her quiet resolve, she didn't take the easy route of vilifying John, but she was unswerving in the protection of her daughter and all children in the family.

- **John** cannot be called a hero. He abused the very child who was his to protect. He conned himself and his daughter. For years he did bad things to his daughter and lied to the rest of the family. In spite of these terrible things, however, he didn't take the easy route out. Though it was so painful for him to admit to the horror of the acts he committed that he wanted to kill himself, John at last did hold himself responsible. By doing this, he helped his daughter shed some of her guilt. And, he helped himself begin the process of change.

For some child molesters, that process of complying with a treatment that extinguishes their arousal to children, that rips away their denial, that requires them to take responsibility, is more than they are willing to endure. Some won't give up the idea that they are right. In order to keep their denial, some molesters terminate all contact with their children, wife, and family, move elsewhere, and start a different life.

John faced up to the severe damage he had caused Kerrie. While we can't call him a hero, we can say he began to walk in the right direction.

THE STOP CHILD MOLESTATION PLAN IN ACTION
— CHAPTER 5 —

1. Tell others the facts.	**Tell your children:** • They have permission to come to you for help — even if their molester is in the family. **Tell your family and friends to support the child's healing by:** • Saying they don't know if the family member did it but they accept that pedophilia is a possibility. • Never trusting a family molester to be alone with children. • Understanding denial. Explain how a man with diagnosed pedophilia and more than 50 acts can still believe that he is not a child molester. • Holding the child innocent, because children are children and have no power to give consent to adult-child sexual interactions. • Refusing to speak of the child's father as an evil monster, while continuing to state zero toleration for molestation acts.
2. **Save the greatest number of children in the shortest possible time.**	• Consider the possibility that a boy is molesting his much younger sister or brother. • Identify him and have him tested for a sexual interest in children. • If the boy tests positive, have him treated
3. **Focus on the cause: Start saving children at the beginning — before a child becomes a victim**	• A man's long-standing sexual interest in children may lead to his molesting his own child or another child in his home or his family.

6

THE MAGIC OF EARLY DIAGNOSIS:
THE NEW THERAPISTS AND THE NEW TESTS THAT
SAVE CHILDREN

FACT

Early diagnosis saves children. Had early diagnosis occurred with the admitted pedophiles in our Stop Child Molestation Study, we could have saved nearly 28,000 children from being molested. W e could also have saved many of them from being molested repeatedly—preventing over 168,000 acts.

YOUR OPPORTUNITY TO SAVE CHILDREN:

You can be a force to stop child molestation if you tell your family and friends that the power to bring about the child-saving magic of early diagnosis is in their hands.

6

—— *ALEX, BRIAN, JAKE, AND JOHN* ——

EARLY DIAGNOSIS

The families of three teenagers, Alex, Brian, and Jake are all seeking answers.

Alex's mom and dad want to know if the sexual incident with his young cousins in the bathtub is indicative of anything more serious. Aunt Kathie believes her sister is ridiculous to take Alex to a therapist over anything so trivial. When Alex's first visit to the sex-specific therapist results in a call from a caseworker asking to interview her daughters, she hits the roof.

Brian's parents want to find out if the sliding-down-the-pole incident and their son's pre-occupation with sex thoughts of very young girls are leading to anything that could make Brian a danger to little children.

Jake's mother refused to believe her 14-year-old son when he told her he might have molested the seven-year-old boy next door. Jake himself was molested at seven. He couldn't have molested another seven-year-old boy, could he?

His mother wants the therapist to answer that question. And she wants the answer to be "no."

The family of the adult, John, want a resolution.

John, the father who committed incest with his daughter, believes the tests he's being asked to take are nonsense. He knows he loves his daughter so he knows nothing on heaven or earth would cause him to hurt Kerrie. Nonetheless, his family is in turmoil. His younger brother, who has always looked up to John, stopped speaking to their mother and their little sister. The younger brother hopes the therapist will do something to clear John's name.

John wants everyone to trust him. He wants everyone to do like his brother, and take it on faith that he is not a child molester.

—— In This Chapter ——

"The Magic of Early Diagnosis: The New Therapists and the New Tests that Save Children," describes the new kind of therapists and therapies that effectively treat a patient's sexual interest in children and the tests that assess for a sexual interest in children. In it you will learn:

- the differences between traditional therapies and the new sex-specific therapies;

- how to find the best sex-specific therapist;

- why therapists, social workers, and teachers report suspected cases of child molestation;

- answers to the six frequently asked questions about sex-specific tests;

- the diagnoses for Alex, Brian, Jake and John.

Alex's mother, Susan, took the lead in finding a sex specific therapist. She called therapists' offices and asked questions of either the therapist or the office manager.

Brian's Dad found a sex-specific therapist by phoning his local mental health center.

Neither Jake's family nor John had that luxury. Both had accusations against them, their cases were under investigation, and they both faced criminal proceedings. The juvenile judge referred Jake for a sex-specific evaluation by a therapist whose work she knew. The child-prevention caseworker referred John.

—— Choosing A Therapist ——

If you are concerned that a child in your family may have a sexual interest in children, finding the best therapist for that child is the most important thing you can do. Why? A good sex-specific therapist is important because not only will he or she have the state-of-the-art skills to best evaluate and treat your teenager, but he or she will also have the best ability to move forward immediately to insure the safety of all the children in the family and in the molester patient's neighborhood.

What does a sex-specific therapist do? A sex-specific therapist evaluates and treats men, women, and teenagers with suspected paraphilias. The patients may be voyeurs (window-peepers), exhibitionists (flashers), or pedophiles (child molesters). They may have a fetish (a sexual obsession with objects such as women's shoes or lingerie). The therapist may be a psychiatrist (M.D.), a psychologist (Ph.D.), a licensed clinical social worker (L.C.S.W.) or a master's level counselor (M.S., M.A., L.P.C.)

It's essential that you proceed with caution. Why? Because today anyone can simply say he or she is a sex-specific therapist. No credentials are required: no degrees, no certification. So, the variance between the 20-year-veteran therapist—who keeps up with the field and uses the tests, medicines—and sex-specific therapies that are proven effective and are now a part of standard practice, and the "therapists" who make up their own treatments is extreme.

As you have learned, there is one immense difference between you and the teenager, friend, or family member who is sexually attracted to children—the direction of your sex drive. So when you look for a therapist, you are looking for one who knows how to teach the techniques that alter sex drive.

First, before you make one phone call, it's important that you realize that sex-specific therapists and sex-specific therapies are extremely different from traditional therapists and traditional therapies.

What you want is an experienced, sex-specific therapist who uses sex-specific tests, medicines, and therapies.

What you *don't* want is the best general therapist in town. Why? Because the best general therapy available in your town doesn't help people such as Alex, Brian, Jake, or John. That's why the best general therapy in town, when given to teenagers or adults with pedophilic interests, leaves the family's children, who might become victims, unprotected.

The sex-specific therapist differs from a traditional therapist in that he or she is skilled in evaluating sex drive and in using treatments that directly reduce or extinguish the sex drive toward children.

——Why Traditional Therapies—— Don't Alter Sex Drive

Dynamically oriented therapy, the kind where you tell a therapist about your childhood experiences and your feelings, is what most people think of when they think of therapy. It is the most widely used form of psychotherapy, and it has proven effective with many types of emotional problems.

However, wanting to be sexual with a child is *not caused by the pedophile's emotions*. It's also *not caused by problems of family dynamics*. Alex's mother, Susan, had educated herself enough to know this. That's why she had so many problems with her sisters.

One sister, Alex's Aunt Kathie, gave Susan the name of a therapist, whom she knew to be brilliant and had helped a troubled teenage boy accomplish a wonderful transformation. When Alex's mother refused this offer, Aunt Kathie became furious and called to tell her so. She said she believed her nephew was fine, but that Susan was overreacting to "this trivial childhood sex thing."

Secretly Susan's three sisters had plotted to get Alex to this therapist, not so much for Alex, but for his parents. They hoped the therapist might help the parents get off this "stupid sex kick," before they damaged Alex beyond repair.

If his parents insisted on "dragging him to a shrink," Aunt Kathie was completely opposed to having her favorite nephew see someone whose specialty was child molesters. She felt Alex might be hurt irreparably by being exposed to "those disgusting people." She'd heard an M.D., an expert on TV, say therapy didn't work with child molesters. Before she slammed the phone down she said, "Alex is no child molester. And therapy doesn't work anyway."

John's younger sister, unlike the rest of the family, had never been a great admirer of John. She was angry when she heard he was going for group therapy and was going to see a therapist whose name she'd never heard. "He'll talk his way through this like he does everything else. Big deal. He'll just get away with it again." She was frustrated, because she believed there was a real chance he'd molest another little girl and she felt powerless to stop it. Also, she had no faith that this unknown therapist would do anything but be sucked in by her charming brother John.

Aunt Kathie makes one good point when she says, "therapy doesn't work."

John's little sister makes another good point, when she expresses frustration and fear concerning the therapist's ability to keep little girls safe from her brother.

When people — including psychiatrists and psychologists — say that therapy does not work for patients with a sex drive directed toward children, they are right if they are referring to traditional, dynamically oriented psychotherapy, family therapy, or general counseling. Most therapies are useless with teenagers or adults who have a sexual interest in children. Why? *Because traditional therapies don't alter sex drive.*

And because traditional therapists lack the specialized training to focus on preventing future acts that would harm children.

What family members like Alex's aunts and John's younger sister cannot imagine is the differences between sex-specific therapy and what *they* think of as therapy.

First of all, sex-specific therapists are intensely protective of children. They have a double focus: protection of potential child victims, as well as evaluation and treatment for the molesting patient. And it's in that order. Children first. Molesting patient second. In contrast to traditional therapists, whose first concerns are their patients' welfare, these sex-specific therapists are immediately active to protect children.

A sex-specific evaluation always includes an assessment of the patient's immediate risk to children. That's the first part of the evaluation given to Alex, Brian, Jake, and John. How much risk do they present to the children around them? In some instances, the molesting patient must wear an electronic monitor on his ankle, which tracks his whereabouts 24 hours a day. In cases where the risk is especially severe, the therapist prescribes medicine that chemically castrates the patient. Those extreme measures are useful in five percent of cases. (For details about the various medications, see the next chapter.)

Most patients are like Alex, Brian, Jake, and John; they pose considerably less threat to the children around them, once they are involved in a sex-specific program that includes medicines, sex-specific therapy, and various levels of supervision. Alex's aunt fears her nephew's association with "disgusting people," because she, like most people, doesn't know what actually causes the sexual interest in children or that it can happen in ordinary families like hers. In fact, most patients, like Alex, come from ordinary families.

As for John's sister's disdain for group therapy as part of her brother's treatment, it would help her to know that group therapy in a sex-specific practice is nothing like what most people have experienced as group therapy. In a sex-specific therapy, the patients with paraphilias meet in groups. The group setting is helpful for two reasons, group confrontation from molester-patients farther along in treatment helps to break the new patient's denial and the group setting lowers treatment cost. The therapist teaches them specific behavioral techniques to lower or extinguish their paraphilic sex drive, and they have assignments to practice that actually extinguish their sexual interest in children.

To protect children, the therapist—rather than relying on the patient's word—retests patients at six-month intervals to *measure* their success. And there's yet another facet of this therapy that protects children: Molester patients are forbidden to be around children. This is monitored outside of the therapy hours by a supervision network that may include family members, social workers, and probation or parole officers. In fact, the sex-specific therapist is often more protective of a family's children than is the family itself. The therapist outlines protective policies and insists that any family member with sexual interest in children be separated from children, regardless of how "trivial" a known incident might be in the eyes of the family.

—— HOW EFFECTIVE ARE THE NEW —— SEX-SPECIFIC THERAPIES?

The families of teenagers or adults who have a sexual interest in children can expect an 89 percent to 99 percent treatment success rate. The range occurs because of the differences in the complexity of the cases. How is success defined? No more child victims. No more sexual abuse acts.

Notice we said "the new sex-specific therapies are effective to stop teenagers and adults *with a sexual interest in children.*" We did not say "child molesters." The new sex-specific therapies are effective in making the sexual desire for children inactive. That is the focus of the new therapies—and their strength.

However, these therapies don't work for the molesters who commit 5 percent of the acts and molest 12 percent of the children. They don't work when the child molestation is caused by: an older child's sexual curiosity and experimentation; an adult's severe medical or mental problem; or by a child molester with the general disregard for other people that is associated with an antisocial personality disorder. The treatments are exceptionally effective, however, in stopping the future acts of child molestation *caused by a person's sexual interest in children.*

Who are these people who can be treated so effectively? The ones who have developed the sexual desire for children by having it happen to them in childhood (Alex), by pairing adult-child sex thoughts with orgasm (Brian), and, by being in the group of boy victims who are handling their fear and anxiety by becoming molesters themselves (Jake). In other words, these therapies are most effective for pedophiles and for boys most likely to become pedophiles. And these are the child molesters who molest 88 percent of the child victims.

—— FINDING A SEX-SPECIFIC THERAPIST ——

Sex-specific therapies bear little resemblance to traditional therapies. It's for that very reason that they are effective. And, of course, it's also for that reason that you must be sure you find a well-trained experienced sex-specific therapist for your family member or friend. In Table 6-1, we highlight some basic differences between the two forms of therapy.

Proceed with caution

Alex's mother is over the biggest hurdle. She knows the difference between the two therapies, and she is determined to find not only a sex-specific therapist, but one of the best.

Now she faces two more hurdles. Because of the general public's lack of education, most people are horror-struck by the idea that a child molester might be sitting in the same waiting room with them, or pained by the idea that a child molester might be in a therapist's office in the neighborhood where their children go to school. They believe in the *not-in-my-family/ stranger with a candy bar* myth of the child molester.

And so, therapists who do this work usually keep a low profile. Molesting patients whose lives have been turned around never tell anybody about their sex-specific therapy. Families whose children have been protected never tell anybody about the molester's sex-specific therapy. The patients keep their treatment a secret from their friends. The families keep their problems a secret. The therapists keep the fact that they specialize in treating people with paraphilias a secret.

TABLE 6-1

Contrasts: Traditional vs. Sex-Specific Therapists

Traditional Therapist	Sex-Specific Therapist
Offers dynamically oriented therapies (talking therapies) that don't directly reduce sexual interest in children.	Offers sex-specific treatments that use cognitive-behavioral techniques to drastically reduce or eliminate the pedophile's sex drive toward children.
Knows little about the development of pedophilia and frequently reacts emotionally to a patient with this disorder.	Trained to deliver sex-specific therapies to pedophiles and to maintain objectivity.
Not trained to proceed with those molesting patients who habitually lie, deny, conceal, and state that they don't want or need therapy.	Trained to proceed with the treatment of pedophiles, irrespective of their denial.
Has one focus, the patient's welfare.	Has a double focus: The children who must be protected *and* the pedophile's extinction of sexual interest in children.
Trained to assess whether a patient is a danger to himself (suicide risk) or to others (murder risk).	Trained to assess murder risk, suicide risk, and the risk that the patient will molest a child.
Usually delivers outpatient therapy that begins and ends in the therapist's office.	Organizes a plan to monitor the patient's activities outside the treatment setting.
Tests: Rarely uses objective measures to monitor treatment success.	Tests: Uses objective measures to prove treatment success.
Medicines: Not trained in use of SSRIs and Provera to alter sex drive.	Medicines: Trained in use of SSRIs and Provera to alter sex drive.
Success: partial degrees of recovery are acceptable.	Success: Sex-specific therapy must stop sexual desire for children and protect potential victims.
Patient determines when the therapy ends.	Therapist determines when therapy ends.

THE STOP CHILD MOLESTATION BOOK

Having read this far, you have a great deal of education, so you know most things that the therapists know: That child molesters are already in the neighborhoods where our children go to school, that they live next door, attend our churches, and are in our families. More than 90 percent of them never touch a child outside of their family or social circle. They are seldom reported *and* they seldom make it to a sex-specific therapist.

The take-home message: Your family's children are far safer from the child molesters in a sex-specific treatment program in their neighborhood than they are from the undetected child molesters already near them.

So, if you are a concerned family member, where do you start?

Help with finding a sex-specific therapist

Your state maintains a list of psychiatrists, psychologists, social workers and counselors available in your city. Your local mental health center probably has the listing of the respective organizations and how to contact them.

To find a sex specific therapist, say this: "I'm concerned that my son (or daughter) is sexually attracted to young children. Can you direct me to a therapist who can evaluate a sexual attraction to children?" You can also find a list of sex-specific therapists by state in the appendix at the end of this book. (Note: Inclusion on this list does **not** indicate an endorsement by the authors. Readers should carefully evaluate each therapy practice that they contact.)

Going beyond the lists

These lists are all useful. However, inclusion on a list does not, by itself, give you enough information to distinguish one sex-specific therapist from another.

If you, like Alex's mother, come to the last hurdle: finding the best sex-specific therapist for your child, at this point you will need to proceed with extreme caution.

Remember, that anyone can simply say: "I am a sex-specific therapist." As long as that is the case, should someone in your family need an evaluation or treatment, your ability to choose the best therapist is crucial.

Sex-specific therapy has thus far been an orphan field for three reasons, and all three center on the family's general lack of education.

1. Having no knowledge about the causes of pedophilia or that effective tests, medicines, and therapies exist, family members and molesting patients are unable to judge the quality of the therapists' evaluations and treatments.

2. The molesting patient is so vilified that little attention is paid to therapists who provide inadequate evaluations or ineffective treatments.

3. Many people fail to make the connection between state-of-the-art evaluations and treatments for pedophiles and the protection of children.

We believe this will change. It will change because the families that read this book will have enough knowledge and enough skill to seek out the best. The most important change will occur when early diagnosis becomes a nationwide reality: The public will look at sex-specific therapy patients differently. In the future, most sex-specific therapy patients will be like Alex and Brian, young people whose parents seek an evaluation out of concern that what's happening with them might lead to children being harmed. Few patients will be like George from Chapter One, the 20-year molester who has hurt 23 little girls. And, of course, with greater education, families will demand high quality evaluations and treatments to protect all children.

However, until that happens, if you are like Alex's mother, Susan, you want your son to have the best evaluation and, if necessary, the best treatment. Only one thing separates the teenager with a pedophilic interest from everyone else in the family—a sex drive directed at children. That sex drive is the force within the pedophile that erupts to harm children. Therefore, you want your son's therapist to concentrate on that sex drive.

Here again, you have to be careful. The therapist may have credentials as a general therapist and may treat a number of patients with sexual interest in children, but he or she may provide no medication or cognitive behavioral treatment to directly reduce or eliminate the patient's sexual interest in children. Although such general therapists believe they are capable of treating a sex problem like Alex's, they may actually feel uncomfortable when dealing with such a patient's sex drive and prefer a talking therapy. So they try to help the patient by dealing with the patient's emotions and family stresses. *This type of therapy is not effective against a sex drive directed toward children.*

To help you find the best sex-specific therapist, we've given you six questions to ask the therapist or the therapist's office manager *before* you make the first appointment. (See Table 6-2.) Should the therapist be unwilling or unable to answer these questions, seek out a therapist who is willing to give you this information. Do not be bashful about asking such questions, since having a competent therapist is essential not only for a competent evaluation and for effective treatment, but also for the protection of the children in the molester's family and social circle.

If, after your first or second contact with the therapist, you are still confused about his or her methods of evaluation and treatment, you shouldn't assume that you absolutely must stay with that therapist. Having a "good fit" with the therapist is important for effective therapy.

——Testing and Evaluation—— The First Visit to the Sex-Specific Therapist

Once you've chosen a therapist, what can you expect to happen at your first appointment?

The sex-specific therapist follows a procedure that is in some ways similar to what happens in most doctors' offices.

—— Alex's Family At The Therapist ——

Since Alex is a minor, in the waiting room his parents are asked to fill out general papers about who the patient is and who is responsible to pay. Next, both Alex and his parents are asked to sign consent forms. Then the therapist meets with Alex (and later with his parents) and completes a clinical interview, orders some tests, and makes a second appointment to go over the test results. And there the similarity to other doctors ends.

Alex's parents find some striking differences between this experience and what happened with other doctors they've taken Alex to see. The first one has to do with the reporting laws.

TABLE 6-2

Questions to Ask When Selecting a Sex-Specific Therapist

Question	What You Want to Hear	Why
How many pedophiles do you treat in a year?	20 or more cases	Generally, the more experienced the therapist, the more knowledgeable he or she is about effective treatment.
Do you use sexual interest testing, plethysmography or polygraphs as part of your evaluation?	Yes	Without objective testing, the therapist has to make recommendations based on incomplete information
If you are a psychiatrist, do you prescribe medications such as SSRIs or Provera for some of your patients with paraphilias? * If you are a social worker or a psychologist, do you have a working relationship with a physician?	Yes	Ideally, you want a therapist who can prescribe medication if needed, or who works closely with a physician who can prescribe. *
Do your treatments include covert sensitization, aversion, or satiation to *directly* reduce sexual interest in children?*	Yes	Sexual interest in children is associated with child molestation; therefore, a sex-specific therapist should have this skill.
Do you use cognitive-behavioral and relapse-prevention therapies?	Yes	Cognitive-behavioral therapies are the most effective means of preventing child molesters from molesting again.*
Do you belong to ATSA, the Association for the Treatment of Sexual Abusers? This is the national association for sex-specific therapists.	Yes	Membership suggests a greater likelihood that the therapist has had appropriate training.

You will find details about these medicines and therapies in chapter Seven.

THE STOP CHILD MOLESTATION BOOK

—— REPORTING LAWS ——

What families tell therapists is usually confidential. However, confidentiality between therapist and patient only works if the things that are kept confidential are not dangerous to anybody. Therapists have always broken confidentiality, if the patient is a danger to himself (a suicide risk) or to others (a murder risk). Now, state law adds a third instance in which the therapist must break confidentiality: if the therapist suspects that a known child is being sexually abused. For instance, if a patient says to a traditional therapist, "I am in such a murderous rage, I just want to murder everybody," the traditional therapist does not have to report that general feeling to the authorities. However, if the patient says, "I'm going to murder John Smith," then the therapist must break confidentiality to notify the authorities and to notify John Smith. It's the same process in interviewing and treating people with pedophilia. If the patient says—like Alex and Brian—"I have continual sex fantasies of little girls, I have strong urges to do sex things with little girls," the therapist has nothing to report to Child Protection Services. However, if—like Alex—the patient says, "I sexually touched my cousin," then the therapist must report.

Before Alex and his parents' appointment, they are asked to sign a consent form that outlines the state reporting laws and clarifies that the family understands the law that requires therapists to report child sexual abuse. Similar laws exist in all 50 states requiring therapists, physicians, schoolteachers, and other professionals to report to Child Protection Services or the police if they suspect that a known child is being sexually abused.

Since Alex is a teenager, both Alex and his parents are asked to sign. This is important, because this consent form outlines the child sexual abuse reporting laws in Alex's state. Alex doesn't know these laws. Neither do his parents. This is their chance to learn the reporting laws. It is also their opportunity to make informed decisions about their interactions with the therapist.[43]

—— REPORTING LAW CONSENT FORM ——

All information obtained from this evaluation will become part of my son's, stepson's, or ward's psychiatric or psychological record and, as such, is confidential. However, there are three conditions under which information about him may be revealed to others:

1. He reveals that he might harm himself.

2. He reveals that he plans to harm someone else.

3. He reveals that he has committed sexual interactions with children.

All state laws require that when a patient reveals to a therapist that they have victimized a specific child, this *must be* reported to appropriate protection agencies. This means that if my son, stepson, or ward reveals the name of a specific child he has victimized, such victimization will be reported and he will be investigated by appropriate protection agencies, which could lead to his being charged with the commission of a sex crime.

The benefit of this evaluation is that my son, stepson, or ward may receive a detailed evaluation of his sexual interest and sexual behavior. The staff will also be able to recommend to me and my son, stepson, or ward, what steps might be taken in response to accusations of his participating in sexually inappropriate behavior.

The information that my son, stepson, or ward, and I provide the staff will be kept confidential unless mandatory reporting is required.

Because understanding the law is crucial to the family's decisions at the first session, most sex-specific therapists not only have the patient sign a consent form acknowledging the law, they also explain the law again at the beginning of the session. Why? Because the reporting laws are important, and a patient should never be surprised that they exist.

After explaining the reporting laws to Alex and his parents, the therapist spends some time talking to Alex alone.

After that first hour of clinical interview, the therapist — because Alex told him he had "touched his five-year-old cousin in her crotch" — informed Alex's parents that he would report the incident to Child Protective Services.

Why does the therapist report such a trivial incident? *It's the law.*

And it is an excellent law because:

1. The therapist has no way of knowing the actual extent of a patient's sexual interaction with a child.

2. Molesters sometimes lie. Molesters are often in denial and have done more than they say.

3. Molesters often present themselves as good, responsible people —like John, the incest father, or the teenagers, Alex, Brian, and Jake—but the therapist never assumes that this responsible appearance means that they are incapable of doing irresponsible acts.

4. It is not the therapist's job to investigate a specific act.

—— THE REASON FOR REPORTING LAWS ——

People like Aunt Kathie are the reason we have mandatory reporting laws. She hit the roof when Child Protective Services called to make an appointment to interview her daughters. Besides her firm belief that Alex could not possibly be a pedophile, she also believed—even though over five million men molest children—that she'd never met a pedophile in her life. And she was unaware enough to believe that she would know immediately if she met one.

If Aunt Kathie had her way, if Alex was her son, she'd make sure this incident was never reported. What's more, she'd never seek an evaluation. What she'd do is handle this herself. She'd tell him he shouldn't do that. He'd say he never would, then he'd be left to deal with his testosterone-fueled sex drive toward little girls by himself. Being such a good kid, with such a strong sense of right and wrong, most likely he'd have quite a bit of success with his control over those urges—for awhile. Of course, he'd also have some failures. And the children around him would be left to deal with cousin Alex, and eventually Uncle Alex's sexual urges, all by themselves.

The caseworker's investigation centered on finding out if there was more to the incident. Did the behavior happen more than once? Were both little girls molested? Were there other occurrences that happened to their friends?

The caseworker discovered that the incident was exactly as presented—one child sexually touched for a few seconds. They listed the case as one in which no further action was needed, beyond the teenager's completion of his sex-specific evaluation and any recommended treatment.

Laws are good

Nora Harlow: Family members often remain unaware of the laws. Or they call for harsher laws, believing that no one in their family could possibly molest. Even if caught in the act, the family sometimes goes on believing that because the molester is young, or just because he is in their family, the act wasn't actually sexual abuse and so the laws do not apply to him.

Laws are good. They were written in the first place because families wrapped themselves in denial and left their young children unprotected. Or if they did react, they simply got angry, made the molester promise "to never touch that child again," and so they left the molested child and other children close to the molester unprotected.

To protect children we have to convince our own family members that the laws do apply to them, that sexual abuse can occur in any family—even in ordinary families, and that pedophilia is a serious medical condition. To save the greatest number of children in the shortest possible time all of us need to know the facts, teach them to our children, create a safe place in our homes to discuss the disorder, and *act* to stop it at the beginning.

Sex-specific therapists have a major advantage over Aunt Kathie: Sex-specific therapists realize that neither the family's money, nor education, nor strong moral values, protects a teenager from developing pedophilia. Most importantly, they know that child molesters are often in denial: Molesters often minimize or dismiss sexual acts against children as trivial and, too often, they are believed. Once child advocates realized that the Aunt Kathies of this world left children unprotected, they encouraged the passing of laws that took child sexual abuse decisions away from the family.

The question that has often plagued family members, neighbors, teachers, school counselors, and even general therapists, "Is this sex incident of *sufficient importance* to be reported?" is now easily answered. The answer is always "Yes." It is no longer the job of the family, the neighbor, the teacher—or even the therapist—to decide which incident to report. Mandatory reporting laws require that *all* suspected child sexual abuse be reported. *It's the law.*

What's good about this is that reporting laws shift this serious public health problem into the hands of professionals. Professional care is the key to the protection of our children, especially from public health problems that have serious consequences.

We don't expect either the patient or the patient's family to decide if a cough is a common cold, bronchitis, pneumonia, or tuberculosis. That's a clinical judgment made by a physician who takes a history, analyzes test results, and comes to a conclusion. Should the family decide that the child's pneumonia is too trivial to warrant the recommended hospitalization, the court may step in to protect the child. In suspected cases of child sexual abuse, where family denial and failure to protect the child are common, the authorities step in quickly.

—— THE THREE SYSTEMS OF PREVENTION ——

Earlier we said, "It is not the therapist's job to investigate a specific act." Alex's therapist reports to Child Protective Services so *they* can investigate.

Both the teenager, Jake, and the adult, John, are in the therapist's office following accusations that they sexually abused a child. The two families come to their first session with a burning question for the therapist: Did he do it? Did Jake molest the little boy next door? Did John molest Kerrie, his daughter? Did they do the specific act of which they are accused? Guilty? Or innocent?

This is *not* the therapist's main responsibility. What the therapist

---

wants to know is: *Does this patient have a diagnosable disorder that can be controlled with medicines and therapy?*

The professionals who can answer the question, "Did he do it?" are the ones who investigate and collect evidence: Child Protection Services and the criminal justice system.

It's about the child's life

Dr. Gene Abel: Since families have little knowledge of pedophilia, what causes it, and what tests, medicines, and therapies are available, they frequently get caught up in arguing about patient-therapist confidentiality and the reporting laws. The therapist's job is to train the family so they understand the law. That training is what maintains the patient's trust in the therapist.

The criminal justice system's job is to investigate the act and make a decision about guilt or innocence, and if the decision is guilt, to decide on the punishment. That's all they do.

The mistake families make is to believe that their son's possible inappropriate sexual behavior is only an issue related to the criminal justice system. It's much more than that. It's about the child's life.

The criminal justice system has no ability to change the teenager's sexual interest in young children. Just knowing that sexual behavior with young children is against the law is not enough. It's like saying it's against the law to get pneumonia.

Since there are three systems that use decidedly different methods to prevent child molestation, families often get confused about who does what.

Sara, Jake's mother, saw her son, even when he was 14, as a boy needing protection. She wanted to know why Child Protective Services was so concerned about the neighbor boy, but did nothing to help her boy. The answer is: It's not their job.

Families find the three systems particularly confusing because the three systems so often work together.

Caseworkers, as they did in John's case, order sex-specific evaluations. Judges sometimes do the same.

Probation or parole for the molester often exists with the condition that the convicted molester agrees to sex-specific treatment. Often a probation or parole officer not only monitors supervision procedures designed by or in cooperation with the sex-specific therapist, but also monitors the molester patient's compliance with treatment. Is he taking his medication? Does he comply with all aspects of therapy?

Since navigating through the three systems presents a dilemma for so many families, we thought we'd help you see who does what, in Table 6-3.

John and his family have to navigate through all three systems. So do Jake and his family.

Alex is in a much better position. The incident with his five-year-old cousin is determined by Child Protective Services to be minor. The interest of their system, as well as that of the criminal justice system, stops there.

Brian has no victim. That puts Brian in the most enviable position of all. His family has no reason to learn to negotiate through the three systems. Since he has no victim, reporting laws don't apply, there is no call to Child Protective Services and no call from them to the criminal justice system. Best of all, no child has been sexually abused.

This is what we call *primary prevention*. (It's like *never starting* to smoke. It's stopping the cause before it starts.)

Catching the disorder early has profound benefits. All three teenage boys are in a much better position than John. They have fewer victims. Their sexuality is still forming, still malleable.

Gene G. Abel, M.D. and Nora Harlow

TABLE 6-3

Contrasts: Three Methods of Prevention

Medical/Psychological	Child Protection Services	Criminal Justice System
Patient presents a problem • Evaluation for a diagnosable disorder.	**Receives a complaint** • Moves to protect the possible child victim	**Receives a complaint** • Begins criminal investigation
Evaluates the medical basis: • Childhood curiosity • Medical or mental • Antisocial • Pedophilia • Other causes of molestation	**Investigates** • Complaint may be dropped as not a bona fide complaint • Or complaint may be forwarded to the police as a founded case • Sometimes refers accused for sex-specific evaluation	**Investigates** • Complaint may be dropped as unfounded or for insufficient evidence • Complaint may be pursued when evidence exists to bring charges.
Treats the Molester • Reduces or eliminates arousal to children • Teaches pedophile arousal-stopping techniques • Prescribes drugs to decrease sex drive • Tests for recurrence of arousal throughout molester's lifetime	**Counsels victims** • About their physical safety • About their physical health • About their emotional health and refers them to a therapist	**Brings cases to court** • Judges the accused molester on evidence he committed a criminal act • Defendant found innocent or guilty
Prevention of recurrence • Institutes cognitive behavioral treatment component • Possible use of medication • Develops supervision system to ensure success	**Protection of the Victim** • If incest, usually removes accused from the home • If incest, may hold accused to a series of conditions before approving re-entry into the home • Isolates molester from other potential victims	**Punishment** • Sentenced to probation or prison • Serves time, then paroled or released to receive sex-specific therapy **Prevention** • Isolates molester for a period of time
Weaknesses • Less effective with molesters who are opportunists or anti-socials	**Weaknesses** • No focus on prevention of recurrence by the molester	**Weaknesses** • No ability to change the molester's sexual interest in children • Releases untreated pedophiles after punishment fulfilled

──── THE THERAPIST FOCUSES ON THE CAUSE ────

Although the incident with Alex's five-year-old cousin proved too minor to warrant police investigation, the therapist, nonetheless, needed to determine the cause. What *caused* Alex to do it? What caused 16-year-old Alex to have persistent sexual thoughts of very young children from the time he was thirteen? For Brian, the therapist's question is: What caused 13-year-old Brian to have continuous sexual thoughts about the little girl sliding down the pole and about his little sister's friend?

What the therapist wants to know is this: Is there something invisible working inside the person's body that makes him different? Does he have a sexual interest in children that *causes* him to want to sexually interact with children?

Although the fact that we're talking about sex and children brings out extreme emotions in many people, the *process* of identifying this major health problem is similar to what we do for many diseases and disorders: The physician or therapist conducts a clinical interview, orders tests, and makes a second appointment to discuss the overall findings.

All three teenagers took a sexual interest test. So did John. John also took a sexual arousal test.

──── THE NEW TESTS ────
WHAT THEY ARE AND WHY WE NEED THEM

If there is one reason we can, today, save three million children, it's the new tests made possible by computer technology.

What causes 17-year-old George to molest his ten-year-old stepsister and then 22 more little girls? He has a sex drive directed at children.

Many people will be surprised that we have tests that identify this sex drive. Actually the tests have existed for 30 years and have been commonly used for 20 years. There are two types of objective tests: the sexual arousal tests and the sexual interest tests. Both measure the patient's sex drive toward children against his sex drive toward adults. The question both tests answer: In relation to this patient's sex drive toward adults, how strong is his sex drive toward children? The sexual arousal tests measure the man's erection. The sexual interest tests are visual reaction tests.

Sexual arousal tests

Sexual arousal tests all use some means of measuring the patient's erection. While different kinds have been used for research purposes, mainly in the United States and Canada, one, penile plethysmography, has been in continuous use with patients since the early 1970's. Dr. Abel pioneered the use of penile plethysmography (or P-test). After he built his first pleythsmograph in 1970, he published 16 scientific articles documenting the accuracy and usefulness of plethysmography.[44] [45] Although the basic methodology remains the same, the latest versions of the P-test are computerized and more sophisticated.

During the P-test the patient sits in a chair in a lab setting. A gauge circles his penis and records small increases in circumference as he looks at images of adults and children or listens to audio presentations describing sexual activities with adults or children.

It also tests for aggression during those activities. It's a test suitable for adult men and is rarely used with anyone less than 16 years old.[46]

Sexual interest tests

Sexual interest tests all use some means of measuring the patient's visual reaction to pictures of adults and children. Again, like the sexual arousal tests, several different versions of these tests have been used in research, but one has emerged into common use with patients—The Abel Assessment *for sexual interest™*.

Dr. Abel created the basic methodology behind the new tests in 1988. After seven years of additional research, in 1995, he released the Abel Assessment for use by professionals. In 2001 it is the only sexual interest test available.

The key to saving children: measurement

Dr. Gene Abel: I was a physician in a psychiatry residency at the medical school in Iowa City, Iowa. It was 1970. One day, in came a patient who was a convicted child molester just released from Joliet Prison. I was told to evaluate him, but I had no idea what to do.

I searched the psychiatric literature for help, but I was disappointed. The information on child molestation was sparse. It was psychoanalytic theory, and there appeared to be no practical use for it. Sigmund Freud had hypothesized that a man molested children because he was afraid of adult sexuality and/or was afraid of castration. I was thinking: What could I do with that?

I entered medicine because I wanted to be a scientist. As a practical Iowa farm boy, I saw improvements in the science of medicine as a real and immediate way to help people.

If my evaluation of this child molester was going to help people in a real and immediate way, what I had to do was find out if this patient was still a threat to little girls today. If he was, I had to figure out if the treatment made him less of a threat. And, I needed something beyond *his* saying, "Gee, Doc, I'm doing great. I'm fine now."

After an extensive search, I found an article in an English medical journal by a physician named John Bancroft. Dr. Bancroft, who is now in the U.S. and is the director of the Kinsey Institute, had built a device to measure a man's general sexual arousal.

That intrigued me. Measurement. If I could measure the child molester's arousal to little girls, I might be able to do an evaluation that was of practical use. Although no mention was made of the device's use with child molesters, I reasoned that the child molester's sexual arousal would work the same way — except instead of being aroused to adults; he would be aroused to children.

I gathered materials silastic tubing, mercury, and an amp meter. I followed Bancroft's diagram, built a similar device, and in two days was using that crude technology to measure the molester's current sexual interest in little girls. I made up some descriptions of a man sexually touching a child. I emphasized the child's small, smooth, underdeveloped body.

Before I gave the test, I was half convinced that the patient would fail to respond. He had been adamant in my clinical interview of him that he had no sexual interest in little girls. He was positive. The man said that prison had taught him that it was wrong. After the test, he declared again that none of those descriptions of a little girl's body affected him at all.

The measurements told a different story. That man, on that day, was four times as sexually interested in little girls as he was in adult women.

I was amazed. I had measured a man's sexual interests. The patient was trying to fool me and he couldn't. All I could think was: If we can measure a person's sexual interest in little children, then we can know who is most likely to molest children. And once we know where that sexual interest comes from, we have a chance to control it, perhaps even extinguish it.

99

The test-taker, who remains in street clothes, sits at a desk in front of a computer. The computer measures his sexual interest in pictures of children and adults dressed in bathing suits, as the test-taker would see them at the local swimming pool. The images are ethnic specific, suitable for Caucasians, African-Americans, or Hispanic/Latino Americans. In addition to its major purpose—helping to identify patients with paraphilias—it's also used to help identify patients with a sexual interest in violence or sadism. Called "the Abel," this sexual interest test is suitable for men, women, and teenagers who have concerns about having a sexual interest in children.

Up until the release of the Abel, many sex-specific therapists who regularly did sexual arousal testing combined that objective testing with various sex-specific psychological questionnaires. For this new test Dr.

Abel combined these sex-specific questionnaires and added them to the objective visual part of the test. The results from both sections of the test— the sexual interest test and the sex-specific questionnaire — are combined in a set of formulas that give several kinds of results helpful to the sex-specific therapist. The most recent formulas not only produce a result that measures the patient's sexual interest in children against his or her sexual interest in adults, it also adds a new measure: the probability that the patient matches a large group of men who have molested a child.

The strength of the Abel is its ability to quickly process some 2,000 variables and then match the patient to the variables that most sharply divide people who admit to molesting children from people who report that they do not molest children.

This test is suitable for early diagnosis and is designed to be acceptable to the family of a 12-year-old child.

Polygraph test

The polygraph is sometimes called a "lie detector test." While not a sex-specific test, the polygraph is often used with patients who have paraphilias. For this test, the patient sits in a chair. Bands circle his chest and are attached to his hand to measure respiratory and cardiac rates and sweating. Therapists most often use the polygraph with the P-test or the Abel to get answers to specific questions. They are used as an additional check on the patient's account of his sex history, to verify specific paraphilic incidents, and to verify his ability to maintain his treatment gains. For instance, a sex-specific therapist might have the polygrapher ask a patient: "Have you been honest with your therapist about your sexual history with children?" "Since you entered treatment have you touched a child for sexual gratification?" "Since you've been on probation, have you been compliant with your probation requirements?"

A sexual interest screen

The newest sexual interest test is a screen. In addition to the tests used with patients, this fourth test will soon be available to screen teenagers and adults who are asking to be put in positions of trust with children. The Abel *Sexual Interest* Screen ™ uses the same methodology and the identical adult and child images as the Abel Assessment. During both tests, the test-taker sees 320 images of adults and children in 20 minutes.

The difference between the two tests, the Abel Assessment and the Abel Screen lies in the questionnaire section and the formula for the results. For the Screen, the test-taker answers a short series of questions. None of the questions is directly sexual. The Screen formula matches the test-taker, on approximately 500 variables, to a group of admitted child molesters and to a group of people who have never molested a child. The Abel Screen has been in development since 1988 and will be released to the public in 2002.[47]

——THE MOST FREQUENTLY ASKED QUESTIONS—— ABOUT SEX-SPECIFIC TESTS

How *reliable* and valid are the sexual interest tests?

Plethysmography, the Abel Assessment and The Abel Screen all have high reliability and validity ratings.[48]

Who could find out your son is being evaluated?

Psychiatric test records are confidential. The patient (or the parents of an underage patient) controls the release of his (or her) records and must sign consent for release of records if he wishes someone else—his lawyers, church officials, family members—to have access to them.

For the Abel sexual interest tests, the test-taker's privacy is strictly guarded. A number identifies each test. So neither the people processing the tests nor anyone who happens to see a test printout will be able to link that test to a specific person. The only one who can match the test to the test-taker is the physician or therapist whose office administered the test.

If you test positive, can you be arrested?

No. The sexual arousal tests and the sexual interest tests do not test for guilt or innocence. What most people want is to relieve their anxiety by getting an answer to the question: Did the patient molest that child? Neither test answers that question. The question they answer is: Does he have an ongoing sexual interest in children that could be stopped by medicines and therapies?

Who will pay for the tests?

Insurance companies that pay for psychological testing also pay for these tests. Occasionally, the patient's employer will pay for testing. With destitute teenagers, the state often pays. And, of course, some patients pay for their own tests.

Why are these tests effective?

The reason these tests work so well, as you saw in Chapter One is that there is actually an enormous difference between men and women who have an ongoing sexual interest in children and men and women who don't.

How do these tests help us protect children?

We know that the child molesters who have this unusual sex drive are the ones who molest 88 percent of our children. And we know that this sex drive toward children appears during puberty, and that the majority of pedophiles have their first victim while they are teenagers. With those two facts in mind, the most sensible thing we could do is test early and treat early.

Which teenagers should we test?

We should test:

1. Teenagers concerned that they may have a sexual interest in children;

2. Boys who are victims of molestation;

3. Boys and girls who are the older child in a sexual incident if the age difference is three to five years or more;

4. Any child or teenager accused of sexually molesting a younger child.

Which adults should we test?

1. Adults concerned that they may have a sexual interest in children

2. Adults who report child-centered sex fantasies for more than six months

3. Exhibitionists (flashers)

4. Voyeurs (window-peepers)

5. Adults who have been accused of sexually molesting a child

6. Adults convicted of sexually molesting a child

Who should we treat?

Any patient who, in the opinion of a sex-specific therapist, could benefit.

But will the treatment actually extinguish the pedophile's sex drive toward children? He'll say he's fine, but is he? Here again, the tests give our children protection. We don't have to rely on the pedophile's word—or the therapist's impressions. We can check the test results to see if the treatment has worked to extinguish the patient's child directed sex drive. We can also measure any reoccurrence of the sexual interest in children in the years following treatment. Tests to identify people with a sexual interest in children are all about sex drive.

—— THE BIGGEST OBSTACLE TO —— PROTECTING CHILDREN

So, what's our biggest obstacle here? Most people have never heard of the tests. A sex test scares them. Why? Because they have it backwards. If you tell them that there is an immense difference between pedophiles and all the people who aren't pedophiles, they'll absolutely agree. But they won't talk about a sex drive directed at children.

They'll tell you that pedophiles are immensely different in *their obvious outward characteristics*. They'll say—a mistaken belief—that pedophiles neither look nor behave like any friend of theirs or any member of their family. Pedophiles, they'll say, are single men who have no education, who never date, have no interest in religion, and are unable to support themselves. They'll go on to say—again mistakenly—that they look strange and they act strange. In fact they are strangers. They are strange men who hang around the schoolyard with candy bars to lure our children away.

We showed you that most men who admitted to molesting a child were just like everyone else in their outward characteristics. In fact, they are a mirror image of this country's population. They are married, educated, working, and religious. And perhaps their most confusing characteristic: one part of their sex drive is like everyone else's—their sex drive toward adults. (Only 7 percent of pedophiles have no sexual interest in adults).

The difference for the 93 percent with sexual interest in adults is—and this is immense—that they *also* have a sexual interest in children.

The pedophile is dealing with a sex drive so immensely different from the sex drive of most of us that people who don't have it can barely imagine it exists.

Since most people don't understand what causes a man like George from Chapter One to (in the minds of his neighbors), suddenly sexually molest a child; they don't believe a test could possibly work.

They mistakenly believe that when they hug a child or hold a child on their lap that an evaluator might mistake that act for child molestation. It's a needless worry; a sex-specific physician or therapist recognizes the difference between someone who wants sexual gratification from a child and a person who touches a child to show love.

On a test that measures *sexual* interest in children, someone who hugs and cuddles children as part of a loving family will react radically different from a person who is interested in a child sexually. Why? Because the loving adult who hugs a child has a sex drive that leaves out children, it's directed at adults. The pedophile's immensely different sex drive works to our advantage. We can test for it, we can offer medicines and therapies to reduce or extinguish that child-directed sex drive. It's because that sex drive is so immensely different that the tests work so well.

Alex takes the sexual interest test

What should parents expect? Since the test contains sexual material, parents should examine the testing material and give their consent for testing.

"Before we test your son," Alex's therapist told them. "I'd like you to review the questions Alex will be asked and the slides he will see. I want you to understand the nature of the questions and see what the people in the slides look like."

Then, while Alex remained outside in the waiting room, his parents looked at the visual material and read the questions. The subjects in the slides were clothed and none were in erotic poses. The 300 questions were at the third grade reading level and worded to be easily understood by teenagers.

Interpreting the tests

The results from the P-test and the Abel are powerful. However, they are not the one-stop answer. Everyone wants to know immediately: Is this person a child molester? Did he or she do it? For the therapist, however, the test results yield pieces of information that fit into a big picture of child protection. The answers help with diagnosis; they help with decisions about specific treatments. They never indicate guilt or innocence related to a specific act. What they do is more powerful. They suggest to the therapist the presence of a diagnosable disorder that can be effectively controlled with medicine and therapies.

The therapist is the only one who can interpret the objective measures from the tests designed to reveal a sexual drive toward children. As in other health specialties, it is the professional who not only interprets the meaning of each patient's results in the light of that patient's past health history, but also makes the crucial decision about the best course of treatment.

—— THE DIAGNOSES: ALEX, BRIAN, JAKE, AND JOHN ——
Alex's diagnosis

Alex's parents came to the second session knowing that Alex might have this disorder. Still, they hoped that the tests, along with the interview, would lead the therapist to conclude that Alex's Aunt Kathie was right, that the incident was nothing more than a boy's natural sexual curiosity.

Alex's test results showed he had some sexual interest in teenage girls in his age range; however, he had more sexual interest in girls of pre-school and grade-school age.

Alex reported one act with one victim. He believed he had control over his urges towards these young girls nearly all the time. While he reported that nearly half his sex fantasies were of girls his age, he also reported that slightly more than half were of girls nine and younger.

He had a good appreciation of the inability of very young girls to give consent and registered on the test scale as a generally truthful person. He reported that for the past three years, since he turned 13, he had had persistent fantasies of sexually touching grade-school-age- and pre-school-age girls. He also admitted to using pornography, such as *Playboy*, and to having had alcohol more than 10 times and marijuana twice.

After the therapist gathered information from Alex and his parents in the clinical interview and reviewed the test results, he made his diagnosis: Pedophilia towards girls.

Alex met the following criteria for that diagnosis: he was 16, his victim was more than five years younger, he had sexual fantasies and urges directed at girls at least five years younger than himself for more than six months. He had acted on his urges. (Note: Alex could be diagnosed without committing a sexual abuse act. His ongoing urges and fantasies qualify.)

Because he also was attracted to teenage girls, Alex was diagnosed as a *non-exclusive pedophile.*

An "exclusive" pedophile is a patient who has sexual interest *exclusively* in children. While seven percent of people with the diagnosis pedophilia are *only* interested in children, 93 percent are *also* (like Alex) interested in having sex with people their own age. This overwhelming majority is said to have pedophilia of the nonexclusive type.[49]

Because Julie was his cousin, Alex was further clarified to be of the incest type. His complete diagnosis: Pedophilia, female incest, non-exclusive.

The good news for Alex: He already had a significant sexual interest in young women his age and older. This meant he would be easier to treat. If he had been part of the seven percent exclusive pedophilia type, the therapist would have a difficult job helping Alex establish a sexual interest in people his own age, a sexual interest that previously didn't exist for him.

The therapist recommended treatment to reduce or extinguish Alex's sexual interest in young girls.

Brian's diagnosis

Brian's therapist talked to the 13-year-old boy and to his father. He checked first to see if there was a consistency between what Brian said happened regarding his ongoing sexual interest and fantasies, and his father's knowledge of what had happened. Then he reviewed with Brian what his father had told him concerning Brian's worry over getting rid of these sexual fantasies of the six-year-old sliding down the pole. The therapist asked Brian: "Have you had any situations in which you've been successful in blocking those sex thoughts? Brian could only remember a few times in which he was successful at blocking.

The therapist ordered testing for several reasons. First, he wanted to see if the boy had a measurable sexual interest in children. Second, he wanted to find out more information that might suggest another cause for the boy's reported interest. (Had Brian been molested, for example, and developed these ongoing sex fantasies because he "identified with the aggressor"?)

In addition, the therapist explored the possibility that another boy his age provoked this interest in Brian—a boy who *was* molesting a six-year-old girl. He also wanted to know if Brian might be developing other paraphilias. Was he, for example, becoming a voyeur, secretly spying on very young girls?

Brian's test results showed a slight sexual interest in girls of pre-school age and grade-school age. He had a much stronger interest in teenage girls and adult women, which is common in teenage boys. He had no paraphilias. He had never been molested. He did, however, have persis-tent sexual fantasies—more than half of his sexual fantasies were of sexually touching pre-school age girls. His answer to the question about alcohol use prompted a confession that he'd made off with several bottles of beer from his home to drink with a friend on New Year's Eve.

The therapist's opinion: Brian's problem of fantasizing about young girls has been identified very early. Brian, at 13, is too young to be diagnosed as having pedophilia, and the therapist is also reluctant to label Brian as having pedophilic interest. At his young age, Brian could be focusing sharply on his experience of being aroused sliding down the pole while looking up the dress of a six-year-old girl simply because he lacked other sexual experiences. The therapist believed a brief intervention would be successful.

After the therapist reassured father and son that their decision making was correct (they were right to seek an evaluation), he suggested that Brian meet with him once a month during the next three months for the purpose of sex-specific counseling. Brian's therapy was rather straightforward. The therapist:

- made sure that Brian's initial sexual history was correct;
- helped Brian understand that first sexual experiences sometimes do have a major impact;
- helped Brian block his thoughts of very young girls;
- made certain that he had the opportunity to talk to someone other than his parents about his sexual interests, fantasies, and concerns;
- helped him expand his sexual fantasies to peers and adults;
- explained that if this problem returned, the boy was to call the therapist to get further help.

As the therapist thought, for Brian, this brief three-session intervention was successful. In fact, this sex-specific therapy did Brian a great service. It prevented him early in his life from using fantasies of very young girls that, had he continued them as he grew up, could have produced a catastrophe in the family.

Brian's final diagnosis: No diagnosis.

Jake's diagnosis

Sara was angry that her family, which had gone through so much, never seemed able to get away from the problem of child molestation. She banked on her belief that a boy like her son, who had suffered so much, would never dream of putting another child through that. The therapist agreed that what she suggested might well be the case. Simply because her son was molested, it didn't necessarily follow that the experience would *cause* him to molest a child. Perhaps he was doing what all kids do, displaying a natural sexual curiosity. Or perhaps, since he had been molested, he was modeling—acting out sexually what he had experienced.

During his private session, Jake confirmed to the therapist that he had, indeed, sexually molested the seven-year-old boy next door. He also revealed a long history—two years—of sexual fantasies of and sexual urges toward boys of that age. His test results showed a sexual interest in teenage girls and adult women. However, his greatest sexual interest was in grade-school boys.

On the questionnaire, Jake answered yes to the question, "Have you ever got a turn on by peeping into windows or secretly watching people taking off their clothes or having sex?" During the follow-up clinical interview, Jake admitted that he had spied on the neighbor boy next door, peeping through his bedroom window to see him naked before he put on his pajamas. At the neighborhood public pool, Jake had also stood in water up to his shoulders and masturbated while looking at little boys.

He reported that he had had one victim and that he had molested the boy 11 times. He also admitted that *all* of his sex fantasies were of sexually touching a much younger child. In answers to questions about being a victim, Jake revealed that he had been sexually molested more than 300 times.

Reporting on his own activities as a molester, Jake was unable to see that the seven-year-old neighbor was a victim. He said that the acts were by mutual consent. This meant that, rather than seeing a seven-year-old as easily overpowered by the will of a 14-year-old, he saw his seven-year-old victim as an equal who could make his own sexual decisions. The sex-specific therapist discovered that Jake, now that puberty had hit, was once again of the belief that he had been an equal of Mr. Jones and, from the ages of three to seven, had been responsible for his own molestation.

Although Jake had molested a child, although he had many symptoms that adults with pedophilia commonly reported that they had at Jake's age,

Jake, at 14, did not meet the criterion for a medical diagnosis as a pedophile. A teenager is not diagnosable as a pedophile until he is 16 because psychiatry recognizes that anyone younger than that has a sex drive that is still somewhat plastic, that is still evolving.

Jake's pedophilic symptoms included:

- Molesting a child who was more that five years younger.

  Jake's victim was seven years old.
- Having ongoing sexual urges toward and sexual fantasies of very young boys.

  Jake fantasized continually, especially about the neighbor boy.
- Acting on his urges.

  Jake had acted 11 times
- Mistakenly believing that the younger child was a consenting, equal partner.

  Jake was in denial; he saw himself as innocent
- Having symptoms of the *initial development* of several paraphilias.

  In addition to symptoms of pedophilia, Jake had symptoms of voyeurism (window-peeping) and public masturbation (molesting in public without wanting to be seen).

The therapist's diagnosis: Conduct disorder, adolescent onset type.

Jake, at 12, had identified with his aggressor and started building his sexual desire for a much younger boy. With that came a return of his feelings of responsibility not only for his own molestation but also for failing to stop Mr. Jones from molesting his little sister.

The therapist recommended treatment to reduce or extinguish Jake's sexual interest in young boys. He also recommended further therapy for Jake's issues related to the fact that he had been a victim.

John's diagnosis

John was investigated by Child Protective Services, went to trial and was convicted by the criminal justice system. He served time, and was released. Before his trial, he was referred for evaluation and treatment. The results of his sexual interest test suggested a high sexual interest in adult females and a slightly higher sexual interest in girls of grade-school age. John disagreed with the results, asked for and was given a sexual arousal test. The results were the same. He also took a polygraph test. Among the questions the therapist had the polygrapher ask John: "Since you've been no longer living at home, have you communicated with your daughter?" Test results suggested that John's answer—"no"—was truthful.

He was diagnosed by the medical system, treated with medicine and therapy, and made relapse prevention a permanent part of his life. No more victims. No more acts.

Diagnosis: Pedophilia, female incest, nonexclusive

——The Magic of Early Diagnosis——
No magic for John

The case of John, who committed incest with his daughter, calls up that familiar phrase, "if only . . ."

If only John's sexual interest in children had been identified while he was still a teenager. If only John and his little sister had lived in a home where the parents talked to their children not only about bad touch, but also about what causes people to molest children and how easy it is to get them to stop. Then what? Then John's sister might have felt free to go to her mother the first time her older brother approached her.

Even better, if only one of John's parents had drawn John into a conversation concerning sex thoughts focused on much younger children the way Brian's dad had with him, then John might have been able to get help to stop his sex fantasies of little girls when he was a young teenager, before he ever molested his sister. Then what? Then three little girls would have been saved.

What about the Christian counselor who helped John so much? And, here, we have yet another, "if only . . ." If only he had suspected that a *possible reason* for a 19-year-old boy to move in with an alcoholic woman in her thirties was the presence of her two young daughters and had referred John for testing. Then what? Then Kerrie would have been saved.

The magic of early diagnosis for Alex

Alex's sexual interest in little girls just happened to him when he hit puberty. Luckily, after Alex sexually touched his five-year-old cousin, his dad had a conversation with him; which convinced both parents that their son needed a sex-specific evaluation.

The evaluation led to an early diagnosis that saved Alex from molesting that five-year-old cousin again and from a lifetime of fighting (with some successes and some failures) his sexual urges toward other little girls.

The magic of early diagnosis for Brian

Brian was developing an ongoing sexual interest in little girls in the way so many young boys do—by accident. Following a sexually arousing first sex experience, he inadvertently began to condition himself to have a consistent sexual interest in little girls. Fortunately, Brian's dad had that conversation with his son that gave the boy critical information about the dangers a teenager faces if he allows his sexual fantasies to fill up with images of first-grade girls. That bit of sex education prompted Brian to worry. And that, incidentally, is a critical difference between Brian and John. When John was a teenager focusing on sexual fantasies of girls in first-grade and second-grade, he had no worries about that. He mistakenly believed all teenage boys had those kinds of sexual thoughts.

The other critical difference between Brian and John: Brian's dad opened the door that allowed Brian to share his sexual worries with his dad, but John had no such opportunity. And beyond that, Brian's dad proved himself a strong, capable parent who could get help for his son—even when the help was to combat a concern that his 13-year-old son might have put himself on the track for becoming a child molester. An early, sex-specific evaluation for Brian meant easily stopping the formation of pedophilia before one child was approached. John was unlucky. John was a teenager in the old era, before families knew how to stop child molestation.

The magic of early diagnosis for Jake

Jake, who became a child molester as a consequence of being a severely sexually abused boy, was on track to molesting a large number of children. With the onslaught of that second batch of testosterone at puberty, and his newly awakening sexuality, Jake protected himself from his sexual memories by identifying with his aggressor.

Statistically, Jake fit into that group of child molesters who had been sexually abused as boys more than 50 times. That group *averages* 25 victims and 142 acts. Jake was able to get help. He was able to stop after one victim and 11 acts. With the average in mind, we can say that early diagnosis, in Jake's case, saved 24 children and stopped 131 acts of sexual abuse.

——WHO ARE THE HEROES —— IN THE STORY OF EARLY DIAGNOSIS?

If we are going to save children, we have to move forward, and turn ourselves into heroes like the heroes in this story of early diagnosis. Who are the heroes in these stories?

- **The parents** are the heroes. The parents of the three teenage boys —and Jake's victim's father.

  The heroes of these stories are the parents who stepped forward and acted: the neighbor boy's father who stepped forward to protect his son and *all* the children in the neighborhood; the parents of Alex, Brian, and Jake, who acted to protect their sons.

  Some parents ignore their children's sexual problems. They see sexual behavior as boys being boys. In so doing, they reinforce their mistaken belief that with the passage of time these sex problems will simply go away. This leaves the child to fend for himself at an age when he knows virtually nothing of the potential dangers of sexual fantasies directed at very young children.

The heroes are the parents who step forward to unravel their teenager's dilemmas and allow experts to help sort out what needs to be done.

Early diagnosis saves the teenager. What the adult protectors of Alex, Brian, and Jake have done is truly magic. They've saved all the young children around these three boys *and* they've saved each boy from waking up one day as a man in his thirties or forties to that devastating reality: I am a child molester.

THE STOP CHILD MOLESTATION PLAN IN ACTION
— CHAPTER 6 —

1. Tell others the facts.	**Tell your family and friends:** • Early diagnosis of teenagers will save millions of children from being sexually abused. Only families can make this happen. • Pedophiles are just like everyone in their outer characteristics — but they are immensely different in their sex drive, even as teenagers. • Sex-specific tests are effective because of that immense difference. The tests have been used more than 30 years and have been continuously improved to be acceptable to families of 12-year-olds • Sex-specific therapists teach techniques to directly reduce or eliminate sexual interest in children. • Early diagnosis not only saves millions of child victims, it saves the teenager with the disorder from having to interact with the criminal justice system or, worst of all, from waking up in their twenties, thirties, or forties and having to face the devastating truth: I am a child *molester.*
2. **Save the greatest number of children in the shortest possible time.**	• Take older child-younger child sexual incidents seriously. • Seek evaluation from a sex-specific therapist • If the older child has a sexual interest in children, have the child treated.
3. **Focus on the cause: Start saving children at the beginning — before a child becomes a victim**	• Consider the first fact about pedophilia: It starts at puberty — 70% of pedophiles molest a child while they are teenagers.

7

TREATMENT:
THE MEDICINES AND THE THERAPIES

A FACT

The medicines are effective. The therapies are successful. Families can expect an 89-percent to 99-percent success rate when they seek out treatment by a sex-specific therapist who uses a combination of medicine, testing, and the most advanced cognitive-behavioral therapies, all directed toward eliminating the molester's sexual desire for children.

YOUR OPPORTUNITY TO SAVE CHILDREN

As you go about your everyday life, if you hear someone you know talking about the discovery of an incident of child sexual abuse, you could save many children by giving these suggestions.

To the victim's family: Please insist that the molester be required to complete sex-specific treatment. This is *not* "helping" or "coddling" the molester. This is child molestation prevention.

To the molester: You must commit yourself to a sex-specific program (even if you are going to jail) that will give you the control to stop and to *never* approach another child.

To the clergy and therapists counseling the victim or the molester: Please protect *all* the children by making sure that the molester (even if he's an incestuous father) completes a sex-specific program.

7

—— ALEX, BRIAN, JAKE, AND JOHN ——

GETTING TREATMENT

Alex's Aunt Kathie refused to accept his diagnosis. Pedophiles were the worst of the child molesters. Her dear, dear Alex wasn't even close to being a child molester, he was a curious boy doing what curious boys do. A touch that took a few seconds, and suddenly Alex is called a pedophile. The same woman who had created such a positive environment for her young daughters, the woman who they ran to with the news when cousin Alex was sexually inappropriate, was the same woman who balked and refused to believe that her favorite nephew might have a serious problem. She felt her sister and brother-in-law were the ones who needed to see a therapist. They had "sex-on-the-brain." "If I had my life to live over," she told Alex's other two aunts, "I would pretend what happened to Julie in the bathtub never happened."

Brian felt good when the sex-specific therapist said he didn't have to come back after the third session. He felt comforted to know that many of the things the therapist said were the same that his dad had said. He learned how important it was to prevent his sex fantasies from drifting toward very young girls.

Jake's mother was angry with the sex-specific therapist before she entered his office. Neighbors calling the police on a child like Jake without even talking to his parents. And now this court-ordered therapist. She saw the therapist as just one more person out to get her son.

John spent most of his energy in the first six sessions explaining that he was not a child molester. Kerrie was his daughter; she was the last person he would have sex with. John's brother trusted him. His brother stopped speaking to their mother. Had their mother lost her mind? How could she call the police on her own son? His brother was also suspicious of John's wife: Did she put the little girl up to it?

—— In This Chapter ——

"Treatment: The Medicines and The Therapies" describes the medical breakthroughs that have given us the means to control pedophilia. In it you will learn:

- how family denial—based on two mistaken beliefs—often prevent us from seeking treatment for molesters;

- what familiar medicines are now routinely used effectively to control sex-specific disorders, such as the desire to flash, to window-peep, or to sexually interact with a child;

- what one combination of therapies has proven effective;

- how to handle family members who obstruct treatment or who ignore special treatment conditions designed to protect possible child victims;

- why severely sexually abused boys who become molesters can be difficult to treat;

- why treatment success is virtually guaranteed for some incest fathers.

—— The Power of Family Denial ——

The medicines are effective. The therapies are successful. What stops us from using them to save three million children?

Family denial. A family's fear of disgrace.

Such denial is ironic in two ways.

Irony # 1: When a family member develops a sexual interest in children, the family has nothing to do with it.

Alex developed his sexual interest in little girls all by himself. It just happened to him. Jake developed his sexual interest in boys because of his fear of Mr. Jones. He identified with his aggressor.

John developed his sexual interest in girls in the family as a teenager. Either his sexual interest just happened to him (like Alex's), or it happened by accident (like Brian's). Then John entrenched that sex drive, initially by having sexual fantasies of his little sister and eventually by molesting her.

How can a family feel shame, embarrassment, or disgrace when the mother, the father, the aunts and uncles, and the grandparents did nothing to **cause the** *development* of that boy's or man's sexual interest?

Irony # 2: While the family has nothing to do with a teenager developing pedophilia; family members are the only ones who can stop this disorder from doing harm. The family is the only group that can save three million children.

While families don't **cause** a teenager to *develop* pedophilia, they sometimes do *contribute* to the high incidence of child molestation. How? By refusing to do anything when they know a child in their family has been molested. John's little sister knew from direct personal experience that her brother had molested a child. And yet, as an adult she kept the secret and so she endangered Kerry and the other children in the family. John's mother knew before John married. John's mother and his sister were in denial. The truth was they were embarrassed that this had happened in their family. They didn't want anyone to know—not even John's wife. Telling someone in authority was out of the question. Like many people they were afraid of dealing publicly with a sexual matter. Sex was private.

Just as molesting patients are often in denial, families whose children have been molested are often in denial. John's mother had many denial stories that she repeated to herself: John's repeated sexual touching of his 10-year-old sister when he was 17 was just "little boy stuff"; maybe her daughter's memory was faulty, maybe it wasn't as big a deal as she remembered; John was grown-up now, he was a responsible, well-liked, accomplished adult, so those childhood sex things were the farthest thing from his mind. She also told herself that John probably didn't even remember he did anything with his sister, and if he did, now that he was an adult, now that he knew for sure that it was wrong, he'd surely never touch a child that way again.

And, John's mother and sister had the worst kind of denial: If we talk about it, John and Amanda and others in the family will be mad at us; if we keep quiet, nothing bad will happen.

Besides that, John's mother had a fear of having to deal publicly with private family matters. She said that when—in response to Kerry's molestation—she dialed Child Protective Services "my hands shook so bad I thought I was having a stroke." We've called her a hero because we know how hard it was for her to make that call. What's interesting here: John's mother, when she first heard from her adult daughter about John's molesting behavior, she could have been a force to find out if he had pedophilia and get it controlled right there. And, she could have kept this family matter private. At that time, John's sister was an adult and so the reporting laws do not apply. The reporting laws protect children. Once the child victim becomes an adult, it's her decision alone—not the therapist's—whether or not to report. But John's sister didn't want anyone to know that she had been a child victim. Most of all she didn't want to talk about sex. Too personal.

That's why many families refuse to consider the possibility that sex has anything to do with children being molested. As long as they insist that child molestation is only a question of right and wrong they have the enormous relief of never having to talk about sex.

However, in our efforts to save the greatest number of children in the shortest possible time, we *do* have to talk about sex. The key to drastically reducing the number of child victims is the molester's sex drive. The purpose of treatment—the medicines and the therapies— is to control that sex drive.[50]

—— THE MEDICINES ——

Once the tests indicate that teenagers like Alex and Jake or a man like John have sexual interest in children, then what happens?

The first decision is whether or not the molester needs medication to gain immediate control. Do these teenage boys or John need medications? If so, what kind and what will the medicines do for them?

Alex and Brian do not need medication.

Ethical dilemna:
Save children or keep the secret

Nora Harlow: Many people have told me stories about being caught in what they felt were terrible ethical dilemmas. Their brother, sister, or their close friend told them they were sexually molested, but swore them to secrecy. Forever. Like Helen tried to do for her sister Margaret, they felt — out of loyalty to the victim — that they were honor-bound to take this victim's secret to their grave.

One man told me about his younger brother being molested by his mother's best friend. This woman took the brothers, when they were boys of 10 and 12, on a trip. She — "as a treat" — gave them alcohol to drink and set them up to watch movies of adults having sex. The older brother passed out, she sexually molested the younger one. Neither boy told their parents. The older one did shield his little brother from ever having to be alone with this woman again. His dilemma occurred many years later. On a visit home from the military, he watched this woman going off to her house with three young boys in tow — the sons of one of his older girl cousins. Years later when he told me this story — what he saw that day still haunted him.

The question he might of asked himself: "Is my silence in the best interest of all the children in my family?"

The story of the brothers happened long ago, when, in fact, people felt powerless and were, for the most part, powerless. They had no idea why any adult would molest or what anyone could do about it.

If the same incident happened today, what could the brother do? The first thing would be to talk to his younger brother. When the brothers made their pact of secrecy, they were young. A ten-year-old boy who is embarrassed and begs a 12-year-old boy for secrecy, may not be embarrassed at 18 or 20, especially after his older brother tells him about seeing their mother's friend going off with other boys in the family. And, this is a perfect opportunity to tell the brother the facts: Pedophilia is a disorder; treatment works.

Other points to make with the brother: It was fanciful for us to believe that you were this molester's only victim. When this woman molested you and the two of us kept her secret, she learned it was all right to molest a boy. *It's our secrecy that makes it easier for her to molest other boys.*

As to keeping the secret, the question to ask now: Is it still worth it?

Most likely the victim will join in the efforts to protect the family's children. Suppose he refuses, then, the older brother talks to the three boys' mother without mentioning the victim. When he talks to their mother he simply asks her why this old friend of the family was going off with her sons. He then says he's concerned because he knows she has molested a child in the past and he doesn't know if she has received treatment. (This gives him the opportunity to tell the boys' mother the facts about what's available to treat child molesters.) What the family needs to do at this point is collect information from as many family members as possible about the known molester's activities with other children in the family — past and present. In many cases, it will be the adult survivor who will volunteer to take this role to protect the family's children. If the victims are now adults, the family can (without reporting) demand that she get treatment. If the family finds that some of her victims are children, to protect them, the family must report. Of course, the woman must also get treatment.

Jake needs medication.

John needs medication.

What do families need to know about these medications?

That, first of all, they work directly to reduce the molester's sex drive toward children.

In Chapter Two, "Childhood Beginnings of the Desire to Molest," you saw that testosterone plays a major role in the development of pedophilia. Most of the medicines used to treat pedophilia have an effect on testosterone. Knock out the testosterone, and you knock out sexual desire, which then knocks out the drive to molest children.

But there are problems here. What the physician wants to do is knock out enough testosterone so that the sexual interest in children stops, but the sexual interest in adults stays. Or in the case of teenagers, the therapist would want the teenager's sexual interest in teens of the same age range to remain. And the physician wants to do this without the process creating unacceptable side effects.

Incidentally, there is no evidence that pedophiles, like John or the teenage Alex and Jake, have abnormally high levels of testosterone. They have the same levels as other males, but reduction of their normal level of testosterone allows them rapid control of their sexual desires.[51]

The strongest drug

Until recently, medroxyprogesterone acetate was the only drug prescribed to control testosterone. Marketed under the names Provera© (administered by mouth), and Depo-Provera© (administered by long–acting injection), this drug can knock out nearly all of a male's circulating testosterone. Without testosterone, a male has no sex drive of any kind. This is called chemical castration.[52]

For the five percent of pedophiles—those who enter treatment while they are at extreme risk to molest a child—this medication can be a godsend. Once on it, the pedophile has a degree of control he has never felt before. The medication allows him to attend to the other components of treatment. However, this so-called castrating drug has two drawbacks. It may have to be prescribed at high doses. This increases the risk of serious side effects. Most physicians are uncomfortable administering Provera at such high doses. General physicians usually have no experience with Provera used to treat child molesters (its primary use is for breakthrough uterine bleeding) and are reluctant to prescribe a high dosage of a drug that could cause such serious side effects as diabetes, or blood clots.

Since it interferes with bone growth, it would stunt a child's height, therefore, this drug is rarely prescribed for anyone under 18. However, if the therapist believed that John posed an immediate risk to children, he would place him on Depo-Provera©. That would be appropriate, since John is a fully mature 37-year-old.

The use of medroxyprogesterone acetate drugs has replaced surgical castration (removal of the testes), because the drug is more effective, reversible, and therefore ethical in its use.

SSRIs: Drugs that change sex thoughts

The big news regarding medications to treat child molesters is a brand new use for a familiar group of medicines: the **selective serotonin reuptake inhibitors (SSRIs)**. Not only do they have few side effects, they are also safe for teenagers.[53] What's more, if given in high enough doses, they can selectively inhibit paraphilias, such as the desire to window peep, to masturbate in public, or to molest children. You probably know SSRIs as the group of drugs psychiatrists prescribe most often to combat depression: Celexa (citalopram HBr), Luvox© (fluvoxamine), Paxil© (paroxetine), Prozac© (fluoxetine), and Zoloft© (seratraline).

What you may not know is that psychiatrists also commonly prescribe these drugs in larger doses for patients who have problems such as obsessive-compulsive disorders.

A person with an obsessive compulsive disorder may wash his or her hands more than fifty times a day or check thirty times before leaving the house to ensure that all the lights are turned out, or count things, where counting serves no function, such as counting the number of straight lines in a room. SSRIs prescribed at a higher dosage level than a psychiatrist would prescribe for depression reduce such obsessive thoughts and behaviors.

In dosages at the high end of what psychiatrists prescribe for patients with an obsessive-compulsive disorder, these drugs have a major effect on the paraphilic sex drive. Pedophiles frequently develop a sense of relief on these drugs, because the drugs succeed in reducing their sex drive towards children. The drugs also decrease their obsessive fantasies about children.

The big question about SSRIs at these high doses has been, are they working specifically to change paraphilic sex drive or are they simply reducing *all* sex drive? Studies show that they work specifically on pedophilia, exhibitionism, voyeurism, and the other paraphilias. In a 1995 study using Zoloft©, John Bradford, M.D. and David Greenberg, M.D., found that paraphilic urges, fantasies, and activities decreased substantially, while sexual activity with consenting adults showed only a minor decrease.[54]

Using SSRIs

Dr. Gene Abel: Today, I have about one-fourth of the patients I treat for pedophilia on SSRIs. I find this category of drugs helpful in a number of ways. First, pedophiles often have severe depressions, so the SSRIs work to treat that. Then, for their sex-specific problems, these drugs not only reduce these patients' sex drive, they also reduce their obsessions, the repetitive thoughts and fantasies that are precursors to the pedophile's child molesting.

These drugs appear to substantially curb the paraphilic drive. And they have few significant side effects.

99

SSRIs and teenage pedophilia: A revolutionary advance in prevention

The most exciting thing about this new use of SSRIs to save children from being molested is this: This class of drugs can be used for *prevention*. Not only can we now identify teenagers with sexual interest in young children, we also now have drugs that, when used in combination with cognitive-behavioral treatment, can stop a teenage boy *before* he has a victim.

Why is this a revolutionary advance? For two reasons. Until the SSRIs, the only major way to reduce a teenager's sexual drive was to give him Provera©. But because Provera© would stunt his growth and therapists were very reluctant to use it. Now, that the SSRIs are proven effective, we have a drug that is safe to use with older children and teenagers, one that does no harm to bone growth and that has few side effects.

SSRIs represent a major breakthrough. Using this class of drugs with teenage boys like Jake, who test positive for sexual interest in much younger children, can play a key role in saving kids from ever becoming victims. Jake's therapist prescribed an SSRI, not only to help him gain control over his sexual drive toward very young boys, but also to help him gain control over his urges to window peep and to masturbate in public.

While many people may wish that one could prevent child molestation by simply giving everyone with a sexual interest in children one of these pills, it's not that easy. In standard medical practice in the United States and in Canada, neither castrating drugs nor SSRIs are used alone. They are prescribed *only* **after** a comprehensive assessment, and **in addition to** a cognitive-behavioral treatment program.

—— THE NEW THERAPY ——

In study after study, one combination of treatments has consistently proved effective.[55] This is cognitive therapy combined with behavioral therapy. It is the only approach that, one, changes the pedophile's sex thoughts about children and, two, stops the behaviors that go with them.[56]

These are the two changes that must occur in order to stop 95 percent of child molestation acts and to ensure that 88 percent of today's potential child victims will *never* be molested.

Cognitive-behavioral therapy: What it is and how it works

What is this revolutionary new combination, cognitive- behavioral therapy? "Cognitive" means "thoughts." Cognitive therapy focuses on changing the way the patient thinks about something. When the patient is a pedophile, cognitive therapy is used to change the pedophile's fantasies and urges related to sexually touching kids. It's also used to combat his denial: It works to directly confront those stories (cognitive distortions) he tells himself to justify his molesting behavior with children. Behavioral therapy focuses on changing the patient's *behavior*. When the patient is a pedophile, behavioral therapy is used to *stop* the pedophile from sexually touching kids.

Who gets the new therapy?

When a teenager comes forward to have a sex-specific evaluation, the therapist first suspects the cause is natural sexual curiosity and experimentation. The therapist suspects this even when the teenage molester is a severely sexually abused boy, because natural sexual curiosity and experimentation is the *most frequent* cause of an older child molesting a younger child.

In contrast, Alex, Brian, and Jake, unlike other teenagers, have problems that are serious and need treatment.

Teenagers like Brian, who have a sex-specific problem without the accompanying direct sexual interest in children, form the largest group of cases who need therapy. Fortunately, members of this group are generally very responsive to a brief intervention such as the one described in Chapter Three for Brian. For Alex and Jake, however, the course of treatment is much longer, as it is for the adult, John.

Time frame and cost for cognitive-behavioral treatment

How long will it take and how much will it cost? These are concerns whenever a family member begins any intensive form of treatment, including a sex-specific cognitive-behavioral therapy.

The evaluation, which includes various clinical interviews, testing, evaluation of any previous criminal justice or treatment records, and also frequently includes interviews with other family members, may take one to three days.

Treatment is divided into two parts: intensive treatment and relapse prevention with maintenance. The intensive treatment takes place generally over a one-year period. Relapse prevention and maintenance sessions, depending on the patient's progress, occur weekly, biweekly, monthly, or quarterly.

At this writing the typical cost for such a program is between $6,000 and $8,000 for three years. This includes a comprehensive evaluation, one year of intensive therapy, and two years of relapse prevention therapy. After successful completion, the patient has ongoing yearly costs averaging about $900 for testing and quarterly relapse prevention.

TABLE 7-1

A Comparison of Drugs Used to Fight Pedophilia

	SSRIs (Celexa®, Luvox®, Paxil®, Prozac®, Zoloft®	Medroxyprogesterone (Provera® or Depo-Povera®)
Effects	• Reduces paraphilic sex drive and paraphilic urges, obsessive thought and behavior	• Eliminates nearly all sex drive
Side Effects	• 70 % have reduction in sex drive • 30 to 35 % have delayed ejaculation and lack of orgasm • Less than 10 % have nausea, insomnia, dry mouth, headache, tremors, weight loss • Liver injury • Depression of white blood cells	• 100 % have decreased sperm count • 95 % have decreased sex drive, decreased ejaculation • 58 % have weight gain • 50 % have increased blood pressure • 30 % have nervousness and depression • 29 % have hot and cold flashes • 20 % have headache and nausea • 13% develop gallbladder disease • 4% develop elevated blood sugar • 2% develop phlebitis (blood clots)
Notes	• Appropriate for use with teenagers • Many physicians prescribe with experience • Have been used with children as young as eight years old	• Requires continual medical checks of hormone levels. • Many physicians reluctant to prescribe because they lack experience. • Appropriate only for patients who have reached full growth.

Alex gets treatment

The therapist explains the elements of treatment to Alex and his parents. He also explains that although he sees no need for medication at this time, he will be monitoring Alex's progress and will talk to them again if medication becomes appropriate.

Alex should do exceedingly well in treatment because he was diagnosed early, he is compliant and successful in other areas of his life, and he has concerned parents to support his efforts. Other facts in his favor are that he is willing to admit his inappropriate behavior and he has told his therapist about his sexual interest in young girls. He is an incest offender, having touched his cousin. This group of conditions points toward a good treatment outcome.

Will the new treatment cure our son?

This is Alex's parents' first question. The answer is: No.

In this respect, the treatment for pedophilia is similar to treatments for many serious health problems—diabetes, heart disease, cancer, and kidney failure. The treatment offers no cure; what it does is keep the disease or disorder under control. While the patient often can return to a normal, healthy life, he must continue to follow a well-organized therapeutic regimen. If medications have been prescribed, they will be reduced as he gains control and will eventually be discontinued. He has semi-annual tests. He follows the therapist's recommendations in order to maintain treatment gains.

Patients who have had diabetes, heart disease, cancer, or kidney failure can never be free to blissfully put these conditions out of their minds, but must see them as ongoing concerns to which they must always be attentive. The therapist explains that this process is also true for patients like Alex after they have been treated for having a sexual interest in children.

Since the sexual interest in children may re-emerge, sex-specific therapy is not designed to end with a cure after which the patient has permission to forget he's had a problem. Instead, a sexual interest in children, with its potential for harm, is seen as an ongoing problem to which the teenager or adult must always pay attention. At the end of the treatment's intensive phase, Alex, like each successfully treated patient, will have an acute awareness of the many signs specific to him that signal a return of the sexual interest in children. He'll be equipped with specific techniques he can use immediately to stop any recurrence of this interest.

In view of the potential danger of treatment failure or that the sexual interest in children will recur, therapists who treat child molesters use a conservative approach with their patients. Supervision and ongoing treatment to maintain the therapeutic gains are essential. For patients with poor control, maintenance therapy may occur as frequently as every week. For patients with excellent control, maintenance therapy occurs as infrequently as every three months. To ensure the safety of children, it is recommended that patients who once had a sexual drive toward children remain in maintenance therapy for the rest of their lives.

Requirements vital to treatment success

Because of the serious nature of any failure, the therapist may set many treatment requirements that would be inappropriate in traditional therapy. The most important have to do with children and supervision.

The first condition of treatment: the patient must keep a distance between himself (or herself) and children. This is by far the most important treatment condition.

Before the first treatment session, both Alex and his parents receive a rules-of-treatment consent form to sign. Typically, the parents and the teenager agree that the patient:

- " . . . will avoid proximity to children and will never be alone with a child unless approved by my therapist,"

- " . . . will not view, purchase, or use child pornography."

- " . . . will not use the Internet."

These rules have a single aim: to separate the molester patient from children and to separate him from any pictures of children that might help him maintain his sex drive toward children.

To separate himself from children also means he must avoid places where children congregate: no beaches in summer, no mall arcades, no amusement parks, no Boy Scout outings, no Big Brother mentoring. Occasionally, this requires a job change. For teenage pedophiles like Alex, no jobs as babysitters, lifeguards, or camp counselors, no jobs coaching kindergarten or grade-school soccer; for adult pedophiles, no jobs in homes for emotionally disturbed children, in orphanages, or in daycare centers. No jobs as grade-school teachers or school bus drivers.

Supervision

Individual pedophiles may be monitored by family members, fellow workers, and friends as well as, in some cases, probation or parole officers. Concerned people, such as friends, relatives, or co-workers with whom the pedophile frequently interacts, come to one meeting during which the teenager or adult discusses how he (or she) interacts with children and describes circumstances he encounters in the course of his day that he sees as having led to dangerous situations in the past. The therapist uses the information to design a one-page question-and-answer sheet. These people are then asked to complete this short form every two weeks and return it to the therapist. Rather than following the patient about or spying on him, the friend or co-worker responds according to what he or she observes in the natural course of their being together.

For molesters who are also in the criminal justice system, probation or parole officers often play a key role in protecting children by working closely with the treatment program. Pedophiles who pose a high risk—less than 5 percent of pedophiles—may be required to wear an electronic monitor that sends a signal to the probation officer if the pedophile leaves home. Probation or parole officers may also monitor the patient's compliance with treatment, ensuring that he (or she) attends treatment sessions and complies with the treatment protocol. In addition, these officers make frequent calls to inspect the patient's living situation.

Since Alex has never been accused of a criminal act against a child, his family provides his supervision. This is family support for Alex.

During the first year of treatment, Alex attends weekly sessions in which he learns techniques to reduce or extinguish sexual attraction to little girls. The patient group includes five other teenage boys.

Why ban the Internet for people with a sexual interest in children?

Dr. Gene Abel: I have learned the hard way about patients' misuse of the Internet. The problem is that internet use looks so benign. Families feel that use of the Internet is so important that they are reluctant to prevent the molester in their family from using it. Often patients, including the ones who have faced charges involving use of child pornography, feel the same way.

What is the danger? For a patient with pedophilia, it's the golden road to child sexual fantasy material — to pictures that fuel their sexual fantasies of children. For the patient with a sex drive directed at children, it's tempting. Downloading deviant fantasy material is easy. They are often in their own homes. They feel as though they are anonymous, but they face the problems of impulsivity and arousal.

While a patient may not get in his car, go to a store, and buy child pornography, or submit a resume and go to an interview for a job working with children, for him to just go on the web is nothing. He can do it on an impulse.

One patient, whose internet use was being supervised by his mother, used the minutes his mother was in the bathroom to click to his old child pornography sites. In this case, the patient was 45 and had his professional license, his livelihood, at stake.

A teenage patient's father — while his son was waiting for his criminal charges involving use of child pornography to be resolved — gave his son a computer. Immediately the boy was back on the Internet, back to his child pornography sites, toying with incarceration.

To protect children from becoming victims, our culture has to come to grips with the Internet. Most families are naïve. They will trust the child. They don't understand how easy it is to download images of adult-child sex. All teenage patients, like Alex and Jake, have to do is click.

Therapy techniques
that directly reduce the urge to molest

Four treatment techniques are commonly used to directly reduce the patient's sexual desire for children. Three, covert sensitization, imaginal desensitization, and olfactory aversion, are used with teenagers such as Alex and also with adults. One, masturbatory satiation, is used primarily with adults. The therapists teach members of the treatment group how to do the various treatments to decrease the sexual interest in children. Once these methods are learned in the group setting, the patient applies them in real life situations when desires, urges, or fantasies increase their risk of touching a child.

Covert sensitization directly reduces sexual interest in children. In this technique, the patient pairs thoughts of what he did that led to the molestation act with thoughts of very bad consequences. For example, in one session Alex paired his memories of urging his young cousins to eat their ice cream slowly (which he knew would increase the odds that it would drip on them) with thoughts of his being arrested in school, in front of his school friends.

Imaginal Desensitization is another technique to directly reduce sexual interest in children. The patient talks about the various things he did in the chain of acts that led to the exciting urges to molest. He then uses relaxation techniques to reduce the physical and emotional excitement and beliefs that he must act on these urges.

Alex would have used imaginal desensitization to first imagine the excitement and thrill he had when he saw his young niece in the bathtub. However, once he felt that stage of excitement, he then practiced relaxing his body. As treatment proceeded, he became more effective at reducing his emotional and physiologic reaction to these images. What he learned from this was that he didn't need to act on those reactions; he could simply wait, relax, and the urges and excitement of these images would dissipate.

Olfactory Aversion also directly reduces sexual interest in children. The patient recalls a sexual urge to interact with a child, and then uses a strong odor to interrupt that urge. The patient breaks open a smelling salts capsule (ammonia) and takes a breath of the smell.

Alex, like many patients, carries smelling salts capsules in his pocket.

Gene G. Abel, M.D. and Nora Harlow   257

Once, after his Aunt Kathie urged her girls to go play with Alex and the two little girls were pulling on his clothes, jumping up and down, and begging him for horsy rides, Alex went outside the house and broke a capsule and inhaled. Coughing and teary, he was able to block his sexual thoughts.

Masturbatory Satiation is a technique used *almost exclusively with adults* to directly reduce their sexual interest in children. Essentially, the very actions the molester used to entrench his sexual arousal to children are now used to eliminate that arousal. In the privacy of their homes, patients masturbate while having sex thoughts involving adults. Immediately after ejaculation, they begin masturbating again, only this time they imagine a brief, highly erotic scene of child molestation. They continue masturbating to that brief image until it is boring, then very boring, then aversive, and finally highly aversive.

Initially, for the first five to eight home sessions of satiation, John saw very little change in his sexual interest towards children. However, as he continued repetitively using brief scenes of his most erotic images, they first became boring, then exceedingly boring, and finally quite aversive. John was particularly pleased that he could do this treatment outside the therapist's office. Occasionally, when he saw a child whom he found sexually attractive, that same day he would use this technique and successfully eliminate his interest in the child.

Additional therapy techniques

In addition to the four techniques that a therapist can use to directly reduce a patient's sexual drive toward children, two more techniques can be used to accomplish other goals.

Cognitive Restructuring is a technique to change the faulty beliefs and rationalizations that the patient uses to support his acts of molestation. Typically, the therapist and group members confront the patient about the lies he tells himself as part of his denial. The longer pedophiles, like John, use denial stories, the longer they tell themselves that when they sexually touched a child it was really ok, the stronger their denial becomes.

Alex, because he had so little denial, was good at confronting the other teenagers in his group. By "teaching" the others he strengthened his own sense of the dangers of slipping into mistaken beliefs about how "in certain circumstances" it was "really all right" to sexually touch a much younger child.

Jake, who believed his victim was equally responsible, needed work in this area. So did John, who fiercely held the belief that he was not a child molester.

Victim Empathy Training is a technique to increase the molesters' awareness of their victims' suffering. The patients watch videotapes of sexual abuse survivors who describe the emotional and physical problems they experienced after being molested. Patients also read short pieces written by sexual abuse survivors.

Alex was surprised to learn about the tremendous number of difficulties sexual abuse victims had as children. He was also surprised to learn that these difficulties followed the victims into their adult lives.

Molesters seldom see the negative consequences their acts have for the child. This failure to directly witness the consequences of their acts against children helps them maintain their mistaken belief that they haven't harmed the child. Jake wasn't around when the neighbor boy had nightmares or started wetting his bed. John saw all of Kerrie's problems as normal childhood problems that had nothing to do with his actions. He maintained this belief through the first months of treatment.

—— AUNT KATHIE ——
TALKING TO A FAMILY MEMBER IN DENIAL

While Alex's treatment went smoothly, both Alex and his mother had continued difficulty with Aunt Kathie. She refused to believe Alex had pedophilia. When Alex's mother told her sister about Alex's diagnosis, Aunt Kathie laughed in her face. One thing Aunt Kathie was sure of was that there were no pedophiles in her family.

And she wouldn't stop. "For the life of me, I can't figure out *why* you would want to persecute your own son. You tell Alex for me, that he still has me; he has one person in the family that believes in him. You're doing bad stuff here. You always think you are the one doing right by your kids, I'm sorry, but I think you are out to ruin the life of your own son. Do you have a vendetta against your family? Are you going around now telling everybody that our family raises perverts?"

A history of cognitive-behavioral therapy

Dr. Gene Abel: Many of the techniques of cognitive-behavioral therapy were already in the literature when I first started treating patients with paraphilias, but they were used with other patient populations. Covert desensitization, for instance, was used with bulimics. We borrowed the technique. Since our goal was to stop the pedophile from sexually touching a child, we simply searched for behavioral techniques that had worked to help patients stop wanting to do other kinds of hurtful behaviors, then we adapted some of those techniques to effective use with molesting patients. Satiation has existed since parents of two or three generations ago began using it with any kid they caught smoking. They marched the kid out to the barn, and made him smoke cigars until he got sick. Aversive treatments have been described in the literature for more than 50 years. The aversion-by-noxious-smell that we use is also used with drug addicts to help them interrupt the chain of events that leads to their taking drugs.

The treatment to combat the molester's cognitive distortions is one we designed ourselves — Dr. Judith V. Becker, Dr. William Murphy, and me. As for the social skills training and victim empathy, those are general techniques used in treatment for a variety of disorders.

99

At a family gathering, his Aunt Kathie asked Alex to "look after the girls for a few minutes while I make a run for milk." Alex was so disturbed he couldn't say "yes" or "no." All he could do was stand there. Left with the little girls, he walked them directly to his mother, who told him to go home, call a friend, and play catch with him. Alex's mother tried her best to make her sister understand that Alex had a serious problem and that he needed her support to isolate himself from children, but Aunt Kathie thought the whole thing was silly.

The next week, she appeared at football practice to ask Alex for a special babysitting favor. "This is a one-time emergency," she promised, and she went on to say she'd keep the secret from his mother if he would.

Alex felt terrible when he refused to baby-sit. Early in the course of his treatment, Alex and his parents (without Aunt Kathie) scheduled a session with the therapist to address this issue. His therapist helped Alex learn to assert himself with his aunt and other members of his extended family. Alex's mother also helped him by repeatedly asserting herself with her sister.

—— A CONVERSATION TO HAVE WITH THE FAMILY ——

Alex's mother, Susan, talked to her sister. When she did, she said things that are important to get across to any adult family member in denial. First, she explained the diagnosis.

> **Susan:** Kathie, I want you to understand that Alex has had a serious sexual problem for a while. The diagnosis never hinged on that incident with Julie. Alex has told us things about his sexual drive that would be the last thing anyone in our family could imagine. He's been thinking of sexually touching very young girls, almost exclusively, ever since he was 13. That's three years. Most boys don't have his obsession. He always believed he was like all boys. That's why he never thought to tell us or ask for help. But he isn't like all boys. He has this secret drive to sexually interact with Julie and other girls that young. He's been so upset because he knows he failed to control his sex urges towards Julie.

> **Aunt Kathie:** I still think you're making a mountain out of a little molehill. You're the one that's obsessed, not Alex.

Alex's mother keeps her temper and counters her sister's objections calmly and patiently.

> **Susan:** I wish I was making mountains out of molehills, but I'm not. What Alex has is a serious medical problem. There are tests to identify it and medicines and therapies that are effective. He's been fighting this alone for three years. Now, he's learning techniques to stop his sex thoughts about little girls and to reduce his sexual attraction to little girls. We've got to give him all the help we can.

> **Aunt Kathie:** I still think it's just a boy being a boy.

After all, he's just a kid. I'm sure *we* can handle something like that as a *family*.

Susan: Alex's problem goes way beyond the everyday sex things that kids do. His dad and I could never handle this. And, it's more complicated than you or I, as mothers, can deal with. Kathie, I know you love Alex and want to do what's best for him. But you and I have no experience with a child having this strange kind of sex drive.

Aunt Kathie: I still don't see the harm in letting Alex play with my girls. He's a wonderful boy; I don't care what you say.

Susan: Alex's dad and I have gone to a lot of trouble to find a therapist who has experience treating boys with a sex drive like Alex's. He has a history of success. This expert has been very clear since the beginning about one thing. Alex must *not* be around young children. I should point out, the people at Child Protective Services told us the same thing. Alex *has* to stay away from children. To help Alex, we *have* to do this for him. I know you love Alex; I know he's always been special to you. But now, Kathie, he needs special help. Badly. Please, I'm counting on you to help him keep his distance from children.

Aunt Kathie: Why is that so important? I don't understand.

Susan: It's important for Alex. But it's also important because of the laws. I'm worried about the laws. If Alex re-offends, the criminal justice system will treat him harshly.

Aunt Kathie: That can't happen to Alex.

Susan: It could. I've heard such horror stories. There's one case where a child as young as 10 was sentenced to 10 years for being sexual with younger children. If you ignore the requirements set by the sex-specific therapist and the caseworker, we're courting danger for Alex.

While her sister still believed Alex was neither a child molester nor a pedophile, she reluctantly agreed to help. She would keep her little girls at a distance.

Having a conversation like this one with any family members in denial regarding a family member's pedophilia is important for several reasons. If family members are close, geographically and/or emotionally, it's helpful for everyone if they work together when one or more of them has a crisis. It's also important that families understand the serious implications that go with a diagnosis of pedophilia.

Keeping Alex away from children prevents the possibility of a second accusation. What's happening is a win-win situation. By keeping the teenager with a sexual interest in children away from young children, the family protects the children while at the same time they protect the teenager.

Alex makes excellent progress. He is able to use many of the treatment techniques in his day-to-day life. After 60 sessions, he enters the maintenance phase of his treatment. He meets with his group every two weeks. With continued treatment success, measured every six months by objective testing, he eventually moves to monthly sessions. Finally, all Alex must do is attend relapse prevention four times a year and return every six months for testing.

—— JAKE'S FAMILY AT THE THERAPIST ——

Jake, the 14-year-old, who was severely molested at seven, needed medication and two kinds of treatment. His mother, Sara, had much more trouble with his therapy than he did.

When Jake's mother brought her son to the therapist, she was in a foul mood. She had been ordered there by a social worker from Child Protective Services. Once she and Jake signed the consent forms and listened to the therapist's explanation of the law, the first thing she wanted the therapist to know was that this was a terrible misunderstanding — terrible because her Jake, himself, was a child molestation victim. She characterized the neighbor as a nervous nelly whose son twitched every time you looked at him. Jake quickly said, "I didn't do anything to him."

Jake, like most 14-year-olds, is no fool. He knows his mother doesn't want to hear that he's done anything sexual with the neighbor boy. He knows this is a big deal. He's been pulled out of school and brought to a therapist.

He's had to talk to a child protection caseworker. His parents have hired a lawyer. He may go to jail.

The therapist first talks to the mother alone to get the facts about the accusation, then he talks to Jake alone. During the clinical interview, Jake reveals that he did more sexual things with the neighbor boy than the caseworker had in her report. He also reveals that he masturbates thinking about sexual interactions with boys of ages six or seven. He does this especially in the middle of the night after he has a nightmare that Mr. Jones is doing sex things with him. In the dream, Mr. Jones appears bigger than the house Jake lives in. Jake tells the therapist he wants his mother to know he did touch the boy, but he doesn't want to tell her. And he adds, "Please don't tell her I touch myself."

When the therapist tells Sara that her son did exactly what he is accused of, she is quiet. A few moments pass, the belligerence falls away, her body relaxes, and then she says, "What can you do to help him? What do you want me to do?"

Jake's objective test results show he has no attraction to girls of grade-school age or to children of preschool age. He is, however, sexually attracted to boys of grade-school age. In fact, his sexual interest in them is quite strong, while his sexual attraction to boys his own age is nonexistent and his sexual interest in girls his age is barely existent. In his self-report on the questionnaire, he says that *all* of his sexual thoughts are of six- and seven-year-old boys. He also says that he masturbates to orgasm thinking of little boys. He responds on the questionnaire that he is able to control his urges to molest less than half the time. What's more, he has symptoms that accompany two additional paraphilias: voyeurism (window-peeping), and public masturbation. He has done both. He window-peeped on the boy next door and he masturbated in public in the swimming pool where he believed no one could see him, while he was looking at young boys.

In the interview, he also tells the therapist about his scrapbook of cutouts of very young boys in their underpants. To questions about his own victimization, he says it was his fault. All 300 molestations. This reflects his answer on the questionnaire about his sexual interaction with his own victim. He reports it was "by mutual consent."

Denial in the family

Dr. Gene Abel: In our society, commitment to the family looms big. Unfortunately, although family support can provide tremendous help, families can also unite to ignore a problem.

Family members sometimes think they are doing a good thing to paint a picture that everything is ok. Say, Alex's problem was (instead of pedophilia) juvenile-onset diabetes. If his Aunt Kathie insisted that he was healthy, that diabetes didn't run in their family, that a healthy-looking athletic boy like her nephew couldn't possibly have that disease, and if she also, when he was with her, continually offered him sugar-filled treats to prove her point, and ignored his need for timely insulin injections, everyone would see Alex's health fail. Everyone in the family would see the consequences of such poor advice.

However, when Aunt Kathie denies that Alex has pedophilia, say if she succeeded at obstructing treatment, the failure might not appear so quickly. Perhaps Alex could control his urges (or not get caught) for months or even years. If treatment is never instituted because of this family obstructionist, and Alex relapses, the repercussions would be severe. The worst thing that might happen is that he would have molested a number of little girls. Also at a later age, he would be treated harshly by the criminal justice system for two reasons: he would be older and he might have a number of victims or molested a number of times.

It is the therapist's job to muster the forces in the family to combat the single obstructionist member. Indeed, Alex's family was eventually successful at showing Aunt Kathie the potential dangers to Alex and his young cousins if he was left to handle his disorder on his own, without receiving the benefits of treatment. Such conversion of the denying family member generally does not occur with a single talk, but is a product of weeks of education.

99

—— FOR A BOY LIKE JAKE ——
TWO KINDS OF TREATMENT

In the case of a severely sexually abused boy who at puberty begins to molest young boys, therapists might differ on what to do first. They would agree that Jake needs two kinds of treatment. He needs treatment to reduce or eliminate his sexual interest in little boys. And, he needs treatment once again to help him deal with having been sexually abused. While Jake's previous treatment was helpful, at 14, he needs more treatment because the two conditions interact. In Jake's case, the decision is to have him treated by a therapist who specializes in victim recovery at the same time he is continuing with his sex-specific treatment.

Sara says: "Ok, what did I do wrong? I know in some way this is all my fault."

But it isn't. The sex-specific therapist does *not* look to family dynamics as the cause of pedophilia. He or she knows how a sexual interest in children develops and that the parents have nothing to do with it. It is generally known that parents in nearly all cases have no role in the development of pedophilia. The only exceptions are fathers or uncles or mothers or aunts who sexually abuse the children in their families.

Although Sara wants to be co-operative, she has a difficult time. The truth is that her son is dangerous to little boys. Of the three patients we're looking at in this chapter, Alex, Jake, and John, 14-year-old Jake presents the most danger to the children around him. The risk that he will lose control over his urges and molest the neighbor boy again or molest another little boy is great.

What his mother sees is a dear son who has been through so much that she worries about how his being a victim will affect him through his whole life. To his mother, Jake's actions as a molester are only a mild concern. She sees his actions as what lots of children do. Her benchmark is Michael Jones. Her denial hinges on this fact: Her son's acts are not as bad as the acts of *her son's molester*. Like parents in many families, she is in denial. And, that denial continues after she knows that Jake did sexually abuse the boy next door.

At 14, Jake is too young to be diagnosed as a pedophile. So why is he such a risk?

- He was molested more than 50 times. As you saw in

Chapter Four, this group of child molesters, who were themselves molested as children, as molesting adults molest five times as many children as other child molesters.

• He repeatedly deals with his fear of being molested by identifying with the aggressor and masturbating to orgasm to sex thoughts of seven-year-old boys. He is conditioning his sex drive to direct it solely to seven-year-old boys.

• His greatest objectively measured sexual interest by far is his interest in grade-school boys. That sexual interest has continued for more than a year.

• He has acted repeatedly.

• He says he has little control over his urges.

• His sex drive directed at seven-year-old boys now includes behavior in two additional paraphilias — voyeurism (window-peeping) and public masturbation.

——PATIENTS AT GREATEST RISK——
MULTIPLE PARAPHILIAS AND SEXUAL BOUNDARIES

The higher the number of sex-specific diagnoses, the greater the chance the patient will repeat one or more of the behaviors.

In the 1980's, while Dr. Abel and Dr. Judith V. Becker were engaged in a major research project for the Center for Studies of Antisocial and Violent Behavior of the National Institute of Mental Health (NIMH), they and their colleagues looked for the answer to the question: Which group of child molester patients was the most likely to fail treatment?[57][58]

What does "failing treatment" mean? It means another child victim. Another act.

Dr. Abel thought the answer would be the molester with either the most victims, the most acts, the most years as a molester, or the greatest tendency to use force. Those are the criteria for the criminal justice system in decisions about punishment.

What he found was unexpected: *None* of these facts predicted treatment failure. A pedophile who had been molesting for 20 years was just as likely to be a treatment success as a patient who had been molesting for one year. A molester with ten victims was just as likely to succeed as a molester with one victim.

Treatment failure was most likely to occur when the molester had a number of different paraphilias or what therapists call "cross-diagnoses."

The term describes a situation where a patient has multiple paraphilic diagnoses that signal he or she needs an intensified treatment, usually needs medication, and often needs closer supervision. That's an important difference between Alex and Jake. Alex has one diagnosis: pedophilia—limited to girls of grade-school-age. Although Jake, at 14, is too young for a *medical diagnosis*, he, in fact, like some young teenagers, has paraphilic fantasies and urges, has a sex drive directed toward much younger children and has repeatedly molested a young boy. To protect the children around him, all of those symptoms must be evaluated and treated. What makes him a particular risk—above other teenagers? He has shown behavior in three potential paraphilic areas: pedophilia, voyeurism, and public masturbation.

While the finding that patients with multiple paraphilias were the most difficult to treat successfully was unexpected, it nonetheless made sense. What it suggested was that relapse had to do with sexual boundaries. The more sexual boundaries a patient violated, the less control he had over his sex drive. The less control he had, the more likely he was to relapse. For people with pedophilia or pedophilic symptoms relapse is unacceptable. Relapse means molesting again.

What do we mean by sexual boundaries? A sexual boundary is a line you are not supposed to cross. It separates you from another person who is off-limits to you sexually. You are on one side of the line, your mother, father, brother, sister, minister, therapist, and all children are on the other side of the line. You are limited to people your age or older who are not in your family and who consent to being sexual with you.

In addition to multiple paraphilias, cross-diagnoses include the gender, age, and family relationship of the child target. This means that a molesting patient may also cross-sexual boundaries by molesting boys *and* girls, children of preschool age *and* grade-school age, children in the family and children outside the family.

In fact, treatment failure was directly correlated with *the number of boundaries the patient crossed.* The take-home message: Treatment success or failure is determined by the patient's ability to control his sexual behavior. Most men who molest children cross several sexual boundaries. The ones who cross the most sexual boundaries are the most likely to molest again—even with treatment. For instance, Michael Jones molested boys of pre-school age, boys of grade-school age, girls of pre-school age, girls of grade-school age, his own daughter. That's five sexual boundaries he crossed. Patients like Mr. Jones need the most frequent relapse prevention sessions, the most medication, and the most supervision.

Table 7-2 from The Abel and Harlow Stop Child Molestation Study shows the likelihood that adult males who molest children age 13 or younger outside the family will cross other sexual boundaries.

TABLE 7-2

Crossing Multiple Sexual Boundaries

Pedophiles who molest girls
*21% **also** molest boys*
*17% **also** are exhibitionists or flashers*
*36% **also** are voyeurs or window-peepers*
Pedophiles who molest boys
*53% **also** molest girls*
*20% **also** are exhibitionists or flashers*
*33% **also** are voyeurs or window-peepers*

Source: The Abel and Harlow Stop Child Molestation Study

Another place to look for molesters: Since we now know that some men who molest children also window-peep, flash, and masturbate in public, we know to test teenagers and adults who window-peep, flash, or publicly masturbate for the possibility that they also have pedophilia.[59]

A patient like Alex, who broke *one* sexual boundary—sexually touching a very young girl—but who has control in all other sexual areas, has the best chance for treatment success. A patient like Jake, who broke three sexual boundaries—sexually touching a young boy, window-peeping on a young boy, and public masturbation while watching young boys at the swimming pool—will have a tougher time succeeding in treatment.

For Jake, there are additional factors that lead to the therapist's concern. Every time Jake feels scared that he, himself, will be overwhelmed by an adult molester, he masturbates to sex thoughts of molesting a seven-year-old-boy. His fear is a force that leads Jake to reinforce his drive toward little boys. Molested molesters are a particularly difficult group to treat. Sometimes, even though molested boys seem to be successful in their treatment for being molesters, their old fears overwhelm them and they molest again.

While most patients being evaluated report (whether it's true or not) that they have complete control over their sexual urges toward children, Jake reports that he has little control over his urges. When a sex-specific therapist gets this information, when the patient himself says he has little control, the therapist believes him. Jake has such poor sexual control that the therapist immediately prescribes an SSRI.

—— Jake's Therapy Begins —— Separating A Teenage Molester From His Victim

The sex-specific therapist moves to separate Jake from his victim and comes up against Jake's mother. While she had vowed to be supportive of sex-specific therapy, Sara feels what the therapist is asking is extreme.

Sara sees no reason why her son should make himself scarce. "He has a right to play in his own backyard. Let the neighbors keep their son inside if they don't like it," she tells the therapist. Sara thinks, like many mothers, that she can help her son most by believing in him. "Jake says he'll never do it again," she tells herself. "If his own mother doesn't show him she believes in him, who will?"

With a son who molests, believing in him is not the answer. The answer is medicine, therapy, and intense supervision. As you've seen, sex-specific therapy is nothing like what most people think of as therapy. This therapist has a double focus: the victim or potential victims first, and the patient second.

Jake's therapist is quick to clarify. He does not mean that Jake should stay indoors, what he means is that Jake should move to a living situation at a distance from his victim.

Sara is stunned.

Her problem, like that of many parents, is denial.

She knows her son, she has had 14 years of experiencing his good traits, and she can recall thousands of situations where he has performed good deeds. His tenderness and caring of his little sister have been joys to behold. Even his molestation happened as he bravely protected his mother. He fought to overcome that trauma, every year coming more out of his shell, every year his grades improving. He was a worker like his father, the two of them worked together to keep a showcase yard, the two of them repaired the back porch, the gutters, the screens, window frames, and everything that broke in the house. His parents had learned to trust Jake; when he said he was going to do something, he did it. So when Jake says he isn't going to touch the neighbor boy or any kid ever again, Sara believes him.

Here we have apples and oranges. Jake's good behavior—his outward, observable good behavior—has nothing to do with his sex drive. Sara is in denial. She has a hard time imagining that her son's sex drive is different from his father's and different from hers.

And she can't separate the severely molested little boy who had horrific nightmares when Mr. Jones was released from jail from teenage Jake whose biggest current problem is his sex drive directed at little boys. Sara understands the logic of it, but emotionally she feels it's impossible. She has a son who simply wouldn't hurt anybody. And now, now that the molesting behavior is out in the open, now with so many people—like caseworkers, therapists, attorneys—shining lights on that behavior, Jake certainly would never go near that little boy again.

—— A Mistaken Belief Of Many Families ——

This is a mistaken belief of many families. It's part of their denial. Families in denial are drawn back to the idea that child molesting is only about right and wrong. Where do these families go wrong? They staunchly believe: Now that he knows it's wrong, he'll never do it again.

Jake knows it's wrong to sexually touch a much younger child. He has a keener awareness of this than nearly all boys his age. The direction of his present sex drive is not his fault. Or his parent's. It's the fault of his molester, Michael Jones.

Let's add up the things that happened that got Jake into the position he's in today: Take the acts of Michael Jones, add Jake's parents' insufficient knowledge about molested boys becoming molesters, which prevented them from acting early to get professional help for Jake, as a potential molester, and you get this result: the neighbor boy sexually molested.

Today, Jake presents a danger to the young children around him. The therapist tells Sara that Jake must live somewhere else. It's non-negotiable.

The therapist is keenly aware of Jake's tremendous difficulty controlling his sex drive. Separating Jake from his victim is a major step to help the 14-year-old achieve total control. It's as important a part of his treatment as the SSRIs and the continuing sex-specific therapy.

At the therapist's suggestion, Jake moves to his mother's sister's house. Her house was chosen for several reasons: Her children are all older than Jake; her house is in Jake's school district; but it's far enough away from the seven-year-old neighbor boy that Jake is unlikely to see him.

—— FIRST PRIORITY ——
THE PROTECTION OF THE VICTIM

Mothers and fathers should *never* make the decision about how close the molesting child should be to the victim. When a child has molested a brother or sister, the parents frequently insist that the molesting child remain in the house with the victim. They believe they'll work through this together as a family. They feel they must not actually reject or seem to reject the molesting child by agreeing to his leaving home. The problem with this is that the adults are ignoring what should be their *first priority*: the protection of the victim.

As with Alex's Aunt Kathie, we again see denial about the serious threat some teenagers present to other children in the family. That denial prevents the adults from protecting little sisters, little brothers, cousins, and younger stepchildren. It may also prevent them from helping their own children: Parents who insist that the molesting child live with or near the victim are often seen as unfit parents.

Again, as with Aunt Kathie, we're looking at a common mistaken belief:

Families believe they know more about how to help the molesting child than they do. The average family member knows virtually nothing about the behavior of a child molester. Furthermore, since such behavior is concealed from family members and since the molesting teenager conceals his sexual interests, thoughts, and behavior from his parents, the family members have little ability to deal with him (or her). Family members are out of their league when they try to evaluate something that is frequently and intentionally concealed by the child.

If Jake's mother attempts to make critical decisions for Jake in an area that she is essentially naive about, she will feel forever guilty if she makes the wrong decisions. Her job is to protect the children around Jake and to help Jake understand and stop his molesting behavior so that it doesn't ruin his life. The family simply cannot make the decision about where the child molester lives, even if he's 10 or 12. It must always be decided first by the caseworker whose job is to protect the victim and second by the sex-specific therapist whose job is to protect both the victim and the molesting child.

—— JAKE'S TREATMENT SUCCESS ——

Jake makes excellent progress in the treatment sessions. He learns why it is dangerous for him to masturbate to sex thoughts of little boys, and he stops. He gives the therapist his scrapbook. He avoids the swimming pool. He learns to avoid all places where grade-school boys congregate. He practices techniques to directly reduce his sexual interest in little boys; he carries ammonia capsules in his pocket.

In the course of treatment, he learns to have empathy for his victim. He learns that the neighbor boy was *not* an equal partner. Jake begins to understand that the neighbor boy had fears about him, just as he had had fears about Mr. Jones. In addition, Jake learns social skills. Alex hadn't needed this treatment component. He had many friends his own age. As a member of the football team, Alex was socially sought after. In contrast, Jake, at the age of seven, withdrew from friendships with boys his own age. The therapist teaches Jake social skills that help him spend more time with other teenagers.

When Jake is adjudicated before a juvenile court judge, the therapist testifies on his patient's behalf. Jake's treatment, so far, is a success. No more victims, no more acts. His latest test results show some reduction in his sexual interest in boys of grade-school age. He learns quickly, is responsive, compliant, and a pleasure to have as a patient. The judge rules that Jake should serve twelve months probation. Continued compliance with treatment is a major condition of the teenager's probation.

—— WHY SARA CAN'T END JAKE'S TREATMENT ——

Once her son has finished probation and a full year of intensive treatment, Sara wants to be done with it. She feels that her family has suffered enough; her son has proved himself, now it is over.

But it isn't.

While the criminal justice system no longer holds a threat over Jake, the possibility of recurrence of his sex drive toward little boys is still a reality. As we emphasized earlier, families need to understand that this is about the child's life. Jake, the therapist says, needs several more months of therapy. But Sara decides her son has had enough therapy.

Sex-specific therapy, however, differs from traditional types of therapy in this regard. The decision to stop therapy does *not* rest with the family. Nor does the decision about how many maintenance sessions per year that the child molester patient will attend.

This is the most difficult part of the therapy for Jake's parents. They are upset that this decision about when to end therapy is not theirs to make, that it is up to the therapist. The family desperately wants to put this behind them, have it over, move on and never look back. However, once a boy has developed a sexual interest in children, that's not possible.

Just as parents would never make the decision about which antibiotic Jake should have, or whether sputum cultures will be necessary to fight his pneumonia, or how often he sees the pediatrician, decisions about medication and treatment for boys struggling with their sexual urges toward little children should be left to the professionals.

In contrast to most teenage molesters, Jake needed an extra six months of intensive treatment. Jake finished the intensive part of therapy in 18 months. At the end of the 100 sessions, his test results showed that his sexual interest in seven-year-old boys was insignificant next to his sexual interest in teenage girls and adult women.

Jake began an ongoing relapse prevention program that was designed to help the 14-year-old maintain his treatment gains.

Because he had responded so well, following an extra six months of intensive treatment Jake met with his relapse prevention group once a month. After the first year, tests still showed his greatest sexual interest was in girls his own age. The therapist reduced his relapse prevention sessions to four times a year. Tests every six months showed no sexual interest in children.

The length of time and frequency of relapse prevention sessions varies with the case. Of course, if the teenager has molested many children, and/ or his sexual interest tests show continued sexual interest in children, relapse prevention is more frequent.

—— AN INCEST FATHER —— IS EASY TO TREAT SUCCESSFULLY

Amanda heard from the sex-specific therapist that, although John had an ongoing sexual interest in children, he would probably be easy to treat successfully.

Sex-specific therapists sometimes say incest cases are a cinch. For the most part, it's true. Incest molesters are the easiest type of molesters to treat successfully. The success rate, following treatment, is 95 percent. No more victims. No more acts.

These heartening statistics, however, apply only to the incest *molester*. The incest *victim* is another matter. This is an important point but it can give rise to some confusion.

Incest victims, seen from a clinical perspective, often suffer the greatest and most long-standing damage of any category of molestation victims. They, as children, are defenseless. They are children betrayed by the very adult they love and idolize. They are betrayed by the adult that they have to depend on for their very survival.

While Kerrie has a life-long struggle ahead of her, her father can be stopped from his sexual interest in children in the family with medicines and therapies more easily than other child molesters. For some incest victims this constitutes a bitter irony.

Another irony: The high rate of treatment success among incest molesters means that a family living in the new era can expect that by putting an incestuous molesting family member in treatment, the molesting behavior will be stopped. Had John's parents lived in the new era, had they taken him for treatment *the first time he touched his little sister*, his chances to rid himself of his sexual interest in children would have been excellent. And Kerrie would never have become an incest victim.

Even now, John is likely to be completely successful in treatment. This is true for several reasons, most of them having to do with the typical incest father's control. John enters treatment with several built-in sexual controls in place.

- He molests only in the family.
- He molests only children that he's known a long time who are living in the home with him.
- He limits his sexual touching to fondling.

Amanda is encouraged when she finds out that John already has some built-in controls over whom he will molest. Those controls give John a tremendous advantage. Those controls are also an advantage to society, to us: Since John limits his molesting to young girls who live in his house, we can limit the number of children we have to protect. Our job is reduced. We don't have to protect all the children in the world from John. We only have to protect the little girls who might live with him.

It's easier to control John because his family — once they have been educated — will be able to pull together to protect the family's children.

Another advantage for John: He enters treatment with a pronounced sexual interest in adult women.

It might seem that John would be more difficult to treat because he's been molesting little girls in the family for 20 years. He started with his little sister when he was 17, and he's now 37. However, research studies suggest the number of years molesting has little effect on treatment success. John has also had three victims and committed a large number of acts. Research studies also suggest that neither number of victims nor number of acts has a significant effect on treatment success.

That incest molesters are the category of molesters that succeeds best in treatment should in no way trivialize the injury that results from their acts.

Their sexual abuse of the family's children severely damages those children, often for the rest of their lives.

—— WHY SOME INCEST MOLESTERS FAIL TREATMENT —— AND MOLEST AGAIN.

We said earlier that, *generally*, incest molesters are the easiest type of molester to treat successfully. This is true for most incest molesters—but not all of them. Let's look for a moment from a treatment standpoint at two of our cases to find out why this is true.

It's dangerous to generalize, to say that all incest fathers are sure treatment successes. A few incest fathers are just the opposite—likely treatment failures, likely to molest again. Who are they? They are incest fathers who have many diagnoses, who cross many sexual boundaries, who enter treatment with few controls in place.

Remember Michael Jones, Jake's molester? He had a history of accusations for which he was never convicted. Among them was one from his daughter. If his daughter's accusation is true, this makes Michael Jones a prime example of an incest molester who is the opposite of John. He comes into treatment with a decided lack of built-in controls. How many sexual boundaries does Michael Jones cross? He molests: girls in his own family, girls outside his family, boys, children of preschool age, children of grade-school age.

That's five separate sexual boundaries he's crossed. Those are only the ones evident from court records of depositions. An actual evaluation might well reveal several more.

Another part of Mr. Jones' daughter's accusation, if true, would add to the probability of his molesting again: She accused her father of having sexual intercourse with her. While most incest fathers are treatment successes, this group does *not* include fathers who have had actual sexual intercourse with their daughters.

—— JOHN'S TREATMENT ——

John provides a good example of an incest molester who, in most respects, proved an easy case to treat. The most difficult part of his treatment was dealing with his denial. However, the fact that two different tests produced the same results softened John's denial.

Test results, in most cases, have a big impact on the pedophile. Just as many people may deny they have a serious illness until the doctor shows them their test results, pedophiles like John are often in denial until the therapist shows them their test results. Faced with objective results, pedophiles will, in over 60 percent of cases, admit they have a problem and enter the treatment process in earnest. The therapist confronted John with the results from his plethysmography-test, which showed he had sexual arousal to girls Kerrie's age, and the results from his Abel Assessment, which also showed he had sexual interest in girls Kerrie's age.[60]

After seeing his test results, John admitted that he did have sex fantasies about little girls, but said he hadn't done anything terrible because of them. Other members of his therapy group, who had once been in denial themselves, confronted him. That helped. The cataclysmic break in his denial occurred, however, when his own victims confronted him. This was not a face-to-face confrontation. John's sister and his daughter both wrote him letters about their painful experiences being molested. By the time he finished reading those letters, he was a broken man.

A period of depression followed. For a while, John saw his own death as the only suitable resolution to his past behavior. When that crisis passed, he focused his efforts on being the good father Kerrie deserved—even when that meant staying away from her and the rest of his family.

In the midst of this terrible sadness, there was one fact that brought John hope. As an incestuous father with a high sexual interest in adult women and many sexual controls in place, John knew his treatment was highly likely to be a success. And it was.

—— WHO ARE THE HEROES —— IN THE STORY OF TREATMENT?

Who are the heroes in these stories of treatment? The heroes are the parents who moved forward to act. The parents who stood up against their families' denial.

> • **Alex's mother** is a hero. She insisted on protecting her sister's little girls in the face of Kathie's strong denial that there was a problem. She moved forward to get professional help for her son, even though she knew her sister would be extremely angry. Alex's mother had to suffer through her sister's accusations that she was a bad mother. She had to hold her ground when she knew her

angry sister was telling their other two sisters and their mother that she was hurting her son and their family. She held her ground on the importance of getting treatment for Alex. Then, she went beyond that. Alex's mother took on a new role: She became the family teacher. She helped her angry sister learn about diagnosis. She helped her learn enough about the importance of separating a pedophile from children to get Kathie's help in protecting the little girls *and* Alex.

- **Jake's mother,** although she was in denial, made sure her son took his medication, made sure he was on time for every treatment session, made sure he did his treatment homework. She also took on the role of family educator with her extended family. She even stood up to her difficult brother-in-law, refusing to let him trivialize Jake's experience of being a child victim.

- **Brian's father** moved forward to talk to his 13-year-old son —even though he felt his son acted too immature to engage in such a serious talk, even though in his heart he was positive Brian was one kid who would never have this problem. Why is he the greatest hero? Because he overcame his own denial, didn't take the easy path of ignoring the presence of child molestation as a serious problem in our country. He proved himself a strong parent capable of helping his son with *any* sexual concern. He didn't have the struggles with family that made Alex's mother and Jake's mother and John's wife such wonderful heroes. That's because he moved early to help Brian, early enough so that Brian's problem was easily stopped. Less than three hours of a therapist's time stopped any development of the boy's sexual interest in children dead in its tracks. Brian's father is our model for the super-heroic family member, because he got professional help for his son *before* his son had one child victim.

- **John's mother** stepped forward to protect her grand-daughter. Faced with the near-certainty of her sons' anger and the uncertainty as to what would happen to John and his family after she reported him, her hand shook when she picked up the phone, but she still made the call. She ended her granddaughter's days of being a victim.

THE STOP CHILD MOLESTATION PLAN IN ACTION — CHAPTER 7 —	
1. Tell others the facts.	**Tell your family and friends:** • Families do not cause a teenager or adult to develop a sexual interest in children. • Families often fail to protect their younger children because they deny the importance of sexual abuse when it's in the family. • Medicines exist that are used routinely to reduce a teenager's or adult's desire to flash, window-peep, or sexually abuse a child. • Research advances have led to the use of a series of treatments — called cognitive-behavioral therapies — that have an 89-percent success rate. • Some sex-specific treatments come with special conditions imposed that protect child victims and all children. • Some men even though they molested a number of children over 20 or 30 years have an excellent chance of treatment success. • For many incestuous fathers, uncles, and older brothers, their treatment is virtually guaranteed to be a success.
2. Save the greatest number of children in the shortest possible time.	**Take your teenager to a sex-specific therapist for an evaluation if he or she has:** • sexually touched a much younger child. • ongoing sex thoughts about or sex urges directed toward a much younger child. • has been molested as a child, particularly if he is a molested boy.
3. Focus on the cause: Start saving children at the beginning — before a child becomes a victim	• Pedophilia caused by a sexual interest in children can be successfully treated. The sexual interest in children can be reduced or extinguished.

8

How Many Children Can You Save?

THE STOP CHILD MOLESTATION BOOK

8

──── BOBBY'S STORY ────

Bobby thinks he was four when he was first molested. What he says is he can't remember a time when he was not having sex. His father and his uncle sexually touched him from as early as he can remember. Before he got out of fifth grade, when the two men stopped molesting him, he had been a victim for at least seven years. Although he can't remember a lot about what happened when he was four and five, Bobby believes that by the age of eleven, he had been sexually molested at least 900 times.

He had his first victim when he was seven. By the time someone stopped him he was 35. Who was the hero? A six-year-old boy. Bobby's son.

One day at school he started crying. He told his teacher that his daddy was "coming into my bedroom and touching my pee-pee." The teacher, following the reporting laws, called Child Protective Services. The caseworker took the boy into the custody of the state, while she began to sort out the family situation.

The family was already under considerable stress. Bobby's wife—who was only 42—had breast cancer. New test results showed the cancer had metastasized. Bobby was removed from the house, and because his wife could not handle a rambunctious little boy without her husband, the son was put in foster care.

The family's many friends in the community and at church were horrified. They knew Bobby. They believed it couldn't be true. They believed Bobby was just like them. They knew his parents as good people, and so they imagined his childhood as just like theirs. They believed good people like Bobby could not possibly molest a child. The fact that he was accused of molesting a boy, and his own son at that, made the accusation doubly laughable if it hadn't been so cruel. Bobby,—everyone knew—was heterosexual and he adored his wife. As one neighbor said, "If you could see him caring for his wife—the devotion, the tenderness—you'd know Bobby is not the type of person who could have done this.

Actually, Bobby fit the profile of a child molester. At 35 he was a happily married heterosexual man with one son and a baby daughter. He had a good job, made $40,000 a year, and was in line for a promotion. He went to church and was active in the Kiwanis and the Masons. Bobby was outgoing and popular; he was one of those guys everyone likes.

One man from church, who called immediately to tell Bobby he would stand as a character witness, told everyone in the congregation that they shouldn't blame the little boy. "He was so obviously trying to get attention. He knows something is terribly wrong with his mother and he's scared." He also advised everyone to give all their support to Bobby. "It's what every man fears," he said, "a false accusation."

He didn't blame the son, he blamed the teacher: "Boys that age tell all sorts of made-up stories." He was truly shocked that a teacher who was supposed to know something about six-year-old boys didn't know that. What he'd heard is that she didn't even call Bobby or his wife before she reported this ridiculous story to the authorities.

These are people who, unfortunately, are operating on the mistaken belief that they know who is and who is not sexually abusing children. They also have the mistaken belief that the teacher has a choice about reporting. She doesn't. And this is a good thing. Since there is no possible way she or any other layperson could know whether or not this six-year-old's father has a sexual interest in little boys, it's protective of the child to report to professionals who can make that judgment.

In sympathy with the mother's illness, the case worker did everything she could to rush the evaluation process; she made an immediate appointment for Bobby with a sex-specific therapist whose office did objective testing.

Though there were no charges against Bobby, he surprised the therapist by admitting that he did molest his son. "I did it," he said. "Now, just tell me what I have to do to get my family back together. I'll do anything."

Bobby's therapist takes up the story at this point:

"Very rarely do I have someone come into my office with no charges and say, 'I did it.' Bobby was a big guy, very jovial, and when he started talking you couldn't shut him up. He expanded on his initial admission by confessing that

he had two additional male victims, adults now, that he had molested years ago when he was a teenager and they were in grade school.

"In the first few weeks of Bobby's therapy, I was feeling very pleased with his progress. He was revealing more and more. Out of the blue, he started talking about 15 victims. I have to admit I was so pleased, because it was a blessing not to have to fight the usual patient's denial, or concealment, or outright lies.

"Then I got Bobby's sexual interest test results. At first I thought there had been a mistake, that maybe his test had gotten mixed up with another patient's. His objective results showed his greatest sexual interest was in pre-school age girls, *then* grade-school girls, *and only third in rank were grade-school boys.*

"I had already questioned him about girls, and he'd said. 'No, no interest in girls.' When I confronted him with his test results, saying I was puzzled and confused, he laughed. By the end of the session he was telling me about the three nieces, who were his female *victims.*

"The results from the sexual interest assessment opened the door. From that moment, his treatment went into overdrive. First, I called the caseworker to set her in motion to protect the little girls. Then, I put him on an SSRI to reduce his sex drive. In addition to the group training sessions that had begun to reduce his sex drive toward boys, I scheduled him for individual sessions directed at lowering his arousal to boys and girls.

"Then I immediately set him up with a second objective test, a polygraph, to see what he was doing now. And this first set of test results from the sexual interest test helped me focus some specific questions. I found out that even when he was molesting his son he was fantasizing about little girls.

"Finally, I called Bobby's son's therapist to talk to her about the possibility that the boy might later molest smaller children because of modeling or because he would 'identify with the aggressor.' I suggested the boy get tested yearly, starting at age 12."

By the time Bobby arrived for evaluation and treatment, he had a history:

- He had been sexually abused for seven years.
- He was the victim of more than 900 molestations.
- He had had 56 girl and boy victims.
- He had committed 400 acts.

Bobby's son is the hero in this story. His first grade teacher is another hero, as is the caseworker. And so is the therapist, who moved quickly to protect all the children in Bobby's family.

Since sexual stimulation was his earliest memory, Bobby's whole life was one of denial. Bobby never thought of himself as a victim. And he never thought of his son as a victim. That's why he was astounded when his son told the teacher. Sex was private. And his easy confession, "I did it," came from the same place.

Bobby's open manner with the therapist came straight from his denial. He believed he hadn't hurt his son, since he only fondled him. The men in his family had done worse to him and he never said anything. He thought that probably half of the families in the world did it. He survived it and he was fine, so what was the big deal?

In Bobby's mind, sexually touching little boys wasn't child molesting; it was what grown men did, what fathers and sons did. What he felt bad about, what he had been hiding, were the little girls.

——WHO COULD HAVE SAVED BOBBY?——

By the time his six-year-old son stopped him, Bobby had been a child victim for eight years and a molester for 28 years. Who could have saved Bobby from this life? Who could have saved his 56 child victims? In his early years there were several people.

Bobby's Mother

Bobby's mother could have saved him and his 56 future child victims— including her own grandson—if she had stopped it right there when Bobby was 4 or 5 or 6. All she had to do was *consider the possibility*. If she could have done that, she could have had a talk with her son using the same techniques that Jake's mother used with Jake in Chapter Four.

Unfortunately, Bobby's mother was like most people. She could not possibly imagine that her son (or her husband or her brother-in-law) had a sex drive different from that of most boys and men.

She ignored the fact that child molestation existed. If she ever thought about it, she had a fleeting thought that some low types of in-bred backwoods people had sex with the young girls in their families. These were the kind of people no one in her family was ever likely to know. So she failed Bobby's 56 child victims, including her grandson, and she failed Bobby.

The parents of Bobby's school friend

When Bobby was eight, he bragged to his friend, Sammy, another eight-year-old in his class, that he "jacked off" every day, and so did his dad. His dad did it to him; then he did it to his dad. The friend asked his teenage brother about this. Did their dad ever "jack off" with him?

When the teenage brother told their parents, the uproar was so gigantic that Sammy, for the rest of his life, never mentioned anything about sex in front of his older brother or his parents. His parents forbade him to go to Bobby's house ever again. They also said that, as for Bobby's sexual behavior, it was none of their business.

His eight-year-old friend's parents, who said it was none of their business, could have saved Bobby and 53 of his future child victims.

How? All they had to do was pick up the phone and call Child Protective Services. With one phone call they could not only have saved 53 children, they could also have saved Bobby from three more years of sexual abuse.

Bobby says he had his first victim when he was *seven*. The victim, he remembers, was walking, but a little shaky on his feet. He was the son of a close friend of Bobby's mother. The boy was too young to tell, so no one suspected. At eight, Bobby was a sexually experienced little boy. By that time, he had three victims. These molestations were most likely the result of modeling. He was copying what his father did to him.

Bobby's mother's friend

As a sexually abused little boy, Bobby felt out of control and powerless. When that second batch of testosterone hit him at puberty, just like Jake, the boy who was sexually abused by the daycare owner, Bobby did a 180-degree turn and handled his fear and anxiety by becoming the one in the powerful position. He identified with his aggressors. Also, like Brian, he repeatedly paired orgasm with fantasies of sexually touching a much younger child. After that second batch of testosterone made his voice deepen and hair grow on his face, Bobby increased his sexual molestations.

When he was a high school sophomore, Bobby volunteered to help his mother's best friend with her Cub Scout troop. Her own son started acting up so badly during meetings that she had to send him to his room. Then her son said he wouldn't come out of his room to go to the meeting if Bobby was there. When questioned, the little boy refused to say why.

Although his mother guessed it was something sexual, what she worried about was what to say to Bobby and his mother. She wasn't going to let Bobby help any more, but she had to think of a good excuse. She made up an excuse, then after Bobby was out of the Cub Scout meetings, she got her nerve up to tell his mother.

His mother's friend could have saved Bobby. And here, Bobby's mother had a second chance. Although his mother had failed to have ongoing discussions with her son so that he had permission to talk with her about bad touch, this complaint from her best friend gave her another chance to consider the possibility that her son needed help.

But Bobby's mother ignored the warning. When the friend told her that she thought "sex stuff" was going on between the two boys, Bobby's mother refused to consider the possibility that her son might need help. "All boys do sex play," she said.

The saddest thing about this case? Nobody rescued that little boy—at four, at seven, at sixteen. The best friend told herself she had done what she could, but both she and Bobby's mother could have done more. These two women could have saved so many children.

How? The friend could have told Bobby's mother that she was reporting her son's molestation to Child Protective Services and then made the call. Bobby's mother could have talked to her son the same way Alex's dad talked to his son in Chapter Two. Then she could have taken him to a sex-specific therapist for testing and an evaluation. With that one act, Bobby's mother could have saved her son, her grandson, and 46 other children.

By the time he was 16, Bobby had had nine victims. With those nine victims he had committed 79 acts of child molestation.

Bobby's employer and a victim's parents

The summer between his senior year and college, the summer he was 18, Bobby worked as a camp counselor. Now an expert swimmer, he taught the children to swim.

By the end of that summer, he had had three more victims. That made twelve victims.

After the season was over, a parent wrote to the camp director complaining that Bobby had made some sexual advances to her son. Although Bobby had molested the boy repeatedly, when questioned he said that he absolutely had not made advances. He told the camp director that he had a girlfriend he'd been going steady with for six months before he began work at the camp. He told the camp director to ask his parents if he didn't believe him.

Afraid that Bobby's parents would sue him for falsely accusing the boy, the camp director said nothing to Bobby's parents or anybody else. The camp director was at a loss. He eased the camp out of it by simply not inviting Bobby back the next year.

The camp director could have stopped Bobby right there. How? All he had to do was make a call to Child Protective Services and report the parents' accusation. In fact, the molested boy's parents could have made the same call.

The mistake the camp director—and the parents—made was to believe he should be the investigator. Thinking a camp director has the ability to deal with a possible case of pedophilia is as silly as believing he could determine if Bobby had diabetes or TB. And because of that mistake, these three people failed Bobby, Bobby's son, and 44 other children.

—— HOW MANY CHILDREN CAN YOU SAVE? ——

How many children can one person save by taking one simple action? How many people can *you* save?

To find out, put yourself in the place of Bobby's grandparents. They had two sons who grew up to be pedophiles. They were like most parents: They taught their sons right from wrong, gave them religious values. The younger one was considering the ministry as his life's work; the older one, who became Bobby's father, was set on engineering.

When the boys were fifteen and sixteen, their mother got a phone call from an angry neighbor who told her to keep her sons away from her little girl. The girl was ten. The neighbor accused the older son (Bobby's father at 16) of pulling her daughter's panties down with a no-good purpose in mind. She also said she was telling her husband and, "If he sees your boy within six blocks of our daughter, he'll beat him to within an inch of his life."

Bobby's grandmother defended her son, she defended her family, and she defended herself as a good mother who knew how to raise good boys. She was so mad at this woman for slandering her son, herself, and her family that she determined to cut her dead every time she saw her. She warned her son — after saying she believed in him — to walk in the opposite direction any time he saw that girl or the girl's mother or father.

And so her two sons became successful, well-respected men in their communities, each free to molest more than one hundred children.

At that moment, if Bobby's grandmother had all the advantages you have today, she could have saved her two sons, her grandson, her great-grandson, and more than 350 innocent children—all the victims of her sons and grandson.

How? All she had to do—all any parent has to do, all any friend has to do—was to allow a *possibility* to enter her mind: Could this child have a problem?

And if you want to take your place as a hero that's all you have to do, too. When you get that phone call from a neighbor, when your sister calls, when a tearful child comes to you—at that moment you have the power to save.

You have the power to save your family from generations of heartache. You have the power to save hundreds of children besides your own. It's so little to ask. A slight shift in thought: **Could this child have a problem?**

REFERENCE NOTES

[1] American Psychiatric Association, Diagnostic *and Statistical Manual of Mental Disorders*, 4th Edition, Text Revision, American Psychiatric Association: (Washington, D.C.: 2000).

[2] Kenneth V. Lanning, SSA, "Sexual Homicide of Children," in *The APSAC Advisor* 7, no. 4 (Winter 1994).

[3] David Finkelhor, A *Sourcebook on Child Sexual Abuse* (London: Sage, 1986).

[4] Gail L. Zellman and Kathleen C. Faller, "Reporting of Child Maltreatment," in *The APSAC Handbook on Child Maltreatment*, ed. John Briere (Thousand Oaks, CA: Sage Publication, 1996): 359-381.

[5] Lisa Jones and David Finkelhor, "The Decline in Child Sexual Abuse Cases," Juvenile *Justice Bulletin* (Office of Juvenile Justice and Delinquency Prevention: January 2001): 1-10.

[6] U.S. Department of Health and Human Services, Public Health Service: Office of Disease Prevention and Health Promotion and Centers for Disease Control and Prevention. *For a Healthy Nation: Returns on Investment in Public Health.* [20497] (U.S. Government Printing Office, 1995): 390-173.

[7] Vincent J. Felitti, et. al., "Relationship of Childhood Abuse and Household Dysfunction to Many of the Leading Causes of Death in Adults: The Adverse Childhood Experiences Study," American *Journal of Preventive Medicine* 14, no. 4 (1998): 245-258.

[8] Lucy Berliner and Diana M. Elliot, "Sexual Abuse of Children," in *The APSAC Handbook on Child Maltreatment*, ed. John Briere (Thousand Oaks, CA: Sage Publication, 1996): 55-60.

[9] Sandra L. Bryant and L.M. Range, "Suicidality in College Women Who Were Sexually and Physically Punished by Parents," *Violence Victims* 10 (1995): 195-201.

[10] F. Springs and William N. Friedrich, "Health Risk Behaviors and Medical Sequelae of Childhood Sexual Abuse," Mayo Clinic Proc 67 (1992): 527-32.

[11] J.R. Conte and John R. Schuerman, "The Effects of Sexual Abuse on Children: A Multidimensional View," in *Lasting Effects of Child Sexual Abuse*, eds. G.E. Wyatt, and G.J. Powell (Beverly Hills, California: Sage Publications): 150-170.

[12] U.S. Census Bureau, U.S. Department of Commerce, Economics and Statistics Administration, Statistical *Abstract of the United States: The National Data Book 1999.* 119th Edition. (Washington, D.C.: October 1999).

[13] Gene G. Abel, Joanne L. Rouleau, and Jerry Cunningham-Rathner, "Sexually Aggressive Behavior," in *Forensic Psychiatry and Psychology: Perspectives and Standards for Interdisciplinary Practice*, eds. W.J. Curran, A.L. McGarry, and S.A. Shah (Philadelphia: F.A. Davis, 1986): 289-313.

[14] Gene G. Abel, et al., "Pedophilia," in *Treatments of Psychiatric Disorders,* Third Edition, eds. G. O. Gabbard and S.B. Levine (American Psychiatric Press, 1995): 1981-2005.

[15] American Psychiatric Association, *Diagnostic and Statistical Manual of Mental Disorders*, 4th Edition, Text Revision, American Psychiatric Association: (Washington, D.C.: 2000).

[16] David Finkelhor, L.M. Williams, and N. Burns, *Nursery Crimes: Sexual Abuse in Day Care* (Newbury Park, CA: Sage, 1987).

[17] Gene G. Abel and Candice A. Osborn, "The Paraphilias," in *Oxford Textbook of Psychiatry* vol. 1, eds. M. G. Gelder, J.J. Lopez-Ibor, Jr., N.C. Andreason (Oxford University Press: 2000): 897-913.

[18] Stacey C. Zolondek, Gene G. Abel, William F. Northey, Jr.,

Alan D. Jordan, "The Self-Reported Behaviors of Juvenile Sex Offenders," *Journal of Interpersonal Violence* 16, no. 1 (2001): 73-85.

[19] Jay R. Feierman, ed., *Pedophilia: Biosocial Dimensions*, (New York: Springer-Verlag, 1990).

[20] Ibid.

[21] Gene G. Abel, Suzanne S. Lawry, Elizabeth M. Karlstrom, Candice A. Osborn, and Charles F. Gillespie, "Screening Tests for Pedophilia," in *Criminal Justice and Behavior*, 21, no. 1, (Thousand Oaks, CA: Sage Publications, March 1994).

[22] Gene G. Abel, Candice A. Osborn, and Deborah A. Twigg, "Sexual Assault Through the Life Span: Adult Offenders with Juvenile Histories," in *The Juvenile Sex Offender*, eds. Howard E. Barbaree, William L. Marshall, and Richard Laws (New York: Guilford Publications Inc., 1993): 104-116.

[23] Gene G. Abel, John M. W. Bradford, and G.G. Glancy, "The Assessment and Treatment of Child Molesters (CME Workshop)," Presented at the One Fifty-Fourth Annual Meeting of the American Psychiatric Association, New Orleans, LA, May 2001.

[24] Ibid.

[25] Ibid.

[26] Gene G. Abel, "Behavioral Treatment of Child Molesters," in *Perspectives on Behavioral Medicine*, eds. A.J. Stunkard and A. Baum (New York: Lawrence Erlbaum Associates, Inc., 1989): 223-242.

[27] Jay R. Feierman, "A Biosocial Overview of Adult Human Sexual Behavior with Children and Adolescents," in *Pedophilia: Biosocial Dimensions*, ed. Jay Feierman (New York: Springer Verlag, 1990): 8-68.

[28] Gene G. Abel and Candice A. Osborn, "Pedophilia," in *The Psychology of Sexual Orientation: A Handbook*, eds. L. Diamant and R. McAnulty (Connecticut: Greenwood Publishing Group, Inc., 1995): 270-281.

[29] Stacey C. Zolondek, Gene G. Abel, William F. Northey, Jr. and Alan D. Jordan, "The Self-Reported Behaviors of Juvenile Sex Offenders," *Journal of Interpersonal Violence* 16, no. 1 (2001): 73-85.

[30] Alfred Kinsey, William Pomeroy, and Clyde Martin, "*Sexual Behavior in the Human Male*" (Philadelphia and London: W.B. Saunders Company, 1948): 654.

[31] Gene G. Abel and Candice A. Osborn, "The Paraphilias," in *Oxford Textbook of Psychiatry* eds. M.G. Gelder, J.J. Lopez-Ibor and N.C. Andreason (Oxford University Press: Nov. 2000).

[32] Gene G. Abel, "Behavioral Treatment of Child Molesters," in *Perspectives on Behavioral Medicine*, eds. A.J. Stunkard and A. Baum (New York: Lawrence Erlbaum Associates, Inc., 1989): 223-242.

[33] Gene G. Abel and Edward B. Blanchard, "The Role of Fantasy in the Treatment of Sexual Deviation," *Archives of General Psychiatry*, 30, no. 6 (1974): 467-475.

[34] Lucy Berliner and Diana M. Elliott, "Sexual Abuse of Children," in *APSAC Handbook on Child Maltreatment*, eds. John Briere, Lucy Berliner, J.A. Bulkley, C. Jenney and T.Reid (London: Sage Publications, 1996): 51-71.

[35] David Finkelhor, *A Sourcebook on Child Sexual Abuse* (London: Sage, 1986).

[36] Gene G. Abel, Candice A. Osborn, and Deborah A. Twigg, "Sexual Assault through the Life Span: Adult Offenders with Juvenile Histories," in *The Juvenile Sexual Offender*, eds. H.E. Barbaree, W.L. Marshall and D.R. Laws (New York: Guilford Publications, Inc., 1993): 104-116.

[37] Gene G. Abel, Judith V. Becker, Jerry Cunningham-Rathner,

Mary S. Mittelman, and Joanne L. Rouleau, "Multiple Paraphilic Diagnoses Among Sex Offenders," *Bulletin of the American Academy of Psychiatry and the Law* 16, no. 2 (1989): 153-168.

[38] National Grant #MH36347, "The Treatment of Child Molesters," August 1, 1981 – July 31, 1984.

[39] Judith V. Becker, Linda J. Skinner, and Gene G. Abel, "Treatment of a Four-year Old Victim of Incest," *The American Journal of Family Therapy* 10 (1982): 41-46.

[40] Judith V. Becker, Linda J Skinner, and Gene G. Abel, "Sequelae of Sexual Assault: The Survivor's Perspective," in *The Sexual Aggressor: Current Perspectives on Treatment,* eds. J.G. Greer and I.R. Stuart (New York: Van Nostrand Reinhold, 1983): 240-266.

[41] Gene G. Abel, Judith V. Becker, and Jerry Cunningham-Rathner, "Complications, Consent and Cognitions in Sex Between Children and Adults," *International Journal of Law and Psychiatry* 7, no. 1 (1984): 89-103.

[42] Gene G. Abel, Charles L. Holland, Nancy L. Camp, Judith V. Becker, and Jerry Cinningham-Rathner, "The Measurement of the Cognitive Distortions of Child Molesters," *Annals of Sex Research* 2, no. 2 (1989): 135-153.

[43] Judith V. Becker and Gene G. Abel, "Methodological and Ethical Issues in Evaluating and Treating Adolescent Sexual Offenders," in *Adolescent Sex Offenders: Issues in Research and Treatment* Department of Health and Human Services Publication No. ADM 85-1396 (Washington, DC: U.S. Government Printing Office, 1985).

[44] Gene G. Abel, Edward B. Blanchard, and David H. Barlow, "Measurement of Sexual Arousal in Several Paraphilias: The Effects of Stimulus Modality, Instructional Set and Stimulus Content on the Objective," *Behavior Research and Therapy* 19, no. 1 (1981): 25-23.

[45] Gene G. Abel, Edward B. Blanchard, William D. Murphy, Judith V. Becker, and A. Djenderedjian, "Two Methods of

Measuring Penile Response," *Behavior Therapy* 12 (1981): 320-328.

[46] Gene G. Abel and Edward B. Blanchard, "The Measurement and Generation of Sexual Arousal in Male Sexual Deviates," in *Progress in Behavior Modification* vol. 2, eds. M. Herson et al. (New York: Academic Press, 1976): 99-136.

[47] Gene G. Abel, Suzanne S. Lawry, Elizabeth M. Karlstrom, Candice A. Osborn, and Charles F. Gillespie, "Screening Tests for Pedophilia," *Criminal Justice and Behavior* (Sage Publications) 21, no. 1 (March 1994): 115-131.

[48] Gene G. Abel, Jeffery Huffman, Brent W. Warberg, and Charles L. Holland, "Visual Reaction Time and Plethysmography as Measures of Sexual Interest in Child Molesters," *Sexual Abuse: A Journal of Research and Treatment* 10, no. 2 (1998): 81-95.

[49] Gene G. Abel and Candice A. Osborn, "The Paraphilias," in. *Oxford Textbook of Psychiatry*, eds. M.G. Gelder, J.J. Lopez-Ibor, Jr., and N.C. Andreasen (Oxford University Press, 2000): 897-913.

[50] Gene G. Abel, Candice A. Osborn and A.M. Phipps, "Pedophilia," in *Treatments of Psychiatric Disorders*, Third Edition, 2, eds. Gabbard, G.O. and Levine, S.B. (American Psychiatric Press, 1995): 1981-2005.

[51] John M. W. Bradford, "The Treatment of Sexual Deviation Using a Pharmacological Approach," *Journal of Sex Research* 37, no. 3 (2000): 248-257.

[52] Richard Krueger and Meg S. Kaplan, "Depot-Leuprolide Acetate for Treatment of Paraphilias: A Report of Twelve Cases," *Archives of Sexual Behavior* 30, no. 4 (2001): 409-422.

[53] Dangerous Sex Offenders. A Task Force Report of the American Psychiatric Association. (Washington, DC © 1999).

[54] John M. W. Bradford, David Greenberg, D, J. Gojer, J.J. Martindale, and M. Goldberg, "Sertraline in the Treatment of

Pedophilia: An Open Label Study," *New Research Program Abstracts 441* (1995).

[55] Gene G. Abel, "The Relationship Between Treatment for Sex Offenders and the Court," in *The Sexual Aggressor: Current Perspectives on Treatment,* eds. S.N. Verdun-Jones and A. A. Keltner (New York: Van Nostrand Reinhold, 1983): 240-266.

[56] A. Gordon, R.K. Hanson, A. Harris, J. Marques, W. Murphy, B. Quinsey, and M. Ceto, "The Effectiveness of Treatment for Sex Offenders: Report of the Association for the Treatment of Sexual Abusers Collaborative Data Research Committee," presented at the 19th Annual Research and Treatment Conference in San Diego, CA November 2, 2000.

[57] Gene G. Abel, Judith V. Becker, Jerry Cunningham-Rathner, Mary S. Mittelman, and Joanne L. Rouleau, "Multiple Paraphilic Diagnosis Among Sex Offenders," *Bulletin of the American Academy of Psychiatry and the Law* (1989): 153-168.

[58] Gene G. Abel, Mary S. Mittleman, Judith V. Becker, Jerry Cunningham-Rathner, and Joanne L. Rouleau, "Predicting Child Molesters' Response to Treatment," *Annals of the New York Academy of Sciences* (1988): 223-234.

[59] Gene G. Abel and Candice A. Osborn, "The Paraphilias: The Extent and Nature of Sexual Deviant and Criminal Behavior," in *Psychiatric Clinics of North America,* ed. J.M.W. Bradford 15, no. 3 (Philadelphia, PA: W.B. Sanders Co., 1992): 675-687.

[60] Gene G. Abel, "Paraphilias," in *Comprehensive Textbook of Psychiatry,* Vol. 1, 5th ed., eds. H.I. Kaplan and B.J. Sadock, Vol. 1, 5th ed. (Baltimore; Williams and Wilkins, 1989): 1069-1085.

—TABLES—

THE ABEL AND HARLOW STOP CHILD MOLESTATION STUDY

By Gene G. Abel, M.D., and Nora Harlow

—— OVERVIEW ——

The Problem

Child molestation, because of its large numbers of victims and because of the extent of its damage to the health of its victims, is a national public health problem. To combat this public health problem we must focus on the cause. People with pedophilia molest 88 percent of child sexual abuse victims. Early diagnosis of this disorder, followed by effective medicines and therapies, has the potential to save children from being molested.

The Study

Starting with a study sample of 16,109 adults who were tested in 41 states in reaction to possible sexual boundary violations, the authors analyzed the reports of 4,007 adults, ages 18 to 95, who admitted that they had sexually molested one or several children. Special attention was given to finding information that could be used to sharply reduce the number of child victims of sexual abuse.

We defined "child" and "child molestation" using the medical criteria of the American Psychiatric Association, as defined in their *Diagnostic and Statistical Manual of Mental Disorders*, Forth Edition, Text Revision, DSM-IV-TR

Definitions

Child: Any girl or boy 13 years of age or younger. To be in the child molester group in this study, the test-taker must have reported that he or she had sexually touched a child 13 years old or younger.

Child molestation: The act of sexually touching a child.

Child molester: Any older child or adult who touches a child for his or her own sexual gratification.

Age difference: To fit the medically accepted definition of a child molester, the person sexually touching the child must be at least five years older. For example, if a 14-year-old child sexually touches a nine-year-old child, the 14-year-old is a child molester.

Findings

1. *Demographics*: Child molesters match the U.S. population in education, percentage married or formerly married, and religious observance.

2. *Ethnicity*: Child molesters occur in various ethnic groups: Caucasian, Hispanic, African-American, Asian, and American Indian.

3. *High-risk children*: Only 10 percent of child molesters molest children they don't know.

4. *Children in the family*: The overwhelming majority of molesters (68 percent) sexually abuse children in their own families — either children whom they parent, nieces and nephews, or grandchildren. As teenagers they molest much younger siblings.

5. *Children in the social circle*: The next largest number of molesters (40 percent) abuse children of families in their social circle. Some molesters molest children in their own families *and* children in their social circle.

6. *Pedophilia*: Pedophilia is the most significant cause of child molestation.

7. *Early onset*: Pedophilia is a disorder that starts

early in life. Child molesters with the disorder pedophilia begin to molest much younger children at an earlier age. More than 40 percent molest before they reach age 15, and the majority molest before age 20.

8. *Influence of sex fantasies*: Molesters who maintain sex fantasies of children (41 percent) have more than three times the number of child victims as molesters who do not fantasize about having sexual interactions with children.

9. *Sexually abused boys who become molesters*: Being abused as a boy appears to increase the risk that the abused child will himself eventually molest a child. More than 47 percent of the admitted child molesters had been sexually abused as children.

10. *Severely sexually abused boys*: Adult molesters who, as children, were sexually abused more than 50 times have triple the number of child victims compared to child molesters who were never sexually molested. Of those sexually abused more than 50 times, 82 percent can be categorized as pedophiles.

11. *Sexual orientation*: More than 70 percent of the men who molest boys rate themselves as heterosexual in their adult sexual preferences. In addition, 9 percent report that they are equally heterosexual and homosexual. Only 8 percent report that they are exclusively homosexual. The majority of the men who molest boys are also married, divorced, widowed, or living with an adult partner.

12. *Crossing multiple sex boundaries*: More than 60 percent of pedophiles have other paraphilias. Many are also exhibitionists or voyeurs. Of the pedophiles who molest girls, 21 percent also molest boys. Of the pedophiles who molest boys, 53 percent also molest girls.

—— SUGGESTIONS TO PROTECT CHILDREN ——

Focus on the cause

Focus on the most significant cause of child molestation: the development in some teenagers and adults of the disorder pedophilia. While not all child molesters have a diagnosable disorder, teenagers and adults who do develop pedophilia molest 88 percent of the child victims and they commit 95 percent of the sexual acts against children. The disorder can be diagnosed. Treatment with medicines and therapies is effective.

Early diagnosis is important

The disorder starts early. Since teenagers may meet all the diagnostic criteria for pedophilia *before* they have sexually touched a child, teenagers who are evaluated at this early stage of pedophilia — if given effective treatment — have an excellent chance of controlling their pedophilia so they never become child molesters. Early diagnosis will significantly reduce the number of children molested.

Evaluate the following people for possible pedophilia

1. Teenagers and adults concerned that they may have a sexual interest in children.

2. Teenagers and adults who report child-centered sex fantasies for more than six months.

3. Children who sexually interact with children at least five years younger.

4. Children who have been molested more than 50 times.

5. Exhibitionists (flashers).

6. Voyeurs (window peepers).

7. Any child, teenager, or adult accused of sexually molesting a younger child.

8. Any teenager or adult convicted of sexually molesting a child.

THE STOP CHILD MOLESTATION BOOK

Setting

The Abel and Harlow Stop Child Molestation Study is based at Abel Screening, Inc., a research and testing company in Atlanta, Georgia. More than 300 medical, psychological and criminal justice sites in 41 states use the standardized testing services provided by Abel Screening, Inc.

Abel Screening's National Sexual Violence Databank is the nation's largest source of detailed information on sexual violence—particularly against children.

Confidentiality and consent

All test-takers sign a consent form prior to testing, which advises them that their data (identified only by a test number) will also be used for research.

Referral sources and presenting complaints

Test-takers are referred for testing by their employers, by their lawyers, by criminal justice professionals, or by mental or medical professionals. Some test-takers are self-referred. Test-takers are referred in response to possible sexual boundary violations that include: professional sexual misconduct (sexual interaction with adult parishioners, patients, and employees by their clergy, physicians, therapists, or employers); exhibitionism (flashing); voyeurism (window-peeping); fetishism (obsessive sexual interest in objects); child molestation; and other possible paraphilias.

Standardized sexual questionnaire

The Abel Assessment *for sexual interest*ä includes completion of a standardized sexual questionnaire that requests demographic, sexual, and paraphilic information and a separate standardized objective measure of sexual interest in males and females of various ages.

A mental health professional, following an interview with the test-taker, adds to the assessment by answering additional questions concerning the test-taker's ability to read and comprehend the testing material. In addition, the professional answers questions as to the probable truthfulness of the test-taker. The mental health professional completes the patient history and reviews the test results with the patient.

All the subjects of *The Abel and Harlow Stop Child Molestation Study* completed the Abel Assessment *for sexual interestÔ* according to these protocols.

Funding

Gene G. Abel, M.D., Nora Harlow, and Abel Screening, Inc., funded *The Abel and Harlow Stop Child Molestation Study*.

—— STUDY POPULATION AND METHODS ——

The Institutional Review Board at West Paces Ferry Hospital in Atlanta, Georgia, approved the research protocols for the study.

The 16,109 test-takers who completed tests between February 14, 1994, and January 22, 2001, were included in *The Stop Child Molestation Study*. Their ages ranged from 18 to 95 years. Their average age was 38.5. Test-takers were from 41 states.

The 16,109 were divided into three groups.

Group one was made up of test-takers who reported that they were *not* child molesters. *Classified as non-child molesters, group one totaled 5,152 males and 304 females.*

Group two was composed of test-takers reported by the mental health professional that evaluated them as either lying or in denial about being child molesters. The mental health professional used three criteria to make this judgment: a) The test-taker had been convicted of child molestation, and/or b) The test-taker was accused of child molestation by more than one family, and/or c) the test-taker's explanation of the reason for the sexual interaction with the child was preposterous. Some examples of preposterous explanations encountered during the study: "When I touched my daughter's breasts while she was sleeping it was for the purpose of sex education." "Yes, I penetrated my six-year-old daughter, but it was an accident. I was coming out of the shower, I slipped on the soap and my penis accidentally went into her vagina." *Classified as liars or deniers, group two totaled 5,138 males and 194 females.*

Group three was made up of test-takers who admitted that they had molested one child or several children. The criterion for admission to the child molesting group was that the test-taker said he or she was a child molester. *Classified by themselves as child molesters, group three totaled 5,218 males and 103 females.*

The three groups—1) non-child molesters, 2) liars or deniers, and 3) admitted child molesters—split nearly evenly, with each group containing over 5,000 people.

We chose to concentrate the major part of our study on the third group, the 5,321 people who said they were child molesters. First, we refined the group so that they matched the American Psychiatric Association's diagnostic criteria for age of the child by limiting it to people who admitted to molesting children age 13 or younger. The admitted child molesters who reported that they had molested a child of 13 years or younger totaled 3,952 males and 55 females.

Exclusions

The following were excluded from our sample:

Adults who Sexually Interact with Adolescents. An additional 1,266 males and 48 females admitted to sexually molesting adolescents 14 to 18 years of age. Data from this group was eliminated.

Adults who sexually interact with adolescents are called ephebophiles. However, there is neither a medical definition nor a medical diagnosis for this group. Ephebophiles do seek and receive therapy. They also are often prosecuted by the criminal justice system for sexually interacting with a minor. Although this group does commit serious acts of sexual abuse, we eliminated them from this study because they do not fit the medical diagnostic criteria for pedophilia.

Women. We also eliminated the women from our final group of admitted child molesters, because the number who admitted to molesting a child of 13 years or younger — 55 — was too small to yield statistically significant results or to make adequate comparisons to the 3,952 males.

Although not all of the males in the child molester group were pedophiles, all did meet two of the medical criteria: They had molested one child or

---

several children who were 13 years or younger, and, being at least 18, were all five years older than the child they had molested.

—— ESTIMATES ——

Prevalence of molested children and adult survivors

Estimates of the number of children who are sexually abused vary so widely from study to study ¾ 3 percent to 54 percent ¾ that they become almost useless.

This wide variation occurs because of the lack of standardized definitions of the terms "child molestation" and "child." For example, one study will define child molestation as touch only and another as touch and non-touch. Also, information-gathering techniques and study populations vary widely, which makes comparisons between studies difficult. The field is further hampered because of failure to standardize the age of the child. One study's directors will use 18 years as the outer limit of "child," another will use 16 years, and others will use 14 or 13 years.

We used the medical definition established by the American Psychiatric Association in their diagnostic manual to define "pedophilia," *Diagnostic and Statistical Manual of Mental Disorders*, Fourth Edition, Text Revision; DSM-IV-TR. We used the sexual *touching* of a child to define the term "child molestation." We used the age of 13 years or younger to define "child."

Number of children

To estimate the number of molested children, we used an analysis by David Finkelhor, Ph.D. from his 1986 *A Sourcebook on Child Sexual Abuse*, page 65. In this table he analyzed six studies of sexual abuse prevalence, which yielded a summated average of sexually abused girls per 100 by age of onset ¾ age one through age 18. We applied those percentages for girls 13 years and younger to the female child population as given in the 1999 U.S. Census Statistical Abstract.

THE STOP CHILD MOLESTATION BOOK

Number of boy victims

To estimate the number of boy victims, we analyzed 13 studies from the same source, pages 20-21, and found the number of boy victims was 45 percent of the number of girl victims. We applied this ratio to Finkelhor's percentages of sexually abused girls by age group, and in turn applied those numbers to the male child population as given in the 1999 U.S. Census Statistical Abstract.

Final estimated numbers: 2,231,372 sexually abused girls and 1,004,117 sexually abused boys.

Number of adult survivors

To estimate the number of adult survivors, we again used David Finkelhor's *Sourcebook*, totaling his summated averages for the year of onset of girls' sexual victimization. By that estimate, 24 percent of girls were sexually abused by the end of their 13th year. Using Finkelhor's percentage of boys who are molested relative to girls who are molested, we estimated the number of male adult survivors using the 1999 U.S. Census Statistical Abstract.

Final estimated numbers: 27,160,752 adult females and 12,222,388 adult males are survivors of childhood sexual abuse.

Comparing the men in The Stop Child Molestation Study to men in the U.S. population

We wanted to show to what extent our complete sample of 15,508 men matched males in the U.S. population, and we also wanted to show to what extent our smaller sample of 3,952 men who admitted to being child molesters matched the U.S. population.

Comparison of 13,476 men age 25 years or older from the complete sample with men in the U.S. population

To get a valid comparison between our sample and the U.S. Census Statistical Report, 1999, on the personal demographics of marriage, education, work, and religion, each test-taker had to be 25 years and older because the Census Statistical Report used 25 years or older for those measurements. Our sample of 13,476 men age 25 and older closely matched the U.S. male population on these demographics.

> **Married or formerly married:** U.S. males, 73 percent *vs.* our sample, 77 percent.
>
> **Some college or higher education:** U.S. males, 49 percent vs. our sample, 48 percent.
>
> **High school graduate:** U.S. males, 32 percent *vs.* our sample, 27 percent.
>
> **Working:** U.S. males, 64 percent *vs.* our sample, 69 percent.
>
> **Religious:** U.S. males, 93 percent *vs.* our sample, 93 percent.

The complete sample of 15,508 men, ages 18 to 95, for the most part also matched the U.S. male population on ethnicity.

> **Caucasian:** U.S. males, 72 percent vs. our sample, 71 percent.
>
> **Hispanic/Latin American:** U.S. males, 11 percent *vs.* our sample, 12 percent.
>
> **African American:** U.S. males, 12 percent *vs.* our sample, 10 percent.
>
> **Asian:** U.S. males, 4 percent *vs.* our sample, 1 percent.
>
> **American Indian:** U.S. males, 1 percent *vs.* our sample, 3 percent.

An additional 2 percent of our sample of 15,508 men reported that they were from none of the above. In terms of the 15,508 males in the complete sample, they were representative of the general male population both in their general demographics of marriage, education, employment, and religiosity, and in representing five ethnic groups. American Indians were over-represented in this large original sample, at 3 percent, as the U.S. Male Population Census reports American Indians as one percent.

Comparison of 3,952 admitted male child molesters to the U.S. male population.

Once we established that our complete sample of more than 15,500 men was representative of the general male population on the above demographics, the question became: How do admitted child molesters differ?

This study's demographic results showed a near match between the 3,952 admitted male molesters of children 13 years old or younger and the general male population in terms of marriage, education, employment, and religion. This finding contradicts sharply the general idea that child molesters are, in the main, unmarried, unemployed, uneducated, and not religious.

Our sample of admitted male child molesters paralleled the U.S. male population on these five demographic characteristics.

> **Married or formerly married:** U.S. males, 73 percent *vs.* child molesters, 77 percent.
>
> **Some college or higher education:** U.S. males, 49 percent *vs.* child molesters, 46 percent.
>
> **High school graduate:** U.S. males, 32 percent vs. of child molesters, 30 percent.
>
> **Working:** U.S. males, 64 percent *vs.* child molesters, 65 percent.
>
> **Religious:** U.S. males, 93 percent *vs.* child molesters, 93 percent.

Just as the larger sample of more than 13,000 men 25 years of age and older closely matched the men in the U.S. Census, the smaller group of 3,952 admitted child molesters also closely matched the men in the U.S. Census. This study found no significant differences between these categories.

Social class of child molesters

While studies of *physical* abuse have shown a link to lower income and lower levels of education, studies of the *sexual* abuse of children have failed to demonstrate that such a link exists.

Study after study of child molestation victims and child molesters has sought to link education or household income level to numbers of victims or numbers of molesters. All have sought to show a link to one class over another. Only one study showed a slight link to a social class, and that class was the highest social class determined by both money and education. See Finkelhor, 1986.

Ethnicity

We also looked at admitted child molesters in terms of their ethnicity. The question: Which ethnic group might produce proportionately more child molesters? Our study sample of 3,952 admitted male child molesters paralleled the U.S. male population in terms of representing five ethnic groups.

> **Caucasian:** U.S. males, 72 percent *vs.* child molesters, 79 percent.

> **Hispanic/Latin American:** U.S. males, 11 percent *vs.* child molesters, 9 percent.

> **African American:** U.S. males, 12 percent *vs.* child molesters, 6 percent.

> **Asian:** U.S. males, 4 percent *vs.* child molesters, 1 percent.

> **American Indian:** U.S. males, 1 percent *vs.* child molesters, 3 percent.

> An additional 2 percent reported that they were "none of the above."

While the Caucasian group seems to produce slightly more child molesters and the Hispanic/Latin-American and African-American groups seem to produce fewer, we found another possible interpretation.

When we looked at group two, men who were lying or denying (from our complete sample), we found proportionately *fewer* Caucasians: 67 percent *vs.* the 71 percent of Caucasians in our overall sample. For Hispanics/Latin-Americans we found proportionately *more* people said to be either lying or denying: 14 percent vs. 12 percent in our overall sample.

In addition, African-Americans were slightly under-represented in our complete sample. They were only 10 percent of that sample, while they are 12 percent of all U.S. men. African-Americans were over-represented in the lying or denying group. They made up 12 percent of that group. That they were both *under-represented* in the large complete sample and *over-represented* in the lying or denying group may suggest that this low number of 6 percent of admitted child molesters as African-Americans may not be as robust as one would wish.

These results (Caucasians admitting to being child molesters in proportionally greater numbers and both Hispanics/Latin-Americans and African-Americans admitting to being child molesters in proportionally lower numbers) may also suggest a greater mistrust on the part of people in ethnic minority groups of the people assessing them.

In general, the admitted child molesters paralleled this culture's social demographics and existed in five or more ethnic groups. These results suggest that the act of molesting a child is prompted by a factor outside of the molester's social status or his ethnic group. It also suggests that, while his high, middle, or low social status or his ethnic group do not *cause* him to molest a child, neither do they *protect* him from becoming a child molester.

——— THE CHILD MOLESTER'S RELATION TO THE CHILD ———

Molesting children in the family

Of the 3,952 men who admitted to being child molesters, 68 percent reported that they had molested a child in their family. Nineteen percent had molested their biological child, 30 percent their stepchild, adopted child, or a foster child. Eighteen percent had molested their nieces or nephews, and 5 percent, their grandchildren.

Pedophilia is a disorder that starts in the teenage years and continues through life. The same molester, in some cases, may have molested several categories of children in the family. He may have molested his own children, a niece or nephew, and his grandchild. Some 12 percent had, as teenagers, molested a much younger brother or sister. For those reasons, the percentages when added are more than the 68 percent of men who molest family members. The 68 percent is based on individual men, while each individual man may have molested one child or several children who were in different family relationships with him.

Molesting children in the parents' social circle

Forty percent of the child molesters reported molesting the children of their friends or their neighbors. Again, we see a cross-over. Nearly 24 percent of the men who were molesting children in their family were *also* molesting the children of their friends or neighbors.

The question about molesting "a child left in my care by an organization" elicited 5 percent of "yes" responses.

The most surprising finding was that only 10 percent of the child molesters reported that they molested a child who was "a stranger to me." This finding is at odds with the popular conception of the child molester as a man or woman who is unknown to the parents. The emphasis on knowing if convicted child molesters live in the neighborhood, while excellent, probably provides less protection for children than was once believed.

To keep these percentages in context, we need to remember, for instance, that while the number of adopted children and the number of foster children is far less than the number of biological or stepchildren, still 129 men (3.3 percent) reported that they were molesting their adopted children and 50 men (1.3 percent) reported they were molesting their foster children. These may be more significant numbers when put in the context of the small overall numbers of U.S. children in adoptive or foster homes.

Males vs. *females as child molesters*

Of a sample of 4,007 men and women who admit to molesting a child 13 years old or younger, 99 percent were male and 1 percent were female.

Although we know that most child molesters are men, the exact percentage of women molesters varies in our own studies from 1 to 3 percent. The percentage of female child molesters may be biased in this study because its 601 women accounted for only 3.73 percent of the total sample of 16,109 people who were tested. Researchers across studies generally agree that the molestation acts of women are under-reported. Studies of women molesters are generally difficult because of the low numbers of women who are either reported to Child Protective Services, present themselves to mental health professionals, or are referred for testing.

While many professionals point out that boys molested by adult women often fail to report their molestation, that alone could not account for the vast difference between the numbers of male molesters versus female molesters. While 15,508 males were referred for testing because of the probability of a sexual difficulty, only 601 females were referred. This discrepancy in numbers supports the premise that testosterone is a substantial contributor to the formation of paraphilias. Further support comes from the medicines, Depo-Provera and the selective serotonin reuptake inhibitors, all of which reduce the effects of testosterone and subsequently reduce sexual interests in children.

——THE PEDOPHILE GROUP——

Selection of molesters with pedophilia

The American Psychiatric Association lists several criteria for a diagnosis of pedophilia.

- *Must be at least 16 years of age.* **Our child molester group ranged in age between 18 and 95 years of age, so all met that criterion.**

- *Must have sexual fantasies or urges or behavior toward a child of 13 years or younger.* **All of our 3,952 admitted molesters reported that they had the behavior. They *all* reported sexually touching one child or several children. Being at least 16 and sexually touching a child of 13 years or younger do *not* by themselves signal a disorder. They may add up to an incident. It is the duration that signals disorder.**

- *Must have had the sexual fantasies, sexual urges, or behaviors described above for more than six months' duration.*

To separate admitted child molesters who fit the pedophilic diagnostic criterion that the behavior must have continued "for more than six months," we used length of time of the continuing behavior. Since the questionnaire defined length in one-year intervals, we defined the pedophile group — 2,429 (65 percent) — as those molesters who were involved in molestation for more than one year.

A total of 1,297 (35 percent) of the original 3,952 admitted to less than a year of involvement and were therefore classified, for purposes of our study, as non-pedophiles. An additional 226 of the 3,952 were eliminated from the pedophile/non-pedophile groups because they gave incomplete or inconsistent information.

Age of onset of pedophilia

Pedophilia starts early. How early depends on whether the pedophile molests boys or girls. Molesters with pedophilia who sexually abuse boys start the earliest. Twenty percent reported that they had their first victim before they were 10 years old, another 43 percent began to molest between the ages of 10 and 15, and a total of 76 percent say they had their first child victim before they were 20 years old.

Although men with pedophilia who molest girls have their first child victim slightly later, a significant number (12 percent) said that they also molested a child before they were 10 years old, another 32 percent began to molest when they were between ages 10 and 15, and a total of 54 percent said they had molested a child before they were 20 years old.

These results strongly suggest that early intervention in the lives of molesters developing pedophilia is a powerful preventive measure that will drastically reduce the numbers of child victims.

Numbers of victims, numbers of acts

Pedophiles molest four times the number of children than do non-pedophile molesters. On average, a pedophile molests 11.7 children compared to a non-pedophile molester, who molests, on average, 2.9 children. The 2,429 pedophiles in our study sample molested 88 percent of the children (28,419), as compared to the 1,297 non-pedophile molesters, who molested 12 percent of the children (3,761).

Pedophiles commit more than 10 times as many sexual acts against children as do non-pedophile molesters. On average, a molester *with* pedophilia commits 70.8 molestation acts. On average, a molester *without* pedophilia commits 6.5 acts. Our group of 2,429 pedophiles committed 95 percent of the acts (171,973). Only 5 percent of the acts (8,431) were committed by non-pedophiles.

These results — pedophiles molesting an average of 12 children and committing an average of 71 acts — suggest that many, if not most, child victims are molested repeatedly.

A possible weakness in the above analysis stems from the obvious expectations that 1) molesters who claim to be molesting children for less than a year will, in terms of length of time available, molest fewer children, and 2) molesters will likely minimize the number of molestation acts they have committed. Since 12 percent of the men in this sample were in prison and many had been charged with a crime, we might assume that they may have reported only the number of victims and the number of acts, that were known by the criminal justice system.

While, we agree this is true, we believe that both groups, the pedophiles and the non-pedophiles, will minimize the number of their child victims and acts. It is unlikely that this minimization alone could account for the huge differences in victims and acts between the two groups.

Sex of victims

Of additional interest in the molesters' reports is that the number of child victims and acts per molester depended on whether the molester targeted girls, boys, or children of both sexes. Those who reported molesting only girls averaged 5.2 victims and 34.2 acts. Those who reported molesting only boys averaged 10.7 victims and 52 acts. Those who reported molesting both boys and girls averaged 27.3 victims and 120.9 acts.

While many more men molested girls, the men who molested boys averaged double the number of victims. The number of boy victims reported by the molesters who targeted only boys is similar to the number of boy victims reported in the six victim studies we analyzed to determine the prevalence of boy victims in the United States. When we excluded the men in our study that molested both boys and girls, the remaining subjects reported a total number of boy victims that was 40 percent of the number of girl victims. The adults who had been child victims reported similar numbers. This gives added scientific validity to the assumption that the number of boy victims is slightly less than half the number of girl victims.

Of the 2,050 pedophiles who molested girls, 21 percent reported that they also molested boys. Of the 804 pedophiles who molested boys, more than half (53 percent) reported that they also molested girls. This finding promises to be helpful in the evaluation of child molesters.

The fact that the men who molested children of both sexes averaged 27 victims is of particular significance in terms of prevention. Although they numbered only 468, these men had more than 12,700 child victims. To intervene early in their lives, test, medicate, and provide effective therapy has the potential to save a large number of children from being molested.

Comparison to an earlier study

The average numbers of victims and acts reported in the *Abel and Harlow* study were far lower than the numbers molesters reported in the *Abel and Becker* study of 1983. The structure of this earlier study may have made possible more reliable reports by molesters regardng their numbers of victims and numbers of acts. The 561 subjects in the 1983 study were guaranteed confidentiality by the federal government, which issued a certificate of confidentiality that prevented any law enforcement body from accessing their records. These molesters also differed in another way: None were incarcerated. They all lived in their communities and volunteered for a free evaluation and free treatment. Guaranteed confidentiality, they reported a far greater number of sexual abuse acts and sexual abuse victims than did the molesters in our current study. The molesters in the 1983 study reported that they *averaged* 49 victims and *averaged* 114 acts. However, the numbers reported in 1983 parallel the numbers of the present study with respect to the various categories of children molested. Most of the men molested girls; fewer men molested boys, but had larger numbers of boy victims. Fewer men molested their biological daughters, but reported a large number of acts against them.

While we acknowledge that the numbers of victims and numbers of acts reported by the 3, 952 male molesters in the current study are at the low end of the spectrum, the basic findings — that more men molest girls; that fewer men molest boys, but have much larger numbers of boy victims — remain valid.

To put *The Abel and Harlow Stop Child Molestation Study* in context, the reader should assume that the reported numbers represent a minimization of what is actually happening in our society. An interesting note: In the 1983 study, one in which money for evaluation or treatment was not a barrier, the 561 men also fit the demographic profile of the 3,952 molesters in the present study. They were mainly married, educated, working, and religious. The men in the 1983 study *volunteered*, 561 of them, for a sex-specific evaluation; and they came on their own, seeking treatment that they hoped would stop them from molesting children. This is important, because it suggests yet another avenue to explore that may save children from being molested.

For more information see: Gene G. Abel, Judith V. Becker, Mary S. Mittleman, Jerry Cunningham-Rathner, Joanne L. Rouleau, and William D. Murphy, "Self-Reported Sex Crimes of Non-incarcerated Paraphiliacs," *Journal of Interpersonal Violence* 2, 1987): 3-25.

—— SEX FANTASIES ——
AND THEORIES OF EARLY CHILDHOOD EXPERIENCE

Many years ago, two groups of scientists educated in entirely different theoretical psychiatric orientations came independently to identical conclusions. One group, the analysts, including Sigmund Freud, and a second group, the behaviorists, both concluded that the fantasies coming from early childhood sexual experiences were critical to the child's development of adult sexual interest. It is a rare scientific occurrence for two groups of scientists from two different perspectives to come to identical conclusions. When this does occur, we say that the finding is of increased scientific validity. Our finding, that the older child's repeated sexual fantasies of much younger children shapes that child's adult sexual interest in children, is yet another confirmation of these earlier theories.

How molesters' fantasies relate to the number of children they molest

We divided the 3,952 male child molesters into two groups: those who claimed to have no sexual fantasies of children (59 percent) and those who reported continual fantasies of touching a child for sexual arousal (41 percent). When members of the second group were asked, "How many of your sexual fantasies are about touching a child sexually?," their answers ranged from "a few" to "all."

Having child-centered sexual fantasies nearly quadrupled the number of children the molester victimized. Men who *did not* fantasize about children averaged 4 victims. Men with child-centered sex fantasies averaged 15 victims. Having child-centered sex fantasies also more than doubled the number of acts a molester committed. Men who *did not* fantasize averaged 30 acts, in contrast to men *with* sexual fantasies, who averaged 73 acts

Statistical significance

To determine if having child-centered sex fantasies prompted men to sexually touch more children than men without those fantasies at a statistically significant level, a t-test was conducted using the Satterthwaite approximation for unequal variances. Results revealed that the differences were statistically significant (t=-7.5, DF=1703, p<=.001). The same methodology used to test the statistical significance of the effect of child-centered sex fantasies on number of acts revealed that the differences between the two groups were statistically significant (t=-9.3, DF=2194, p<=.0001). Although the molesters with child-centered sex fantasies were less than half (41 percent) of the total number of molesters, they molested 66,521 children. The non-fantasizing molesters (59 percent) molested 8,770.

—— ADULT SEXUAL ORIENTATIONS —— OF MEN WHO MOLEST BOYS

While it is a commonly held belief that men who prefer men as adult sex partners molest boys and men who prefer women as adult sex partners molest girls, our study results suggest something different. (Note: Only 7 percent of child molesters show no sexual interest in adults.)

Alfred E. Kinsey, in his landmark study of male sexuality, divided adult sexual interest into seven categories: three categories of homosexuality, one category of bi-sexuality, and three categories of heterosexuality. The *Abel and Harlow* study used this "Kinsey Scale" in its questions about adult sexual preference.

The 1,038 men who molested boys reported a range of adult sexual preferences. Contrary to popular belief, only 8 percent reported that they were *exclusively* homosexual in their adult preferences. The majority of the men who molested boys (51 percent) described themselves as *exclusively* heterosexual in their adult partner preferences. An additional 19 percent reported they were predominately heterosexual, while yet another 9 percent said they were equally heterosexual and homosexual in their adult sex life. As with other characteristics, the group of 1,038 men who molest boys followed the general pattern of the U.S. male population in regard to their adult sexual preferences. As reported by Kinsey, the majority of U.S. adult males (76 percent) described themselves as exclusively heterosexual and an additional 9 percent said they were predominantly heterosexual. In terms of their homosexuality, Kinsey reports that those U.S. males who describe themselves as exclusively homosexual are 6 percent and those that report being predominantly homosexual an additional 4 percent. These findings are in direct opposition to the generally accepted opinion that the overwhelming majority of men who molest boys are homosexual. The majority of men who molest boys (70 percent) are predominantly heterosexual. In general, that large number parallels the number of men in the U.S. population (85 percent) who have reported that they are predominantly heterosexual.

—— Molested Boys Who Become —— Adult Molesters

There was a difference in our molester group between the 53 percent of men who had *never* been sexually abused as children (2,066) and the 47 percent of men who had been sexually abused (1,832). The molesters who had been sexually abused children started to molest at an earlier age, and they molested more children. The most striking difference occurred with the adult molesters who, as children, had been severely sexually abused (molested more than 50 times).

Starting early

In our analysis of 2,294 pedophiles, those who were *never* abused reported that only 9 percent of them molested before the age of 10 years and another 28 percent between the ages 10 and 15. Severely sexually abused pedophiles reported that 25 percent of them molested before the age of 10 and 40 percent between the ages of 10 and 15. In all, 49 percent of the never-abused pedophiles molested before the age of 20, while 76 percent of the severely sexually abused pedophiles molested before the age of 20.

Molesting more children

An analysis of the total group of 3,952 admitted child molesters revealed a dramatic difference between the never-abused molesters (53 percent) and the severely abused molesters (47 percent) in the number of their victims. Never-abused molesters averaged 7 child victims while severely sexually abused victims averaged 25 victims. On average, severely sexually abused molesters committed well over 100 more acts (142 acts) than never-abused molesters (37 acts).

This finding leads us to believe in the importance of identifying molested boys and intervening early in their lives with evaluations and, when necessary, medication and effective therapies that will help them control their urges to sexually abuse much younger children. This is a necessary step to protect children through primary prevention by blocking the development of pedophilia.

——Children's Consent to Sexual Abuse——

Children, because they are children, do not have the ability to consent to interactions of a serious nature with adults. They cannot sign legal documents. They cannot sign consent forms for surgery. They cannot be responsible for their own bank account or consent to an adult's request to drive a car. And, they have no ability — being children — to consent to sexual interactions either with much older children or with adults. Their agreement to such an interaction does not constitute consent. The adult's role is to protect the child from the dangers of engaging in behavior with potentially serious consequences. Many child molesters—65 percent—fail to recognize this important fact.

——Aggression During Molestation——

When the admitted child molesters were asked about the amount of aggression they used during molestation, 15 percent reported that the child initiated the act, and a surprising 50 percent reported that the act was "by mutual consent." Slightly more than 12 percent said they used verbal threats, slightly more than 12 percent said they used physical restraint, and 11 percent said they were physically aggressive.

——Crossing Multiple Sexual Boundaries——

One barrier to the protection of children is the limited classification of pedophiles as sexually interested in one gender of a child only and/or being sexually interested in only the paraphilia of pedophilia. When we analyzed the reports of 2,429 men in our pedophilia group, we found a high percentage of men molesting both boys *and* girls and a high percentage of pedophiles engaging in more than one paraphilia.

Of the pedophiles who molested girls, 17 percent were *also* exhibitionists and 36 percent were *also* voyeurs. Of the pedophiles who molested boys, 20 percent were *also* exhibitionists and 33 percent were *also* voyeurs.

This finding may help in the protection of children by indicating the need for more extensive evaluation of exhibitionists and voyeurs.

It also indicates that patients may present with more than one paraphilia and, following an evaluation, may need a more comprehensive treatment regimen than was originally believed.

An important note: Results from the 1983 treatment outcome study by Gene G. Abel, M.D., and Judith V. Becker, Ph.D., suggested that this phenomenon of a pedophile crossing several sexual boundaries was the greatest predictor of treatment failure.

—— DISCUSSION AND CONCLUSIONS ——

One can arrive at a number of conclusions from these results. First, information is gathered from a huge sample of men and women throughout the United States whose demographics closely match the general demographics of U.S. men and women. This suggests that child molesters occur throughout the United States population and are not isolated to individuals with specific marital, educational, social, economic, or racial backgrounds.

Second, and clearly the most startling finding, is that those who meet the medical criteria of pedophilia molest 88 percent of the victims and commit 95 percent of child molestations. It is clear that, in order to reduce the number of children molested, we must identify the pedophile and implement treatment for the pedophile as rapidly as possible.

Third, we know characteristics of the child molester that are bad prognostic signs. Those molesters who themselves were molested frequently as children, those who frequently fantasize about sexual interaction with children, and those who have several paraphillias: those who molest both boys and girls, those who molest children in several age ranges and those who molest children both inside and outside the home or who are also voyeurs and/or exhibitionists are especially problematic.

Given the sample size and the representative nature of the more than 16,000 participants in this study that included 3,952 males who admitted that they were child molesters, it is now safe to say we know the characteristics of child molesters. We also know the sub-characteristics of child molesters, the characteristics that make them likely to molest again. If we are to have a significant impact on reducing the number of children who suffer from this public health problem, we have to test, medicate and provide effective treatment for people with the disorder pedophilia—especially the teenagers who are developing the disorder.

—ACKNOWLEDGMENTS—

Gene G. Abel, M.D.:

More than 100 people have helped me to understand and complete research to stop child molestation.

I wish to thank four colleagues who were most influential. Judith V. Becker, Ph.D., helped me through the many ethical and political dilemmas that one faces when researching sexual violence. She was co-principal director on several of the early and difficult studies. Thank you, Judith. Thanks to William Murphy, Ph.D., for his contributions. Candice A. Osborn, M.A., has added scientific vigor to recent studies. At the Center for Studies of Antisocial and Violent Behavior of the National Institute of Mental Health, James Breiling, Ph.D., trained me on the intricacies of funding. His support was crucial in the days before there was a sexual-violence prevention field.

A number of individuals have worked at my side investigating sexual violence, including D.H. Barret, Ph.D.; C.L. Holland, Ph.D.; Jeff Huffman, Meg Kaplan, Ph.D.; Joanne L. Rouleau, Ph.D.; Emily Coleman, M.A.; Leonard H. Epstein Ph.D; Jerry Cunningham-Rathner; Brent W. Warberg, L.C.S.W.; and William Allenbaugh, M.A. Thanks to Dennis Steed, M.D., who was so very helpful in the early discussions of sexual interest testing. Statistician Allan Jordan also deserves my thanks.

At the beginning of my studies, John Clancy, M.D., and Donald J. Levis, M.D., at the University of Iowa taught me about the world of research. W. Stewart Agras, M.D. David H. Barlow, Ph.D.; Edward B. Blanchard, Ph.D. and other colleagues at the University of Mississippi continued my education, teaching me how to rigorously pursue and produce valid research.

I also owe a debt of gratitude to a number of sexual violence researchers whose work is inspirational and groundbreaking, and therefore motivates my own investigations: Kurt Freund, Ph.D., who led the field for us to follow; William L. Marshall, Ph.D.; Vernon L. Quinsey, Ph.D.; Richard

Laws, Ph.D.; Mark Weinrott, Ph.D.; Ray Knight, Ph.D.; and Robert Prentky, Ph.D.

And finally, I wish to thank my wife, Nora Harlow, who has so ably translated the dry aspects of my research into easily readable family stories that make the research results usable.

I thank all of you for your support during my many years of research.

Nora Harlow:

First I would like to thank my mother, Ireane Null, for making sure I got an education so that I could write this book.

Early and late in the writing process the Midtown Atlanta Writers Group's enthusiastic responses shaped and reshaped this work. Thanks to Skip Connett, Linda Clopton, Karla Jennings, Anne Lovett, Bill Osher, Jill Patrick, Jim Taylor, Diane Thomas, Anne Webster, Fred Willard, and Gene Wright.

Thanks to Sandra Deer for being a champion for the writing. Thanks to Alice Teeter for her excellent graphics work, to Susan Carroll for her support and sensitivity, and to all the other members of the Atlanta Artists Conference Network who cheered for this work every step of the way: Nancy Cole, Shirley Cox, Maria Helena Dolan, Lesly Fredman, Chantal Gadd, Kathryn Kelly, Ann Tatum, and Libby Eason Sener.

I've received excellent administrative assistance from many people. Special thanks to Elektra Xanadu, Therese de Sandre, Sarah Allen Brown, and Crystal Love.

Both of us would like to thank the following people for their help while we were writing and rewriting. First, we'd like to thank our editor, Diane Thomas, for her suggestions that added so much to the final presentation.

Thanks to our daughters and stepdaughters, Jennifer Abel, Tracy Massimillo, and Laura Abel for their moral support and to Whitney Gabriel for holding a critical public reading in Oakland, California that led to a productive revision.

Judy Weisman's friendship and insights helped us repeatedly from the first days of this book to the end.

Thanks to George W. Counts, M.D., whose friendship and valuable advice made this a better book through the last three revisions and to Anne Topple, Gretchen Turner and Claire Hertzler, whose enthusiastic directions on how to reach more people were invaluable.

Thoughtful critiques by victim advocate, Lucy Berliner, M.S.W., and Brent Warberg, L.C.S.W., led to a more precise writing on several points.

Most of all we'd like to say thanks to two groups of people, the staff of the Behavioral Medicine Institute of Atlanta: Tracey Irvin, M. D., Candice Osborn, Sarah Gregg, Ken Hosier, Roberta Mitchell, Judy Michalek, Carol Stephens, Donna Valentine, and Carlotta McCalister; and the staff of Abel Screening, Inc: Don Jones, Peggy Denby, Trey Miller, Paul Mitchell, Dave Scibek, Clint Reaves, James Watson, and Claudia Brummel for their years of devotion to protecting children. Day after day they create, they innovate, and they stretch what they do beyond the borders of what anyone could define as a job.

—— SEX-SPECIFIC THERAPY SITES BY STATE ——

This list is published as a public service. Therapists and mental health - centers that are members of The Association for the Treatment of Sexual Abusers (ATSA) agreed to be listed in response to a general request. Appearance on this list in no way constitutes the authors' endorsement of an individual therapist or center.

Alabama

Birmingham
UAB-Urology Division
Ms. Jane Forsyth Brown, LRC, MA, 205-879-9970

Huntsville
North Alabama Sex Offender Group Treatment
Frankie L. Preston, Ph.D. 256-534-8161

Tuscaloosa
Clinical Neuropsychology
John R. Goff, Ph.D. 205-553-2851

Alaska

Anchorage
Martin Atrops, Ph.D. 907-272-7600

Center for Human Development
Bruce N. Smith, Ph.D. 907-272-8270

Arizona

Flagstaff
Summit Counseling Services
Konard Kaserer, MA, CPC 520-522-8161

Phoenix
Arizona State Hospital
Judith V. Becker, Ph.D. 602-220-6005 or 520-240-5108

Family Transitions
Tom Shelby, Ph.D. 602-258-9450

Psychological and Consulting Services
Steven R. Gray, Ed.D. 480-777-8807

Mountain Valley Counseling
Marvin Hillyard, MS.Ed. 602-870-0972

Sedona
Terry Scritchlow, Ph.D. 520-282-1357

Tucson
Johnson and Becker Associates, PLLC
Bradley R. Johnson, M.D. 520-297-9878

Psychological and Consulting Services
Steven R. Gray, Ed.D. and Stephen Sadler, MA 520-274-4802

Richard J. Brooks, Ph.D., PC 520-751-8311

Yuma
Yuma County Adult Probation Department

Julie Akiyama, Ph.D. 520-329-2210

California

Eureka
Narum Clinical Associates/Nelson-Kokish Associates
Ron Kokish 707-441-8626 or 707-677-3181

Fresno
Atkinson Assessment Center
Carol H. Atkinson, Ph.D. 559-222-7713

Laguna Hills
La Paz Psychological Group
Ann Dodd, MSW 949-586-6690

Los Angeles
The Sharp Program *(also in San Francisco)*
Craig Teofilo, Psy.D. 213-738-8853

Orange
Orange Psychological Services
Wesley B. Maram, Ph.D. 714-771-0722

Pleasant Hill
Crossroads Psychotherapy Institute
Larry Wornian, Ph.D., Sue Scoff, Ph.D., and Chris Bennett, MFT 925-942-0733

Redding
New Directions to Hope
Gerry D. Blassingame, MA, MFCC, LMFT 530-222-8927

Shasta Treatment Center
Ronald W. Armstrong, Ph.D. 818-785-4700

Roseville
R.E.A.C.H. Clinical Services
Kathy J. Ellis, MFCC. 916-965-1001 or 916-491-4596

San Diego
Corrigan & Associates
Larry W. Corrigan, LCSW, MFT 858-565-8303

Tustin
Clinical and Forensic Psychology
Martha Rogers, Ph.D. 714-731-6155

Colorado

Aurora
The Offenders Group at Aurora Mental Health Center
John J. Murphy, LCSW 303-617-2424

Rick L. May, Psy.D. and Pamela Hines Psy.D 303-369-4200

Boulder
Colorado Abuse Intervention Research Services
Suzanne M. Pinto Bernhard, Ph.D. 303-444-8070

Forensic Mental Health Services (*also located in Ft. Collins*)
Pamela J. Sedei-Rodden, Ph.D. 303-440-8611 or 970-482-8553

Canon City
Colorado Department of Corrections
Peggy Heil and Richard A. Vehar, Ph.D. 719-269-5024

Colorado Springs
Bijou Treatment and Training Institute
Robert C. Warren, Ph.D. and Kathleen Boggess, MSW 719-442-0144
The Family Center
Lisa White, MSW 719-471-1816

Southwest Consulting, Inc.
L. Dennis Kleinasser, Ph.D. 719-442-0144

Denver
Baker Clinic II
Cindy Williams, MSW and Aaron Townsand, Ph.D. 303-871-1944
Brake & Associates
Stephen C. Brake, Ph.D. 303-745-7745

Progressive Therapy Systems
Walter T. Simon, Ph.D. and Greg Fellman, MSW. 303-831-9344

Durango
Ragsdale and Associates, P.C.
J.W. Ragsdale, Ph.D. 970-247-2451

Fort Collins
Child Safe
Cheri Fisher, MA, LPC 970-495-4769

Grand Junction

Offense Specific Treatment Center
Tammy Gaurmer, MA, LPC and Sharlotte Fox-
Clayton, AAS 970-245-9840

PsycHealth Associates, P.C.
Carolynn S. Sanda, MA 970-241-6500

Greeley
Davsel Ventures, Inc.
A. Mervyn Davies, MA, LPC 970-353-8171

Individual and Group Therapy Services
Deana Davies, MA, LPC and Kim R. Buybal, MA,
LPC 970-353-8171

St. Aurora
The Offenders Group at Aurora Mental Health Center
John J. Murphy, LCSW 303-617-2424

Connecticut

Lyme
Griffin and Associates
James C. Griffin, Ph.D. 860-434-5976

Middletown
Center for the Treatment of Problem Sexual Behavior
David D'Amora, MS 860-343-5515

New Haven
Campagna & Associates LLP
Anthony F. Campagna, Ph.D. 203-789-8435

Delaware

Milford
Community Counseling Associates, Inc.
Alan R. Southard, MHS 302-424-4121

Florida

Bradenton
Insight Counseling Services, Inc.
Lisa M. Davis 941-755-4782

Gainesville
I.T.M. Group
Ted Shaw, Ph.D. and Astrid Hall, Drs. 352-379-2829

Orlando (Groveland)
GFC Counseling Center
Joseph Nussbaumer, Ph.D. 352-429-5600

Sarasota
Child Protection Center: Sarasota Sexual Abuse Intervention Network
D. Ross Thompson, LMHC 941-365-1277

Tampa
Center for Rational Living, Inc.
Robert W, Whitford, Ed.S. 813-872-1530

Georgia

Atlanta
Behavioral Medicine Institute of Atlanta
Gene G. Abel, M.D. 404-872-7929

Paula Hanson-Kahn, MBS, MA/CP 770-350-0777

The Highland Institute for Behavioral Change, Inc.
Delores T. Roys, Ph.D., LCSW 770-455-0835

Conyers
Rockdale Professional Counseling Associates
James Morton, LPC 770-860-8549

Cumming
Family Recovery, Inc.
Gary Holstad, MS 770-207-1147

Gainesville
Family Recovery, Inc.
Gary Holstad, MS 770-535-1073

Lafayette
Randall Fannin, LSCW 706-638-2998

LaGrange
Dunlap Enterprises
Lloyd E. Dunlap, MS, LPC 706-322-2204

Lilburn
B.L. Schaller & Associates
Bonnie L. Schaller, MA, LPC 770-314-1440

GracePoint Counseling Associates, LLC
Michael J. Brissett, Ph.D. 770-638-1577

Marietta
Psychological Forensic Associates
James E. Stark, Ph.D 770-541-9988

Milledgeville
GDOJJ/ Bill E. Ireland YDC
Linda J. Allen, Therapist *478-445-7266*

Monroe
Family Recovery, Inc.
Gary Holstad, MS 770-535-1073

Smyrna
Robert Mathis, LCSW 678-305-0606

Stockbridge
Medlin Treatment Center
Julie C. Medlin, Ph.D. 770-507-6044

Hawaii

Honolulu
Forensic & Behavioral Sciences
Gary Smith, M.Ed., MFCC and Jack S. Annon, Ph.D.,
808-537-2149

Honolulu Family Therapy Center
Carol P.M. Tyler, Psy.D. 808-941-5869

Jack S. Annon, Inc.
Jack S. Annon, Ph.D., ABFP 808-396-5450

Idaho

Boise
SANE Solutions
David R. Ferguson, MS 208-345-1170 ext. 115

Myers Counseling
Richard J. Myers, MS 208-528-6853

Idaho Falls
New Beginnings, Inc.
G.L. Snowden, PA, LPCP 208-522-1935

Illinois

Aurora
PsychCare Associates
George Hotchkiss, Ph.D. and Roger P. Hatcher, Ph.D.
630-851-6100

Chicago
Adelante, PC
Karen Stanbary, LCSW and Evaristo Ruiz, LSW,
M.Div. 773-486-0031

Affiliated Psycologists, Ltd.
Ray Quackenbush, Psy.D. 773-286-3100

H.E.L.P. Inc. (Human Effective Living Programs)
Gabriella Cohen, MA 312-939-6633

Isaac Ray Center, Inc.
John Walker and James L. Cavanaugh Jr., M.D. 312-
829-1463
Johnathan Kelly, M.D. 312-942-2832

Latino Family Services, PC
Arturo Hurtado, LCSW 847-593-7077

Rom-Rymer & Associates

Beth N. Rom-Rymer, Ph.D. 773-880-8786

St. Joseph's Carondelet Child Center
Saralynn W. Reedy, LCSW, ACSW and Gerald J.
Gripshover, LCSW, ACSW 773-624-7443

Elgin
Larkin Center
Craig Shifrin, Psy.D 847-695-5656

Elk Grove Village
Latino Family Services
Arturo Hurtado, LCSW 847-593-7077

Galesburg
Bridgeway, Inc.
Tom McKinnon 309-344-2323

Grayslake
Blain and Associates, PC
Gerald H. Blain, MS, LCPC

Joliet
Will County Mental Health and Addictions Services
Randall Bultman 815-774-7326

Lombard
Clinical Behavior Consultants
Patricia E. Porter, Psy. D. 630-663-4002

Moline
Robert Young Center for Community Mental Health
Scott W. Stange, LCSW, Lisa Curry, LCSW., and
Mark Raskie 309-779-2167

Mundelein
Alternative Behavior Treatment Center
Bruce E. Bonecutter, Ph.D., Ron Ercoli, Psy. D.,
Thomas Kim M.Div., MSW and Robin McGinnis
847-487-8727

Quincy and Springfield
Clinical Systems, Inc.
Terry B. Brelje, Ph.D. 217-529-2142

Rockford (Woodstock)
Community Counseling & Diagnostic Center
Jeffrey A. Martin, MSW and Frank Elmodesi, Psy.D.
815-338-7749

Woodstock
Community Counseling and Diagnostic Center
Jeff Martin 815-338-7749

Indiana

Indianapolis
Indianapolis Counseling Center
Ron Smith MS, LMHC 317-549-0333

Iowa

Oakdale
CUSO Program
Jim N. Gardner, Ph.D. 319-665-6601

Kansas

Kansas City
Wyandot Mental Health Center

Nancy Baldwin, MSW, LSCW

Lawrence
Bert-Nash Mental Health Center
Tom Bates, MS, MLT 785-843-9192

Pittsburgh
Crawford County Mental Health Center
Mike Willis 316-232-3228

Louisiana

Baton Rouge
Greenbriar Hospital Medial Management Options
Mary Marrs, BCSW 504-893-2970

Lafayette
Lafayette Psychology Center
Larry Benoit, Ph.D. and M. Maueen Brennen, Ph.D.
318-234-4912

Lake Charles
Professional Counseling Specialties, Inc.
Troy E. Mire, BCSW 337-477-0079

Shreveport
Behavioral Intervention Services of Northwest Louisiana, Inc.
Anthony Jerome Wilson, LCSW 318-861-4067

Maine

Bangor
Behavioral Health Center
William L. Donahue, LCSW 207-941-0879

Jonathan H. Siegal, Ph.D., PA 207-942-2627

Maryland

Annapolis
Criminal Justice Resource & Consultation
Stephen E. Price, MA 410-349-3220

Hagerstown
Paul F. Kradel, Ed.D. 301-790-1022

Catoctin Counseling Center
Larry Stauter, LCPC and Nancy Gilleo 301-745-6687 or 866-236-2254

Parsonsburg
Eastern Shore Psychological Services
Kathy Seifert, Ph.D. and Eric Ritterhoff, Ph.D. 410-334-6961

Silver Springs
St. Luke's Institute
Steve Montana, Ph.D. 301-422-5429 or 301-445-7970

Massachusetts

Arlington
New England Forensic Associates
Carol Ball, Ph.D. 781-643-0610

Boston
Adult and Child Consultation Center
Lionel Lyon, Psy.D. 781-391-3266

Cambridge (Wareham)
New Directions for Men
Josephe Doherty, Ed.D. 617-864-5434

Somerville
New England Associates for Psychological Services, Inc.
Anthony Traniello, Ph.D. 617-625-9600

Michigan

Kalamazoo
Western Michigan University
Lester Wright, Ph.D. 616-387-4472

Traverse City
Wedgwood Christian Youth and Family Services, Inc.
John F. Ulrich, Ph.D. 231-922-2885

Minnesota

Fergus Falls
Lakeland Mental Health Center
Esther Johnson, MS, LMFT 218-736-6987

Pelican Rapids
Kertin Counseling, Inc.
Esther Johnson, MS, LMFT 218-863-1499

St. Paul
Project Pathfinder, Inc.
Janis F. Bremer, Ph.D. and Gerald H. Lilja, MSSW
651-644-8515

Missouri

Belton
Brel White, Ph.D., LCSW and Julie Pitensberger, LPC 816-818-1720

Clayton
Duncan-Hively P.C.
Ann Duncan, Ph.D., J.D. and Wells Hively, Ph.D. 314-862-2305

Technologic Behavioral Enterprises
Marie Clark and Priscilla E. Grier, Ph.D. 314-725-2667

Jefferson City
Yvette Phillips Professional Counseling, L.L.C.
Yvette Phillips, M.Ed. LPC 573-893-8579

Kansas City
Midwest Clinical Forensics
Bret White, Ph.D., LCSW 816-318-1720

Wyandot Mental Health Center
Nancy Baldwin, LCSW 913-328-4600

St. Louis
Behavioral Science Institute, Inc.
Priscilla Grier, Ph.D. 314-361-2662

Montana

Billings
Northwest Counseling Center
Robert G. Bakko, MA, LCPC 406-259-6161

South Central Treatment Associates
Michael D. Sullivan, MSW 406-245-4566

Missoula
Michael J. Scolatti, Ph.D. 406-549-4870

Nevada

Las Vegas
Family and Child Treatment
Vicki Graff, MSW, LCSW 702-258-5855

Reno
Marriage and Family Therapist
Robert Stuyvesant, LCSW 775-827-7500

New Jersey

Kearny
Special Offender Treatment Center/Northern
Regional Unit
Mark Mollick, Psy.D. 973-491-2510

New Mexico

Santa Fe
Santa Fe Rape Crisis Center, Inc./PARE Program
Denise Johnson, Ed.S. 505-988-1951

New York

Brooklyn
Ohel Children's Home & Family Services/Sexual
Abuse Treatment Program

Barry Horowitz 718-851-6300

Corning
The Choice Program/Family Service Society, Inc.
Candice Cleveland, CSWR 607-962-3148

Courtland
Courtland County Mental Health
Charles T. Capanzano, Ph.D. 607-758-6100

Garden City
Association for Human Development and Law
Hillel Sternstein, CSW 516-293-4665

Katonah
Four Winds Hospital
David Pogge, Ph.D. 914-763-8151

Middletown
Potter Counseling & Evaluation Service
James H. Potter, MSW, CSW 845-344-4091

New Hampton
Mid-Hudson Psychiatric Center
Charles Smith, M.D. 914-374-3171

New York
Richard B. Krueger, M.D. and Meg Kaplan, Ph.D.
212-517-6624

Syracuse
Damian S. Vallelonga, Ph.D. 315-426-2805

North Carolina

Asheville
Family Relations and Intimacy Center
Robert D. McDonald, Ph.D. 828-258-8365

Durham
The Center for the Assessment and Treatment of Sexual Disorders (CTSD)
Donna M. Peaslee, Ph.D. and Bob Fox 919-490-7909

William Burlingame, Ph.D.
William Burlingame, Ph.D. 919-967-5383

Goldsboro
Waynesborough Psychological Services
Christopher Boyle, MA 919-736-7900

Greensboro
Carolina Counseling Associates
Wendy L. Davis, MS, LPC, and Christie A. Cornwell, M.Ed., LPC
336-558-7782

Jacksonville
Carolina Psychological Health Services
Jack McFadyen, MA 910-347-3010

Morganton
Foothills Sexual Abuse Intervention Service (SAIS)
John. F. Middleton, MA 828-438-6218

Raleigh
Burkey and Associates
William R. Burkey, LCSW 919-773-4658

Winston-Salem
Exchange Club Child Abuse Prevention Center for NC
Dorothy Walton Walker, MS, NCC, LPC 336-748-9028

North Dakota

Fargo
Kerith Counseling, Inc.
Esther Johnson, MS, LMFT 701-234-0324

Ohio

Beachwood
Althof, Levine, Risen, & Associates
Steve Levine, M.D. and Candace Risen, Ph.D. 216-831-2900

Cleveland
Adult Sex Offender Treatment Program
Alan Dean Fazekas, LSW 216-687-1350

Court Psychiatric Clinic
Michael Aranoff, Psy.D. 216-443-7330

Lakewood
The Mokita Center
Robin Palmer, LSW, BA, MSSA 216-521-1961

Lima
Family Resource Center
Cara Reynolds, LISW and Kelly Huffman, CSW 419-423-9221

Youngstown
Forensic Psychiatric Center of Northeast Ohio, Inc.
Gerald L. Heinbaugh, MS 330-792-1918

Oklahoma

Claremore
Human Skills & Resources
Jim Barton, M.Div. 918-283-1423

Norman
Irwin Hall, Ph.D. 405-447-6188

Oklahoma City
Transitions, Inc.
Bonnie Stapp and Elizabeth Ashton 405-810-0054

Tulsa
Human Skills and Resources
Paul W, Inbody, Ed.D., LPC and Roy A. Thornton
918-747-6377

Randy Lopp & Associates
Randy Lopp, LPC 918-747-2799

Oregon

Ashland
Clinical Psychology/Michael Knapp, Ph.D., P.C.
Michael Knapp, Ph.D. 541-482-9241

Cove
CHOICES
Andrew Lee Ph.D., and Meike Kerper, LMFT 541-568-4893

Hermiston
Counseling Services
Sheryl Geiger, MS 541-567-2224

Ontario
Lifeways Behavioral Health Forensic Unit
Dennis D. Tolman LSW, CADC II, CCJS and Paul S. Smith, MSW 541-881-0957

Portland
Center for Behavioral Intervention
Steven Jensen, MA 503-644-2772

McGovern and Associates
Kevin B. McGovern, Ph.D. 503-644-6600

Roseburg
Correctional Evaluation and Treatment, Inc.
David R. Robinson, MS 541-672-2099

Salem
Beth Doyle, MA 503-391-1300

Pennsylvania

Allentown
Forensic Treatment Services
Veronica N. Valliere, Psy.D. 610-433-1529

Bradford
The Guidance Center
Matthew W. Roy M.Ed. 814-362-6535

Broomall
Tri-County Fountain Center, Inc. – STAR Program

J.P. West, BSW 610-270-9120

Carbondale
Tri-County Human Service Center
David a. Humphreys, MSW, LSW 570-282-1732

Clarion
Clarion County Children and Youth Project Point of Light
William G. Allenbaugh, II, MA, CAC
(Clarion) 814-226-1159 (DuBois) 814-371-5566

Ford City
Ministries of Eden, Inc.
Herbert E. Hays, MA 724-763-7600

Lancanster
T.W. Ponessa & Associates Counseling Services
T.W. Ponessa, M.Ed., MS 717-560-7917

Meadville
Community Abuse Response Team
Audrey Smith, MA 814-333-5600

Mechanicsburg
TresslerCare
Jane A. Yeatter, MHS, MS 717-795-0320

New Castle
Adolescent Psychological-Education & Counseling Services
Domenick A. Lombardo, MA 724-924-9288

Philadelphia
F&P Forensic Associates

Timothy P. Foley, Ph.D. 614-649-2209

Forensic Mental Health Associates
Jules DeCruz, MS 215-683-7562

Joseph J. Peters Institute
Ted Glackman, CEO and Keith Linn, Psy.D. 215-893-0600

Pittsburgh
Robert Coufal, Ph.D. 412-362-8817

IELASE Forensic Center
Rita Lukas, MS 412-261-2817

Reading
Reading Specialists
Robert Gill, Ed.D. and Susan E. Kraus, Ph.D. 610-372-7960

Scranton
Tri-County Human Services
David A. Humphreys, MSW, LSW 570-282-1732

Torrance
Cove PREP
Robert Coufal, Ph.D. 724-459-9700

West Chester
Chester County Adult Probation and Parole Department
Timothy M. Waltz 610-344-6290

South Carolina

Fountain Inn
Generations Group Homes
Jeff Cohen, M.Div. 864-243-5557 ex. 270

North Charleston
Family Violence Center
Thomas R. LaRoche, MA, LCSW 843-745-9111

Summerville
New Hope Treatment Center
Robert E. Freeman-Longo, MRC, LPC 843-851-5010

Southeastern Offender Assessments
William Burke, Ph.D. and Helen Clark, Ph.D. 843-821-2124

South Dakota

Huron
Our Home, Inc.
David Kauffman, Ph.D. 605-352-1554

Rapid City
Donald A. Janz, Ph.D. 605-341-8647

Tennessee

Johnson City
Counseling and Consultation Services, Inc.
Jo Michael Adler, Ph.D. 423-282-2892

Memphis
University of Tennessee Medical Group – Department of Psychiatry

William D. Murphy, Ph.D. 901-448-5481

Nashville
Luton Mental Health Services
G. Samuel Jones, Ph.D. 615-279-6733

Texas

Austin
The Orion Treatment Center
Vivian L. Heine, LMSW-ACP, RSOTP and Diana
Garza Louis, LPC, LMFT, RSOTP
512-495-9917

Beaumont
Ray Coxe, Ph.D. 409-833-7946

Bedford
Lozano & Associates
Arthur T. Lozano, LMSW-ACP, RSOTP 817-282-
1911

Belton
Adult & Adolescent Counseling Center
Fred Willoughby, Ph.D. 512-868-9644

College Station
Brazos Valley Christian Counseling
Roy R. Luepnitz, Ph.D. 409-764-0698

Dallas
Adapt Healthcare, Inc.
Marilyn Stewart-Smith, M.D. 214-826-1000

Galaxy Counseling Center
Joyce Webb, Ph.D. 972-272-4429

RSP Counseling Center
Ronald s. Perrett, MSSW, LMSW-AACP 940-382-0823 or 800-825-4693

The Counseling Institute of Texas
Maria T. Molett, M.A., LPC, RSOTP 972-494-0160

El Paso
Reed & Associates
Norma W. Reed, LMSW-ACP 915-542-1582

Fort Worth
Don't Touch!
John Loggins, LPC 817-738-9539

Psychotherapy Services
Ezio D. Leite, M.Ed. 817-338-4471

Professional Associates Counseling & Consultation Center (PACC)
Deborah L. Moore, MA, M.Ed., LPC, LMSW-ACP, RSOTP 817-496-9796

Identity Counseling, L.L.P.
Will Kantz RSOTP 817-921-2870

Galveston
Family Service Center of Galveston
Sandra S. Sullivan, Ph.D. 409-762-8636

Project Oasis
Celia G. Slingluff, MA 409-762-8636

Georgetown
Center for Cognitive Education
Frederick W. Willoughby, Ph.D. 512-868-9644

Houston
Adult Psychiatric Center
Houshmand Tirandaz, M.D. and Randall C. Black, LMSW-AP 281-286-0000

Dr. Crismon & Associates Inc.
Richard R. Crismon, Ph.D., and Sharon Burns 713-697-0776

·Lubbock
The Bears Den Recovery Center
John Newton, Jr., MA, LPC, LCDC 806-749-0801

Marriage & Family Therapy Associates
Richard N. Mack, M.Div., LMFT 603-484-8105

Solutions
Chuck Hansford, Ed.S. and Welborn K. Willingham, Ph.D. 806-744-7169

Midland
Linda L. Patterson, LMSW-ACP 915-684-4540

San Antonio
Professional Associates for Counseling & Evaluation (PACE)
Mark Steege, LMSW-ACP, LPC and Marty Tavino 210-524-9402

South Texas Offender Programs (S.T.O.P Programs)

James B. Keedy, LCDC, LMFT, LPC, RSOTP 210-366-2288

Seguin
Seguin Family Institute
Janice K. Hull, MS, LMFT 830-372-4909

Sherman
Paul Shearer. LPC 888-616-5110

Texarkana
Rafael F. Otero, Ph.D., Inc.
Rafael F. Otero, Ph.D. 903-838-3711 or 903-838-9943

Utah

Logan
Alternative Perspectives
D. Kim Openshaw, Ph.D., LCSW, LMFT 435-753-7332 or 435-797-7434

Salt Lake City
Adolescent and Adult Treatment Center
Roger Read, LCSW, BCD 801-450-0999

International Specialized Abuse Treatment Center (ISAT)
(ISAT also has several other office locations across the state of Utah)
Becky Valcarce, M.S., NCC, LPC 801-486-9805

Monarch Assessment and Treatment Center
Robert D. Card, Ph.D. 801-363-9017

Virginia

Alexandria
The Augustus Institute
Hans H. Selvog, MSW, LCSW 703-684-0373

Charlottesville
Piedmont Psychiatric Professionals
Evan S. Nelson, Ph.D. and Jeffrey C. Fracher, Ph.D.
804-296-9740

Hampton
Eden Counseling Center
Paul Van-Valin Ph.D. and Jeffery D. Ward, Ph.D. 757-827-7707

Harrisonburg
Shenandoah Valley Sex Offenders Treatment Program
Richard Wettstone, Ed.D. 540-434-9430

Midlothian (Richmond)
Forensic Psychology Associates, P.C.
Evan S. Nelson, Ph.D. 804-739-4669

Newport News
BSP Outpatient Services
C. John McCary, LCSW 757-873-3353

Richmond
The Westwood Group
Dennis R. Carpenter, Psy.D. 804-254-0966

Roanoke
Community Correction of Virginia, Inc.
Deborah D. Smith, LPC, CSOTP 540-562-0112

Portsmouth

The Pines Residential Treatment Center
Gail Castenguay, ACSW 757-393-0061

Virginia Beach
Eden Counseling Center
Jeffery D. Ward, Ph.D. 707-431-3600

Washington

Bellingham
Mitchell Whitman, M.Ed. 360-671-2199

Everett
O'Connell Associates
Michael A. O'Connell, Ph.D. 425-741-1405

Marysville
Fountaingate Psychological & Family Services
Gary D. Smith, Psy.D. 360-653-0374

Seattle
Bellevue Community Services/CoHear
Bill Lennon, Ed.D. 425-454-0616

Griffin Home, Friends of Youth
Carol Almero, MA, CMHC, CSOTP 425-228-5776
ext.113

NW Treatment Associates
Roger W. Wolfe 206-283-8099

Timothy A. Smith Consulting and Therapy
Timothy A. Smith, M.Ed. 206-284-3125

Tim Kahn and Associates
Timothy J. Kahn, MSW. and Carol Almero, MA,
CMHC, CSOTP 425-462-9647

William Satoran Certified Sex Offender Treatment
Provider
William Satoran, MSW, MBA, CSOTP 206-325-
9401

Tacoma
Comte's and Associates, Inc.
Michael A. Comte, MSW, ACSW 253-564-3622

Vancouver
Vancouver Guidance Clinics, P.S.
Christopher K. Johnson, Ph.D. 630-694-2016

Yahima
Crest Counseling Services, P.S.
Julie D. Crest, MS 509-575-8989

West Virginia

Charleston
Charleston Psychiatric Group, Inc.
Ralph S. Smith, Jr., M.D. 304-344-0349

Martinsburg
Paul Kradel, Ed.D. 304-263-3788

Morgantown
Chestnut Ridge Hospital
Gary McDaniel, MSW 304-293-4000
Diane Halbritter, MSW 304-598-6400

Wisconsin

Jamesville
Robert H. Gordon, Ph.D. 608-756-2767

Milwaukee and Wauwatosa
Pathways Counseling Center
Roger Northway 414-774-4111

CANADA

Nova Scotia

Halifax
Center for Psychological Services, Ltd.
Robert J. Konopasky, Ph.D.; Mary McGrath, MS,
CGC; Andrew Starzomski, Ph.D.; Debbie Sutherland,
MS, CGC 902-425-5137

Ontario

Aurora
The Southdown Institute for Clergy
Phillip Dodgson, Ph.D. 905-727-4214

Ottawa
Sexual Behaviors Clinic, Royal Ottawa Hospital
John Bradford, M.D. 613-722-6521 ext. 6364

Quebec

Montreal
Department of Psychology, University of Montreal
Joanne L. Rouleau, Ph.D. 514-343-5603 or 514-343-
6111 ext.4399

Sherbrooke

Centre d'intervention en violence et abus sexuels de l'Estrie

Josée Rioux 819-564-5127

ABOUT THE AUTHORS

Gene G. Abel, M.D. is a physician, psychiatrist, and a scientist. The National Institute of Mental Health has awarded him funding for six long-term studies to investigate sexual violence against women and children and to design new ways to stop it.

Dr. Abel has received several awards for his significant achievements in sex research, including the Masters and Johnson Award presented by the Society for Sex Therapy and Research. He is a member of the International Academy of Sex Research.

A past President of the National Society for Behavioral Medicine, Dr. Abel is a Fellow of the American Psychiatry Association and a diplomat of the American Board of Psychiatry and Neurology. A full professor, he has served on the faculty of several medical schools including Columbia University College of Physicians and Surgeons, Emory University Medical School, and Morehouse Medical School.

Nora Harlow founded a day care center in New York City and taught there while getting a graduate degree from Columbia University.

She has published two books, one on childcare, *Sharing the Children*, and one on sexuality, *Lover to Lover*. She is the former editor of two publications for physicians, *Sexual Medicine Today*, and *Frontiers of Psychiatry*.

They are married and live in Atlanta, Georgia. In 1995 they founded Abel Screening, Incorporated, a testing and research company devoted to stopping sexual violence. In 2001 they founded The Stop Child Molestation Group, a non-profit organization that helps families stop child molestation.

SUPPORT AND RESOURCES

You will find a list of resources and the latest scientific and family-oriented information at our website. We would also like to hear your ideas to prevent child molestation or to help other families who are dealing with child molestation. You are welcome to contact Gene G. Abel, M.D. or Nora Harlow through the website: www.stopchildmolestation.org.

TO JOIN THE STOP CHILD MOLESTATION GROUP

For information about what you can do to help protect children through our non-profit organization check our website: www.stopchildmolestation.org.

TO ORDER *THE STOP CHILD MOLESTATION BOOK*

Contact The Stop Child Molestation Group.
Web: www.stopchildmolestation.org
Email: stopcmbook@aol.com